JUL - - 2012 SE

D0691301

Working with Microsoft® Office 365: Running Your Small Business in the Cloud

Brett Hill

Published with the authorization of Microsoft Corporation by:
O'Reilly Media, Inc.
1005 Gravenstein Highway North
Sebastopol, California 95472

ISBN: 978-0-7356-5899-8

1 2 3 4 5 6 7 8 9 LSI 7 6 5 4 3 2

Printed and bound in the United States of America.

Microsoft Press books are available through booksellers and distributors worldwide. If you need support related to this book, email Microsoft Press Book Support at mspinput@microsoft.com. Please tell us what you think of this book at http://www.microsoft.com/learning/booksurvey.

Microsoft and the trademarks listed at *http://www.microsoft.com/about/legal/en/us/IntellectualProperty/ Trademarks/EN-US.aspx* are trademarks of the Microsoft group of companies. All other marks are property of their respective owners.

The example companies, organizations, products, domain names, email addresses, logos, people, places, and events depicted herein are fictitious. No association with any real company, organization, product, domain name, email address, logo, person, place, or event is intended or should be inferred.

Acquisitions and Developmental Editor: Ken Jones

Production Editor: Kristen Borg

Production Services: Octal Publishing Services

Technical Reviewer: Amy Babinchak

Copyeditor: Richard Carey

Indexer: Denise Getz

Cover Design: Twist Creative • Seattle

Cover Composition: Karen Montgomery

Illustrators: Robert Romano and Rebecca Demarest

Contents at a Glance

Contents

What do you think of this book? We want to hear from you!

Microsoft is interested in hearing your feedback so we can continually improve our
books and learning resources for you. To participate in a brief online survey, please visit:

microsoft.com/learning/booksurvey

Chapter 8   Working with Outlook Web App   147

Chapter 9   Working with Mobile Devices   185

Chapter 10 Improving Your Business Image and Productivity with Outlook   201

Chapter 12 Working with Lync Online   287

Introduction

Microsoft Office 365 is taking the small business world by storm. According to Microsoft, over 90 percent of the sales of Office 365 are to small businesses. I can't say I'm surprised. When you look at the capabilities of Office 365 for professionals and small businesses, the offer is compelling.

This book was written for small business owners or consultants to small businesses who want to learn how to:

- Know whether the Office 365 small business plan is a good fit.

- Sign up and deploy the service, including domain name configuration.

- Avoid common problems.

- Use the best features of Office 365.

This book is designed for small businesses and professionals who are familiar with computers but are not technical professionals. While setting up Office 365 can be quite straightforward, there are technical aspects to deployment, particularly around custom domains. This book describes in a step-by-step fashion how to move a custom domain to Office 365 as well as how to set up your desktop. In fact, providing this guidance to owners of the service is one of the primary objectives of the book.

Overall, the book is a guide to anyone who anticipates implementing Office 365 for professionals and small businesses, from early planning, through deployment, to making use of the key features and capabilities. Office 365 is a frequently updated service. Be sure to check the Service Updates wiki at *http://community.office365.com* for changes made to the service since this book was published.

Acknowledgments

The changing nature of online services required significant rewrites and overhauls that extended my time commitment well beyond initial expectations. I'd like to thank my loving wife Ryam for her unrelenting support for this project through the duration. In addition, the Office 365 small business product group at Microsoft assisted at key times by providing information about upcoming changes and implementation details that were essential.

Support & Feedback

The following sections provide information on errata, book support, feedback, and contact information.

Errata & Book Support

We've made every effort to ensure the accuracy of this book and its companion content. Any errors that have been reported since this book was published are listed on our Microsoft Press site at oreilly.com:

http://go.microsoft.com/FWLink/?Linkid=247989

If you find an error that is not already listed, you can report it to us through the same page. The author also maintains a website where he posts about updates to Office 365 services:

Office365answers.com

You will find additional information and services for your book on its catalog page. If you need additional support, please e-mail Microsoft Press Book Support at *mspinput@ microsoft.com*.

Please note that product support for Microsoft software is not offered through the addresses above.

We Want to Hear from You

At Microsoft Press, your satisfaction is our top priority, and your feedback our most valuable asset. Please tell us what you think of this book at:

http://www.microsoft.com/learning/booksurvey

The survey is short, and we read every one of your comments and ideas. Thanks in advance for your input!

Stay in Touch

Let us keep the conversation going! We are on Twitter: *http://twitter.com/MicrosoftPress*.

CHAPTER 1

Office 365: A Big Deal for Small Business

The Cloud is unavoidable these days. Big businesses are talking about it. Small businesses are asking, "Is this for me?" There are conferences, blogs, papers, and even TV commercials about how great the cloud is. But what is all this about *really*, and does it makes sense for a small business?

What Is a Cloud Service?

At its most basic, a cloud service is one that you access over the Internet. A cloud service subscription is not much different from paying for a phone service. In fact, some phone services are Internet-based these days. You might have heard the term "Voice over IP" (abbreviated as VoIP and pronounced just like it looks). If not, you've probably seen Magic Jack™ advertised on TV, which provides a popular way to connect a telephone to the Internet. Magic Jack is a cloud-based telephone service.

Any website you access is a cloud service. Online banking is a cloud service. Amazon.com is a cloud service. There are thousands of examples, and if all of these services are so common, why is the cloud such a hot topic these days? To answer that question, we need to look at how small businesses use online services.

 Note For the purposes of this book, a small business is an organization with 1 to 25 employees. This is the same scale that Microsoft uses for the Office 365 professionals and small businesses plan: organizations from 1 to 25 users. Microsoft allows growth in this plan for up to but not exceeding 50 users.

Current Services vs. the Cloud

Small businesses use many different kinds of online services. One-person shops often use free consumer email such as Google Mail or Hotmail. However, by the time you have five or more employees, you will need to better organize your digital assets, so your business might want to invest in file and email services provided by an ISP or Hosted Exchange. Some small businesses choose to purchase a server and host their own services on-premises by using the Microsoft Small Business Server line of products. Others simply piece together the services they need from different instant messaging, online meeting, document collaboration, and messaging providers.

The patchwork quilt of services used by small businesses creates an opportunity for large companies like Microsoft, Google, IBM, and others to offer service suites that unify the services your business needs in key areas. These companies have the funds, scale, expertise, and capital to build, market, and support the infrastructure needed to offer these services on a massive scale. The result is "The Cloud:" a set of core business services offered by trusted names and delivered at a very attractive price.

Are Cloud Services a Good Deal for Small Businesses?

Consider the responsibilities and resulting costs of providing your own services with servers and software that you maintain on-premises. You have to buy, deploy, and maintain the servers. These servers need software, support, and expertise to operate continuously. This includes spam filtering, server virus scanning, backup systems, uninterruptable power supplies, upgrades, security updates, firewalls, and many other activities, all necessary to keep your on-premises systems up and running.

If you are not using your own services, one option is to purchase services from a variety of other providers. Costs for professionally hosted services can be high. Consumer-based services are often free but lack features and are usually advertising based. In either case, you wind up with a fragmented set of services.

What if you could have email, document collaboration, instant messaging, online meetings, web-based access to your mail and documents, and integration with your mobile phones for only $6 per user, per month, with a 99.9 percent uptime guarantee provided by a Fortune 500 company like Microsoft? That is what Office 365 provides. For many businesses, this is an exceptionally attractive value, and this package deal is why there is so much "buzz" about "The Cloud."

Office 365 in a Nutshell

I vividly remember meeting the project manager for Office 365 for small businesses at Microsoft to review the feature set. Honestly, I was astonished, and I suspect you will be too. More importantly, I learned that Office 365 is more than "buzz"; it's packed with useful features. Here are some highlights:

- 25 GB mailboxes

- Ability to use your company's domain name for your email addresses

- Minimum of one seat available for purchase, if that's all you need

- Month to month payments with the ability to cancel anytime; no long-term contract required

- Spam filtering delivered directly to your junk folder

- All email scanned for viruses before it is delivered to you

- Free/busy status that lets you view other people's schedules, create meeting requests, and reserve resources (such as rooms, vehicles, or projectors) via Microsoft Outlook and Microsoft Exchange

- Ability to publish a basic company website to the Internet

- External sharing feature that allows you to invite people outside your company to work on documents on your Microsoft SharePoint Online site

- 99.9 percent uptime guarantee

- Ability to invite up to 50 anonymous users to your online event, such as a web conference, and talk to them using a microphone on your PC—no dialing in to 800 numbers required

- Instant messaging

- Ability to edit Office documents in a browser (using Office Web Apps)

- Ability to sync email and calendar to a mobile device

- Only $6 per seat (US), per month

And this list is just the beginning. Office 365 is a frequently updated service. Be sure to check the Service Updates wiki at *http://community.office365.com* for changes made to the service since this book was published.

> **Note** When you make a change to your cable TV service, you just call the company and, *voilà*, your new services are updated. With Office 365, it's not that simple. You cannot flip a switch and convert from the plan for small business to another plan that allows for more users. If you think you will be at 51 employees in the foreseeable future, consider starting with the higher-capacity plan. Then you won't have to migrate your content when you reach 51 users. For more advice on choosing the right plan for your business, see Chapter 2, "Choosing an Office 365 Plan."

The Cloud vs. Self-Hosting

If you have your own on-premises servers and are considering a move to Office 365, be aware that moving to the cloud requires some tradeoffs. Although using Office 365 and its many conveniences frees you to focus more on your business than on IT decisions, that freedom comes with limitations in a few areas:

- **Server logs**   Servers keep boatloads of information about what they are doing that you don't typically see. An IT professional can access event viewer logs, performance metrics, web server logs, Exchange server logs, and many others. With an on-premises server, you or your IT team can review these logs when a problem arises to determine the source of the issue. If you move to Office 365, Microsoft will not grant you access to the server logs, because the servers host data for many people, not just you.

- **Server access** With Office 365, you cannot log on to the server by using terminal services, nor can you view, update, or access any server-level settings. You can configure settings related to your account services. In general, this limitation affects people who rely on third-party additions to Exchange or SharePoint on-premises that are not allowed in SharePoint or Exchange Online.

- **Timing to apply updates** Microsoft decides when to apply updates to the services. Suppose that you discover that a specific update to SharePoint Online will enable a feature that will benefit your business. In a self-hosted environment, you could apply the patch right away. For Office 365, Microsoft will apply the patch to the services—or not—based on its own schedule. Microsoft's schedule is determined by a lot of competing issues, including complexity, broad benefits, and importance of other updates that need to be applied.

- **Data location** With Office 365, your data is hosted in a data center that is determined by the address used when you sign up for the services. You have no control over where your data is stored.

- **Security** The security features built in to the service are the only ones available to you. It is absolutely true that some businesses have security requirements that are not available in Office 365, such as the ability to enforce specialized password complexity requirements or specialized auditing requirements. Businesses with a non-negotiable need for security features not available in Office 365 should find another solution.

- **Limited liability** As with most services, if the cloud services fail for some reason, Microsoft is responsible for refunding only the portion of your service subscription fee associated with the downtime. If data is lost, you cannot recover damages from Microsoft. With redundancy in the data center, continuous backups, and fail-over for entire data centers in place, the chances of lost data are low. Even so, for security and compliance reasons, many businesses augment their own on-premises or cloud services with email and document archiving systems.

- **Dependency on Internet connectivity** When your services are cloud-based, if your connection to the Internet is lost, you will experience a disruption. Often you can still work locally with email, due to Outlook's cached mode, and also with locally stored documents that are checked out to you. But you should make plans to have alternative ways to access the Internet in case of a local outage.

As you can see, having your data in the cloud is really quite different than hosting your own services. While you do surrender control and are dependent on the Internet, what are the benefits? Why would you move to the cloud?

How Can My Company Benefit from Office 365?

Office 365 is packaged in a variety of plans, as you'll learn in Chapter 2. The primary focus of this book, called *Office 365 for professionals and small businesses*, or *Plan P1* for short, is aimed at businesses with 1 to 25 employees, but it can accommodate growth up to 50 users. No matter which plan you choose or which name you use for it, the benefits to your company are the same and many. Office 365 can help you to upgrade your image, improve productivity, and leverage your investments in online services and Microsoft Office.

Professional Image

One of the primary reasons small businesses and professionals benefit from using Office 365 has to do with image. Hand someone a business card with your company name and a Google Mail or Hotmail account as an email address, for example, and you just might send the wrong message. Customarily, businesses of substance use email addresses specific to their businesses, rather than using a free online service. With Office 365, you can have all your mail delivered to and sent from your own custom domain, ensuring that your business mail looks business-like.

Do you have a good looking website that explains your business, has a map, and provides a way to contact or locate you? With Office 365, you can start a simple, clean, and professional website at no additional cost.

When you need to meet with a customer, sending her a meeting request in Outlook that includes a link to an online meeting hosted in Lync Online is very impressive. Online meetings are much easier to arrange than you might think, and enterprises use them extensively. In addition, you can host webinars or online conferences for up to 50 people at a time.

These kinds of features are usually available only when you host your own services or purchase online services that have significant associated costs. With Office 365, many small businesses and professionals, as small as one person, can have these impressive capabilities without the overhead of the infrastructure so that they can look and act like a much larger company.

Keep Using What You Know

One of the best aspects of moving to Office 365 is that you can continue to use Microsoft Office much the same way that you do now. The time you've invested in learning about Office and creating Office documents is not only preserved, but enhanced. With Office 365, you can collaborate very easily with SharePoint Online. In Chapter 11, "Working with SharePoint Online," you'll learn that you don't even need to exit Microsoft Word when you want to open and edit documents that are hosted in SharePoint Online.

In fact, I like to think about Office 365 for professionals and small businesses as more of a way of expanding Microsoft Office to have cloud features, rather than buying a pure cloud service. Many features of Microsoft Office just "wake up" when you use Office 365. For example, as you can see in Figure 1-1, Microsoft Word automatically knows when it is connected to SharePoint Online and allows you to check out the document. No configuration, add-ons, or other specialized settings are needed. As a result, you can often benefit from using Office 365 without ever leaving Microsoft Office applications. You keep working in a familiar user interface and get the additional benefits of sharing and document collaboration.

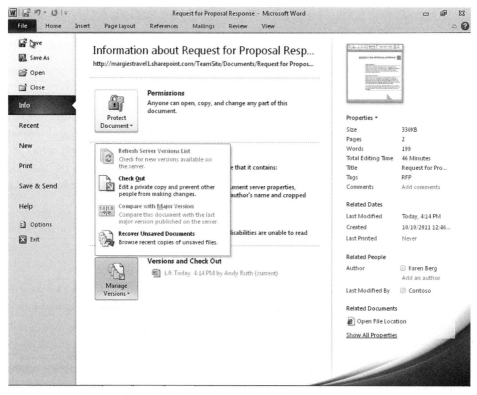

FIGURE 1-1 The Microsoft Word 2010 Version and Check Out features "wake up" when you use Word with SharePoint Online.

Work In or Out of the Office

Because your data is hosted in the cloud, you can work from any location that has Internet access, including your mobile phone. If your office Internet connection goes down, just move over to the local coffee shop Wi-Fi connection, and you're back in business. When you're away from your office and Microsoft Office, you can use any computer browser to access your email or documents. Plus, Office 365 synchronizes your mail with your mobile phone so that you can receive and reply to email directly from your phone.

Security and Availability

Few things impact businesses more profoundly than when email is disrupted. Hosting your own email services gives you total control, but you are subject to outages due to local equipment failures, local ISP connectivity security problems, and unforeseen issues that occur during updates or configuration changes. Any hosted service you obtain will have the same issues, but the procedures and processes for updating services at Microsoft's multimillion dollar data center with millions of mailboxes are generally more rigorous by several orders of magnitude.

Office 365 services are provided with a 99.9 percent uptime guarantee. In effect, if the services are down for more than nine hours annually, you get money back. In practice, this means that if the services are down for an unplanned outage for more than 45 minutes in a month, you are due a refund. Many small businesses have difficulty achieving this level of service availability with their own on-premises solutions. Table 1-1, which is taken from the *Exchange Online Microsoft Exchange Online Service Level Agreement (SLA),* details the credit scale.

TABLE 1-1 Office 365 Uptime Guarantee and Service Credits

Monthly Uptime Percentage	Service Credit
< 99.9%	25%
< 99%	50%
< 95%	100%

The same rationale applies to security. Office 365 provides full virus scanning and spam management in its data centers. In addition, Microsoft data centers have obtained certifications from third parties attesting to the data center compliance with industry-accepted standards and practices.

> **More Info** You can obtain free virus scanning for your local computers from Microsoft Security Essentials (*http://www.microsoft.com/security/pc-security/mse.aspx*).
>
> For more information about the Microsoft data centers, see the Office 365 Security and Service Continuity for Enterprises white paper at *http://www.microsoft.com/download/en/details.aspx?id=13602*. While this paper is focused on the enterprise offerings of Office 365, the enterprise and small business services are hosted in the same data centers.

Using Office 365: A True Story

While consulting with a small mortgage company, I asked its IT Manager whether he was using any online service besides email. As is often the case, he replied that he wasn't, so I went through my usual talk about how SharePoint Online allows you to provide a distributed workforce with access to documents.

He perked up and asked if that meant that they could scan documents and post them on SharePoint. Indeed it did. Currently, he explained, one employee spent up to two hours every day copying documents and faxing them to agents who worked all over the country. Now, with Office 365, the employee could scan the documents, and post the resulting PDFs to SharePoint Online, and then automatically send a simple email notification to prompt the agents to log on and fetch the documents or download them to their phones. "You just saved us a 40-hour work week every month," he said.

This solution was very simple to implement and required no custom code, special applications, or updates (other than the initial Office 365 setup). The mobile devices came into the picture automatically. The owner of the company could have gone with a somewhat less expensive service, but the unexpected benefit from SharePoint Online essentially justified the entire subscription. Applying technology to problems of this sort is where productivity benefits can easily pay off in unexpected ways.

What's Included in Office 365?

In some ways, subscribing to Office 365 is like buying a cable TV plan. Just as the specific cable channels you receive are dependent on the package you buy, the Office 365 features you receive are dependent on your subscription plan. Selecting the right plan is very important, as you'll learn in Chapter 2, which is dedicated to helping you make the right decision. However, all the plans incorporate the three core services—Exchange Online, SharePoint Online, and Lync Online—on some level. Office Web Apps is also a key feature because it's part of SharePoint Online; it is not a stand-alone service. Because you need to know what's on the various channels before you can choose the ones you want, the next sections provide a closer look at Office 365's core services, as well as the Office Professional Plus option.

Exchange Online for Email

Exchange Online is the Office 365 email service (which Microsoft calls "Messaging"). You typically use Outlook 2007 or Outlook 2010 to connect to your Exchange Online mailbox. Also, part of Office 365 is a browser-based version of Outlook called Outlook Web App, often called OWA for short. OWA is a fully functioning web application with which you can manage your mail from almost any computer or even from a mobile device.

With Outlook and Outlook Web App, you can do a lot more than just manage email. You can set up meetings, see who's online now and who's not (via presence indicators), read documents from SharePoint Online, connect to blogs and other services (via RSS feeds), manage tasks, create to-do lists, and more.

Exchange Online is based on Exchange Server 2010, which drives enterprise-class mail services for many of the largest companies in the world. However, don't assume that "enterprise" translates to "way too complicated and big for my small business needs." Just because an enterprise-class service can be complicated doesn't mean you have to use it that way. The small business plan for Office 365 is simplified, and as a result, you have fewer choices in the administration portal. Some of the easiest features to use are also the most useful. We'll focus on these high-impact, easy-to-implement features, such as checking documents in and out of SharePoint Online, sending an online meeting request from Outlook, and creating distribution groups with Exchange Online.

In addition to Outlook 2007 and Outlook 2010, you can use Microsoft Outlook 2011 for Mac and other email clients that support the POP protocol (Windows Live Mail, for example) or IMAP protocol. Outlook 2003 is not supported with Office 365 but was supported with Business Productivity Online Suite (the name for the previous version of the services). If you have Outlook 2003, you must upgrade if you want to use Office 365. See the Office Professional Plus subscription for details about how you can subscribe to Office 2010 rather than purchasing it outright.

Mail features commonly of interest to many small businesses include:

- **25-GB mailbox** By default, you are given a 25-GB mailbox, which is the largest mailbox possible. In practice, this is much more than you need. In fact, if you have a mailbox that is much larger than 1 GB, you should consider reducing the size, because Outlook performance can degrade when searching for specific content.

- **Ad free** Free email services often place advertisements in email as a way to fund their operations. When you use Exchange Online, your email will not be cluttered with any additional messages or "brought to you by" taglines.

- **Spam filtering** Microsoft uses its own product, ForeFront Protection for Exchange (*http://www.microsoft.com/forefront/protection-for-exchange/en/us/default.aspx*), to provide spam filtering at no extra cost. ForeFront is well regarded as a reliable spam filtering system.

- **Virus and malware protection** Also provided by ForeFront, all mail in and out of Exchange Online is always scanned for malware. Remember that virus-scanning software should already be installed on your PCs and is not part of Office 365.

- **Contacts** Contacts are really important to many small businesses. Contacts can be prospects, suppliers, vendors, and contractors—anyone who is not part of your organization about whom you need to keep details. Using Outlook, you can create contacts that are available just to you. With Exchange Online, you can create and share contacts with your entire company. Chapter 8, "Working with Outlook Web App," will teach you how to share contacts.

- **MailBox alias** Frequently, you might need a mailbox to have more than one identity. While the address for a mailbox might be *bill@contoso.com*, you might want Bill to also get mail for *sales@contoso.com*. This is simple to configure in Office 365 and will be covered in Chapter 8.

- **Mobile support** Use your iPhone, Windows Phone, Android, or other device to send and receive email and review documents at no extra cost. Included with Office 365 for Small Business is the ability to configure a mobile device to connect to your services. Having your phone wired up to the information flow for your business allows you and your employees to keep in touch and stay up to date on events as they occur. You can send and receive email, reply to meeting requests, view documents (including Microsoft PowerPoint slides [see Figure 1-2]), receive alerts and notifications, and more.

FIGURE 1-2 Microsoft PowerPoint Mobile showing a PowerPoint slide.

Important Your cell phone service provider might charge for the bandwidth for your email, so be aware of what charges are associated with email to and from your phone. In particular, when traveling overseas, be sure to understand what can happen if you are roaming and receiving email. I know a well-respected member of the IT community who received a bill in excess of $10,000 because he didn't realize his phone was using foreign carriers every couple of minutes to send and receive mail while traveling abroad.

- **Access to mail from the web**   You can access your mail from any computer connected to the web by using the very functional Outlook Web App at *https://portal.microsoftonline.com*.

- **Scheduling meetings**   Exchange Online in Office 365 lets you use Outlook 2007, Outlook 2010, or Outlook Web App to easily find a mutually free time to schedule the meeting.

- **Signatures**   Outlook and OWA offer the ability to add a signature or any one of a set of signatures to your email. This provides a professional and uniform look and turns each communication into a branding opportunity.

- **Rules**   One of the most popular features of Outlook is the ability to create custom rules to manage your mail. Rules can be applied to any incoming or outgoing message, such as "When I receive mail addressed to me from *prospect@mywebsite.com* play the Alarm sound," or "When I receive mail with the phrase 'urgent' in the Subject, mark the message as important and place it in the Urgent folder."

- **Out-of-office messages**   When traveling or unavailable, you can easily set up an automatic reply that informs people about how to reach you or other delegated contacts.

SharePoint Online for Document Collaboration and Websites

Have you ever tried to collaborate on a document with a group of people by sending the document around via email? Microsoft Word provides some helpful tools. For example, by using its Track Changes feature, you and other users can easily see the edits in a document as well as who made them, and accept or reject those changes later. With Word's Comment feature you also can add comments for others to review or read other's comments. However, neither of these features addresses the bigger problem of "versioning issues" spawned by using email to circulate a document.

For example, John sends a document to his team with an email saying, "This is the first draft of the new user's guide. Please comment and return by Wednesday." On Wednesday, John receives three documents via email, each with different comments and edits. He spends a day integrating the changes and sends the new document back out with an email saying "Here is the updated draft, as per your comments. Look it over and let me know by Friday if we're good to go." About three hours later, he gets an email from a team member that says, "John, I sent your draft to Emily, who had some really great additions. Can you add these in?" Emily actually made significant updates to the previous version. The second draft was already in circulation and under review. What's John supposed to do?

Document Version Control Using SharePoint Online

SharePoint Online solves John's problem; instead of sending the document itself to multiple reviewers, he can send them a *link* to the document. To avoid versioning issues, SharePoint Online hosts the "one true copy" that can be checked in and checked out. When a team member checks out the document to work on it, other members cannot edit that version of the document, and all versions of the document are saved in sequence.

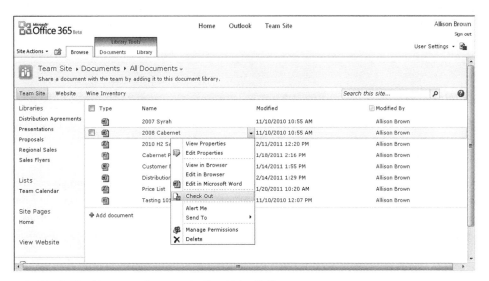

FIGURE 1-3 Checking out a document in SharePoint Online.

Figure 1-3 shows Allison checking out a document in the SharePoint Online site. After she opens it, she doesn't need to go back to SharePoint Online to check the document in or manage versions for the document. She (and you) can do that within Word itself, as Figure 1-1 shows.

Checking out documents helps to manage multiple versions of edited documents because each contributor can mark up and add comments to the same document. In addition, if someone does upload a new document by the same name, you can easily configure SharePoint Online to keep copies of all versions and increment the version numbers automatically. You can also see who has the document checked out and add status information about a document for others to see, showing that any particular document is a draft, in review, final, or out for design work. Plus, it is easy to configure

SharePoint Online to send an email noting whenever a document is changed or updated. These features alone can provide a significant improvement in productivity.

External Document Sharing

In addition to working with your coworkers, you can share your document collaboration site with users outside of your company. Microsoft calls this the external document sharing feature, but the technical name for this feature is *extranet*. An extranet is a computer network to which you can grant access to internal resources to users outside the company.

With external document sharing, you can collaborate on documents with contractors, partners, vendors, or other individuals or organizations. The Small Business plan allows you to invite up to 50 users external to your company at no additional costs.

> **Important** As of this writing, SharePoint Online communications do not include Secure Sockets Layer (SSL) under Plan P1. This limits some of the features and means that documents are not encrypted when being sent across the Internet. Microsoft does include SSL for higher-level plans. This is one of those security considerations that were mentioned earlier.

Public Website

SharePoint Online, as with Office 365 for Small Business, includes the ability to publish a publicly available website. You create your site by using the Site Designer Wizard, which can help you to create an attractive, simple website suitable for many small businesses.

It is not fully customizable because you must use the wizard to create the site, and you cannot run custom code such as a shopping cart or payment system. Even so, for many businesses that simply need to have an identity on the web for reference by customers, suppliers, partners, and others, the site can provide your contact details, description of your business and services, and a few other pages.

Offline Viewing of Files

The term "offline viewing" means "looking at or working with documents hosted online, while not on the Internet." This is similar to watching a TiVo recording of a cable TV show. You can disconnect your cable but still watch the recording.

Some pure cloud service providers have tried to sell the notion that you don't really need offline access to your data. But you and I live in the real world and understand that sometimes you get unexpected calls at inconvenient times. You need to get your hands on an important piece of information (such as the budget for a specific project, a list of phone extensions, or an invoice) in a hurry. Problem is you're in the car, a parking garage, at a baseball game, or some other inconvenient place where you weren't really planning on needing Internet access. And of course, sometimes you are traveling and an Internet connection is not available, but you still need access to work documents. A lot of work gets done on airplanes.

You can edit files that are checked out to you even when you're not online. In addition, SharePoint Online allows you to publish your documents to a folder in Outlook where you can view or work with documents when offline. Finally, there is a SharePoint Workplace, with which you can synchronize files with the SharePoint Online site.

Shared Lists, Calendars, and Contacts

You can use SharePoint Online to share more than just documents. Using Outlook, you can easily create a contact list and publish it company-wide or only to a specific group of employees. You can share a common calendar, as well. Events posted to the calendar appear on the shared calendar, right next to your personal calendar in Outlook. Everyone in the company can see the same events, but they cannot see your personal appointments. The same goes for many tasks or to-do lists.

In Chapter 11, you'll learn how to add shared calendars and create lists. Custom lists can be imported from Microsoft Excel or created by using SharePoint Online for any purpose you require, such as lists of vendors, inventory, sales and marketing figures, tracking the status of various projects, approval cycles for documents, managing sales cycles, and more.

Custom Applications

If you buy a website from a website service provider, chances are that your site is hosted on a server that delivers your site along with many other customers' sites. This works quite well for most small businesses and is one of the reasons that hosting services is relatively inexpensive.

SharePoint Online operates the same way. It is called a multi-tenant service. Your SharePoint Online sites and content are hosted on a server with other people's sites and contents but are separated by security boundaries enforced by the technology.

SharePoint also has the ability to add custom applications to your site. This presents a bit of problem for multi-tenant services. For example, what if someone uploads an application that requires a great deal of CPU time, perhaps trying to predict the path of a hurricane. Or maybe someone uploads an application that attempts to declare a large amount of memory for its own use. The CPU and memory are shared resources needed by everyone on the server. If one site over consumes resources, everyone else's performance will suffer.

To address this problem, Microsoft created the SharePoint sandbox. Applications that run in the sandbox are assigned a specific set of resources that they cannot exceed. You can host applications written for your business or third-party applications that are written to run in the SharePoint sandbox. In contrast, some other SharePoint applications are not designed for sandbox deployment, so if you are considering a custom application, be sure it is built for sandbox deployment. If your developer has questions about this, send him to *http://msdn.microsoft.com/en-us/library/gg317460.aspx* for details.

Office Web Apps

Office Web Apps (OWA)—not to be confused with Outlook Web App, which is also frequently abbreviated OWA—are browser-based versions of Word, Excel, PowerPoint, and Microsoft OneNote. Using Mozilla Firefox, Microsoft Internet Explorer, Google Chrome, or Apple Safari, you can open documents hosted on SharePoint Online (see Figure 1-4 for an example) and do light editing without having Microsoft Office installed.

FIGURE 1-4 Microsoft Word Web App, as viewed in Internet Explorer 8.

You can also access documents by using a mobile device. This is a useful feature when you are asked to review an important document but have only a mobile phone connection to the Internet. Also, turn this situation around and imagine that you need someone to review a document in a hurry and they are available only by mobile phone. That's what I mean by increasing productivity.

Instant Messaging and Online Meetings with Lync Online

As shown in Figure 1-5, Lync Online provides instant messaging, voice calls, online meetings, and presence for users of Office 365. To use Lync Online, you install the Lync 2010 client. Lync 2010 is provided as a part of the Office 365 for professionals and small businesses subscription at no additional cost and should be installed on every computer you plan to use with Office 365.

FIGURE 1-5 Lync 2010.

Lync 2010 has a small footprint, looks attractive, and is straightforward to use. It's easy to instant message people and to use the other basic features. But just because the user interface looks simple doesn't mean it is a basic application! Lync 2010 is packed with features, including a full web conferencing system with voice and video capabilities. Chapter 12, "Working with Lync Online," focuses on the most useful features and offers some best practices for working with Lync Online.

Instant Messaging

Nothing beats instant messaging (IM) when you need to know something right away. Sometimes called "chat," instant messaging is available via several free services, such as Google Talk, Live Messenger, Skype, and AIM. A quick answer using IM can eliminate several emails, so you can get to the next step in your project without waiting on a reply. Once again, this translates to improved productivity.

Using Lync Online and the Lync 2010 client, you can have a private instant messaging system for your organization. You can look up a user's phone number, see whether she is online, chat, and possibly send files and have a voice conversation. In addition, you can also chat with others outside of your organization.

Presence

One of the easiest to use and most beneficial features of Lync Online is a feature known as presence. Presence uses colored dots to indicate a particular user's status. The colors and their associated statuses are: green, available; orange, busy; red, unavailable; yellow, away; or clear, offline.

Presence is, of course, shown in Lync 2010 (see Figure 1-7), so you can see whether someone is available for a chat. However, you can also view presence in Outlook, Outlook Web App (see Figure 1-6), Office Web App, SharePoint Online, Microsoft Office, and other presence-aware applications.

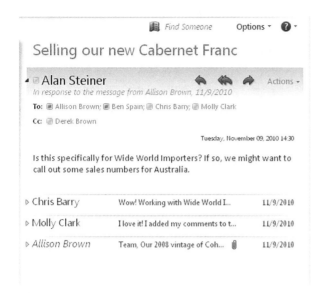

FIGURE 1-6 The presence feature in Outlook Web App (Allison and Ben are online and available).

Presence is incredibly useful when you're typing a message to someone and you notice the green dot next to his name. You can then just double-click on his name and start an instant messaging session.

Online Conferences

Online conferences with Lync Online 2010 can be a lot of fun. Normally, if you are instant messaging with someone and you want to show her a document, picture, or drawing, you'd have to email her the file or place it in an accessible location like SharePoint Online. Because you're both looking at the same document but can't see each other, you have to continually reference landmarks such as "Are you on page 5?" With Lync Online, you can easily just invite your coworkers to an online conference and then share the application in real time. You can all continue to IM while discussing the application, with everyone looking at the same document. You can even give the person you are meeting with control of the application on your desktop!

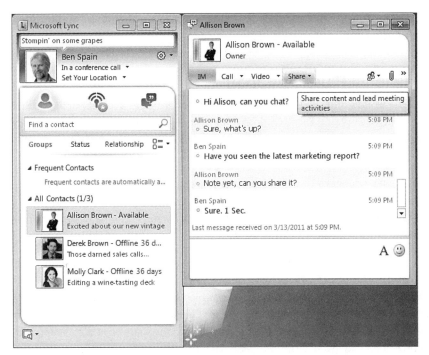

FIGURE 1-7 Presence in Lync 2010 (Ben is showing as busy; Allison is available).

You might recall an earlier reference to enterprise-class applications and how small businesses might shy away from these out of concern that they are simply too complicated or overpowered for a "small" business. Granted, a lot of small businesses are located in a single office or have only one or two employees. In those situations, the use of instant messaging might not be that great a benefit. Even so, many small businesses have a central office with workers or segments of the business out of the office or on the road. Instant messaging and online meetings can be very helpful to these kinds of companies.

Even if you're a one-person business, Lync Online has another important capability that you should know about: Lync Online replaces Microsoft Live Meeting services to provide web conferencing capabilities. It competes with services like GoToMeeting.com, which, as of this writing, is many times more expensive per person than one seat in Office 365.

With Lync Online, you can hold an unlimited number of meetings and invite up to 50 users to any event. Attendees do not need an Office 365 license. They can access the meeting by using Lync Web App or by using an installable Lync client for a richer experience.

In your webinar, you can present to your attendees by using Voice (no conference call bridge is needed when using VoIP) and Video, and you can use a shared whiteboard, take real-time surveys, distribute documents, display series of slides in PowerPoint (annotating the deck in real time) as you lecture and do live demonstrations. Users can ask questions with voice or chat, and you can record the session for distribution (internal library, website, YouTube, and so on). With a service like this, you can really set yourself apart from your competitors by inviting clients and partners into private online meetings to review documents.

Office Professional Plus (Optional)

Microsoft Office is the world's most widely used Office suite and includes a variety of applications, including Word, Access, PowerPoint, Excel, Outlook, OneNote, Publisher, and Visio. You can also obtain SharePoint Designer 2010 for free, and it can be used to customize the appearance of your SharePoint Online team site (not the public website).

Many small businesses would like to use the latest and greatest version of Office, but the price tag can be steep for a small business budget. To make it easier on everyone, Office 365 subscribers can purchase a subscription to Office Professional Plus (*http://office.microsoft.com/en-us/professional-plus/ professional-plus-version-comparison-FX101871482.aspx*).

A subscription has many advantages for small businesses, including reduced initial outlay for upgrading from previous versions of Office; providing a known and predictable cost for your Office software; and ensuring that you have the latest releases, which include new features and capabilities. For example, Office 2010 comes with improved SharePoint Online integrations, a PowerPoint broad-casting service, and the SharePoint Workspace for offline editing for SharePoint files. When sub-scribed, you can download and install Office Professional Plus on up to five computers per user. When installed, Office Professional Plus automatically validates and maintains your licensing (no key codes to keep) with Office 365.

Next Steps

With a better understanding of the advantages and tradeoffs of using Office 365, you're ready to take the next step: choosing a plan. Chapter 2 will help you with that decision; the remainder of the book will provide *immediately actionable* and *practical advice* about how you can set up, deploy, administer, and use Office 365 in your small business.

Choosing an Office 365 Plan

M icrosoft specifically designed the Office 365 for professionals and small businesses and plan, also known as Plan P1, to suit the needs of small businesses and professionals, including the many one-person businesses in the world. For the majority of these businesses, the one-to-50-seat Plan P1 is more than capable and is actually overqualified for the job in many ways. Even so, one size does not fit all, so Microsoft also offers a range of additional Office 365 plans that are aimed at enterprise-level businesses and two plans for kiosk users as well as add-on subscriptions and stand-alone services. Each has specific capabilities, limitations, and requirements.

Which plan or combination of plans is right for your small business? This chapter focuses on answering that question. As you read, consider your own particular circumstances, both now and where you plan to take your business in the future. As described in Chapter 1, "Office 365: A Big Deal for Small Business," and recapped in Table 2-2, Plan P1 is a great choice for most small businesses. But does that include you?

The E Plans

Microsoft classifies its four E plans as the "mid-size and enterprise" plans for Office 365. Although the names of these plans suggest that they are designed for larger businesses, many small businesses find a better fit in an E plan. You can buy an E plan with just one user, and you're not limited on the number of users you can add later. I encourage you to evaluate your choices based on the feature set you require (or foresee requiring as your business grows) and the price you're willing to pay, rather than on Microsoft's named categories.

Table 2-1 outlines the pricing (in US dollars) and basic features of Plans E1 through E4. Each successive plan includes all the features of the lower plans, plus at least one additional service or capability. You can find the Microsoft version of this chart at *http://www.microsoft.com/en-us/office365/enterprise-solutions/enterprise-plans.aspx*. Refer to the Microsoft site for updates because the service prices, features, and plans might change.

TABLE 2-1 Office 365 E Plans

Plan Features	Office 365 Plan (all plans 1–20,000+ users)			
Plan	E1 Current Business Productivity Online Suite (BPOS) customers are migrated to this plan	E2 E1 features plus Office Web Apps with read and write privileges	E3 E2 features plus Office Professional Plus and Office web services for Microsoft SharePoint Online	E4 E3 features plus Lync Server 2010 for on-premises support of Unified Messaging
Price	$8	$14	$20	$22
Voice				●
Office Professional Pro Plus			●	●
Forms, Access/Excel/Visio/Services			●	●
Office Web Apps	Read only	●	●	●
25 GB Mailbox with Exchange Online, including Email, Calendar, Antivirus, Anti-Spam	●	●	●	●
SharePoint Online Collaboration Portal	●	●	●	●
Lync Online Conferencing, IM, and Presence	●	●	●	●

Advantages of All E Plans

Each E plan gives you a little more for your money, but all four share some advantages over the basic Plan P1. The most obvious advantage is that E plans allow your business to grow larger than 50 users. As mentioned in Chapter 1, Plan P1 has a hard stop at 50 users. You cannot call Microsoft and say, "Switch me over to an E plan." It is necessary to download your data, create a new Office 365 account, and reload your data to the new account.

The E plans also allow you to add additional capacity for SharePoint Online storage. Both the P1 and the E plans come with 10 GB of storage plus another 500 MB per user seat you purchase. For example, a 25-seat plan would provide 22.5 GB (10 GB + [500 MB * 25 users]) of file storage on Share-Point Online. If you foresee needing more than this standard allotment, you should consider Plan E, which allows you to purchase additional storage for $0.20 per GB, per month.

An additional major difference is in the area of identity. The E plans allow you to install federation services to allow single sign-on and directory synchronization to replicate users, groups, contacts, and distribution lists into Office 365. Plan P1 does not include federation services.

If you subscribe to the E plans, you can add K plans, which are designed for kiosk users (these are described later in this chapter in the section titled "The K Plans"). Subscribers to Plan P1 cannot add K or E plans to the same company.

Using the E plans, you can configure a rule in Exchange Online to automatically add a footnote to all outgoing mail. Businesses—even small ones—often need to attach a disclaimer or other footnote to every email. In Plan P1, you can add a footnote, but you have to do it by using Signatures in Microsoft Outlook or in OWA, which means that you need to configure it for each user. Because it's a manual process, it can become time-consuming. In addition, you cannot keep users from changing the signature, so you can never be sure that your policy is being enforced. This might not sound like a major issue, but consider the implications for a legal or accounting firm that, for the purposes of legal compliance, must provide a specifically worded privacy warning in every email.

Perhaps the biggest difference between E plans and Plan P1 is the support policy. With Plan P1, you can do research and ask questions in forums (at *http://community.office365.com*), but if you have a technical problem, you cannot call Microsoft. The E1 plan includes 24/7 support by email or phone.

Why no on-demand support for the P1? At $6 a seat, Microsoft simply cannot afford to take calls from small business subscribers. If yours is one of those businesses that won't use a key business service unless support is available when you need it, you need to buy an E plan. Alternately, you can hire a Microsoft Partner to troubleshoot for you and your Plan P1.

Plan E1

Plan E1 is the "basic" E plan, and it replaces Microsoft's Business Productivity Online Suite (BPOS). Customers on BPOS will be migrated to Plan E1 throughout 2012.

Because it is important to start with the right plan, it's important to consider the pricing and the relative merits of Plan E1 and Plan P1, side by side. Plan E1 is $8 per seat, per month, and includes the basic services you'd expect from Office 365: Exchange Online, SharePoint Online, and Lync Online. Why is it $2 per month per user more? Table 2-2 compares key features of Plans P1 and E1.

TABLE 2-2 Comparison of Plan P1 and Plan E1 Features

Features	P1—Small Business	E1—Plan 1
Price	$6 US per seat	$8 US per seat
Number of users	1–50 (no ability to expand)	1–max (tens of thousands)
Number of SharePoint Sites Collections	1	300
Access Services with SharePoint Online	Yes	No
Includes My Site (a SharePoint Online feature)	No	Yes
Office Web Apps	View and edit	View only
Additional SharePoint storage	No ability to expand	Additional storage at $0.20 per GB per month
Document Sharing with external users (extranet)	50 licenses included	50 licenses included
Support	Self and community	Self, community, phone, and online
SSL supported with SharePoint Online	No	Yes
Allows directory synchronization and federation	No	Yes
Can add other plans	No	Yes

> **More Info** For additional comparison details, browse to *http://www.microsoft.com/download/en/details.aspx?id=13602*, download the SharePoint Online for Enterprises Service Description, and then view Table 4.

As you can see, Plan P1 offers capabilities not found in Plan E1, such as the ability to edit using Office Web Apps and the use of Access services with SharePoint Online. You have to evaluate for yourself the importance of these services in your business. For details about editing with Office Web Apps, refer to the "Use Office Web Apps" section in Chapter 11, "Working with SharePoint Online." Having Access Services enabled in Plan P1 opens the door to providing tight integration between Microsoft Access and SharePoint Online.

Although Access services don't steal the spotlight, with them, you can create create integrations and automations that go well beyond what you can otherwise accomplish. In my experience, some well-conceived design and development using Access services can pay big dividends by automating workflows, reporting, and data management in areas that are unique and mission critical to your business. Because these are technical features that often require custom coding, they are not covered in this book. Utilizing these features might require that you work with an IT professional. For more details about publishing Access databases to SharePoint Online, see *http://office.microsoft.com/en-us/sharepoint-online-enterprise-help/build-and-publish-an-access-database-to-sharepoint-HA102435342.aspx*.

Overall, consider Plan P1 if you want phone support, the option to expand SharePoint Online storage, SSL encryption of documents used with SharePoint, or if you expect to have more than 50 users in the foreseeable future. If you want the ability to edit documents by using Office Web Apps but cannot use Plan P1, you must move on to Plan E2. If you require Access services but cannot use P1, you must move on to Plans E3 or E4.

Plan E2

Plan E2 is the next step up from E1. It includes all of the features of Plan E1, plus the ability to view *and edit* Office documents online in a web browser by using Office Web Apps. Using Office Web Apps, you can work with Microsoft Office documents directly in a browser. The ability to read documents using Office Web Apps is built into all Office 365 plans, but the ability to edit them is not. Generally, you would use Office Web Apps only when you don't have a computer available with Microsoft Office installed on it. The question you need to ask is how important is this feature to your business? If you need staff to edit documents from anywhere, anytime, on devices without Microsoft Word installed, you need Plan P1, E2, E3, or E4. If browser-based editing is not essential, Plan E1 is a choice.

In practice, most small businesses have Microsoft Office, and it's equally easy to open a document in a browser or in Word from SharePoint Online. Simply click a Word document stored in SharePoint Online; it will open in Word Web App in your browser, as shown in Figure 2-1. If you have Plan P1, E2, E3, or E4, you can click Edit In Browser. No matter which plan you have, you can click Open In Word and edit your document.

FIGURE 2-1 The Plan P1 Office Word App menu.

Plans E3 and E4

The high-end Plans E3 and E4 include all the capabilities of E2, plus they have Microsoft Access, Business Connectivity Services (BCS), Microsoft InfoPath Forms, Microsoft Excel, and Microsoft Visio Services enabled for SharePoint Online services. For small businesses with only basic needs, these features might be extraneous. For more complex scenarios, this is where the fun is!

Access, InfoPath, Visio, Excel, and BCS services are SharePoint Online features that enable you to do some pretty amazing things. These services bring to life the integration of Microsoft Office and SharePoint Online and provide a high value for streamlining tedious document workflows that are often bottlenecks in many businesses. With this technology, anyone with some imagination and the right expertise can build simple-to-implement but highly productive ways to meet your specific business needs.

For example, with InfoPath Forms Services, you can create forms and post them to SharePoint Online. Office 365 users can then access the page and complete the form without having InfoPath installed. Figure 2-2 shows the Customize Form button, which becomes available when you create a list in SharePoint Online. (See Chapter 11 for details about how to easily create and use a SharePoint list and why you might want to.)

FIGURE 2-2 Add custom forms to SharePoint Online with InfoPath Forms Services in Plans E3 and E4.

Using Access services, you can publish an Access database as a SharePoint list. This gives you the ability to use features of Access to create forms, validate inputs, and perform calculations, and still have the data stored in SharePoint Online, where it is accessible to all.

Add in Excel and BCS services and you have a platform that can be customized to integrate with Office in very precise ways to suit your requirements. The boundaries of what is possible are limited more by your imagination than by the technology.

One key difference between Plans E3 and E4 is that Plan E4 includes a license to deploy Lync Server 2010 on premises. Lync Server 2010 extends the capabilities of Lync Online so that you can make phone calls and provide other services. Installing Lync Server 2010 with Lync Online and integrating with the proper on-premises telephony equipment is a task best suited for specialists in the *Unified Messaging* field, as it is called. As a result, this plan is usually of interest only to larger companies.

For small businesses, the biggest news about Plans E3 and E4 is that Office Professional Plus is included in the price.

Office Professional Plus

Office Professional Plus is a subscription to the best version of Microsoft Office. The subscription is included in the price of Plans E3 and E4 and is available as an add-on for all other subscriptions, including Plan P1. This version has all the bells and whistles, including Microsoft Access and Microsoft Publisher (which is great for newsletters and brochures) and is available only through volume licensing. You can't walk down to your local office supply store and buy this version of Office. The closest commercial equivalent is Microsoft Office Professional, which retails for $499 for one user on two PCs or $349 for one PC on the Microsoft site.

Many small businesses would like to use the latest version of Office, but the up-front costs of buying the software for all the systems can be daunting. Should you buy a version of Microsoft Office outright or pay a monthly subscription fee for Microsoft Office Professional Plus? This question is especially pressing for current users of Microsoft Office 2003 because Office 365 does not work with Office 2003. You must upgrade, but to what?

Many small businesses don't need the full Office suite and find that Office 2010 Home and Business ($279.99 for one user on two PCs or $199.99 for one PC.) is sufficient. However, this version does not include Microsoft Publisher or Microsoft Access and is limited to installation on two PCs per user. Office Professional Plus allows you to install the same software (plus Publisher, Access, SharePoint Workspace, InfoPath, and Lync 2010) on up to five systems per user. To determine whether purchasing or subscribing is the better deal, let's do a little analysis of the costs.

Suppose that you purchase Office Home and Business for $279 per person, plus Plan P1. The cost per user in the first year is $351 ($279 + 12 months* $6). However, in the second year, your cost is only the price of Plan P1. The cost per seat for two years of operation is $17.63 per month, as shown in Figure 2-3.

Number Users	Plan P1 + Office Year 1		Year 2		Total		Monthly Cost Per Seat	
1	$	351.00	$	72.00	$	423.00	$	17.63
2	$	702.00	$	144.00	$	846.00		
3	$	1,053.00	$	216.00	$	1,269.00		
4	$	1,404.00	$	288.00	$	1,692.00		
5	$	1,755.00	$	360.00	$	2,115.00		
6	$	2,106.00	$	432.00	$	2,538.00		
7	$	2,457.00	$	504.00	$	2,961.00		
8	$	2,808.00	$	576.00	$	3,384.00		
9	$	3,159.00	$	648.00	$	3,807.00		
10	$	3,510.00	$	720.00	$	4,230.00		

FIGURE 2-3 Plan P1 with Microsoft 2010 Home and Business—costs after 24 months.

But what if instead you bought an Office Professional Plus subscription for $12 per user per month and added it to your P1 subscription? As you can see in Figure 2-4, the costs are just about the same. Given these assumptions, the Professional Plus subscription is a clear win because you get the latest version of Office for all your users, it allows five PCs per user, and when the next release comes along, you have no additional expense.

Number of Users	P1 Plan with Microsoft Office Professional Plus Year 1		Year 2		Total		Monthly Cost Per Seat	
1	$	216.00	$	216.00	$	432.00	$	18.00
2	$	432.00	$	432.00	$	864.00		
3	$	648.00	$	648.00	$	1,296.00		
4	$	864.00	$	864.00	$	1,728.00		
5	$	1,080.00	$	1,080.00	$	2,160.00		
6	$	1,296.00	$	1,296.00	$	2,592.00		
7	$	1,512.00	$	1,512.00	$	3,024.00		
8	$	1,728.00	$	1,728.00	$	3,456.00		
9	$	1,944.00	$	1,944.00	$	3,888.00		
10	$	2,160.00	$	2,160.00	$	4,320.00		

FIGURE 2-4 Plan P1 with Office Professional Plus subscription.

If you extend this exercise out another year, the cost of buying your own software becomes less expensive because you make use of your investment in Office 2010 for three full years. But when the next version of Office comes along, you will be looking at the same decision again regarding capital outlay. If you have the Pro Plus subscription, you can just automatically upgrade. So when looking at Plan P1, in many cases, the Professional Plus subscription makes good sense.

The only other way to get Professional Plus is with Plans E3 and E4 or through Open Licensing, which requires a minimum of five users. Is it worth upgrading from P1 to E3 simply to gain the Office Pro Plus subscription? Take a look at the analysis in Figure 2-5.

Number of Users	E3 Plan (includes Microsoft Office Pro Plus)			Monthly Cost Per Seat
	Year 1	Year 2	Total	
1	$ 240.00	$ 240.00	$ 480.00	$ 20.00
2	$ 480.00	$ 480.00	$ 960.00	
3	$ 720.00	$ 720.00	$ 1,440.00	
4	$ 960.00	$ 960.00	$ 1,920.00	
5	$ 1,200.00	$ 1,200.00	$ 2,400.00	
6	$ 1,440.00	$ 1,440.00	$ 2,880.00	
7	$ 1,680.00	$ 1,680.00	$ 3,360.00	
8	$ 1,920.00	$ 1,920.00	$ 3,840.00	
9	$ 2,160.00	$ 2,160.00	$ 4,320.00	
10	$ 2,400.00	$ 2,400.00	$ 4,800.00	

FIGURE 2-5 The costs for Plan E3.

In effect, Plan E3 costs only $2 more per user than the P1 with the Microsoft Office Pro Plus subscription added. Considering Plan E3 also comes with support, growth potential, and additional SharePoint Online capabilities, it is worth considering.

In the end, your decision will come down to carefully considering the needs of your business. While you deliberate, keep one more important factor in mind: if your subscription includes rights to Office Professional Plus, you're paying month to month for the right to use Microsoft Office, rather than buying software outright. If you cancel your Office Professional Plus subscription, you lose the rights to use the Microsoft Office software installed from the service. Although there is a generous grace period, you eventually need to uninstall Office and reinstall a different version. If you buy the software, you can use it for as long as you like.

The K Plans

Just to add a bit more to the alphabet soup of Office 365 Plans, Microsoft offers K, or kiosk, plans for specialized scenarios. For example, a factory floor where several people share a single computer would be a good candidate for a K plan. Another example might be a retail store chain where various shifts use a common PC at the counter. In cases like these, each user needs to access email and open Office documents from a web browser but does not have an individual instance of Office to use.

Plan K1 is only $4 per month and includes the following:

- 500 MB mailbox

- Outlook Web Apps to manage email from a browser

- View-only access to SharePoint Online sites

Plan K2 is $8 a month and includes Plan K1, plus read and write capabilities with Office Web Apps.

Note You cannot buy Plan P1 and then add K plans to your order. That is, if you want some users to have a K plan and others to be on a different Office 365 plan and have all those users in the same Office 365 account, you must buy an E plan rather than Plan P1.

Stand-Alone Services

While most small businesses and professionals will likely want to buy a bundled version of Office 365, you can buy just a single service. Briefly, if you want email and nothing else, you can buy the Exchange Online stand-alone plan 1 for $5. Of course, because you can add SharePoint Online and Lync Online for $1 under Plan P1, it's not worth considering for most small businesses. It might seem odd, but the SharePoint Online plan (plan 2 at $10.25), when purchased by itself, costs more than Plan P1 at $6 and has comparable features. See *http://www.microsoft.com/en-us/office365/buy-office-professional-plus.aspx#fbid=278FkQitXzW* for more information about the stand-alone and K services.

Scenarios That Are Not a Good Fit

Office 365 has several services, any one of which could be a big help to a small business. However, a few specific business uses are not good fits for Microsoft Online Services.

Mass Email Companies

If your business needs to send a large number of emails, you should look carefully at the throttles built into Exchange Online to prevent overconsumption of resources. Office 365 has instrumentation that can kick in to constrain mail delivery to maximums of:

- 500 recipients per message.

- 1,500 recipients per user, per day.

- 30 messages per minute, per user.

The key trigger is when a lot of mail comes from or to one account. If any individual email account sends email to more than 1,500 users in one day, it's possible that something is going on besides normal email use. Exchange Online is not designed to be a delivery engine for mass email marketing.

If you have a newsletter or other communication that goes out to many users, no worries. You can create a distribution list in Exchange Online and add the receivers to the list. When you send an email to the distribution list, all users will receive the mail but it counts as only one recipient to Exchange Online.

For more details about limitations built into Exchange Online, see *http://help.outlook.com/ en-us/140/dd630704.aspx?sl=1.*

Businesses with Slow or Unreliable Internet Connections

When you move to cloud services, you should have a reliable and fast Internet connection. If you are in an area where connection is spotty or you have a significant lag in your connection to the Microsoft Online data centers, you might want to acquire a better connection service before moving to the cloud.

> **More Info** You can test your connection speed to Microsoft Online at *http://speedtest. microsoftonline.com.*

Specific Compliance and Security Requirements

One of the facts of life about moving to cloud services is that you have to rely on the provider to take care of security. Microsoft data centers are multimillion dollar operations that are third-party certified to meet or exceed industry standards. You can review the security policies and practices by searching online for "Security Features in Microsoft Online Services."

The point is that, even though Microsoft has specific security practices, you might have legal requirements beyond or different from what Microsoft provides. For example, if you work on content that is confidential and requires encryption when at rest on an email server, Office 365 does not provide that capability. These are technical considerations that are beyond the scope of this book. In any event, if you have compliance or security concerns, consider hiring a Microsoft Partner for assistance.

Significant Investments in Third-Party or Custom Software for On-Premises Servers

There is a very active market for products that enhance the capabilities of Exchange and SharePoint servers. Other than for applications built to run in the new SharePoint Online Sandbox, Microsoft does not allow third-party software to run in its data centers. Consequently, if you have on-premises servers and have invested in custom or third-party software, you cannot integrate it into Microsoft's cloud. This is another situation in which you should hire a Microsoft Partner and consult with the software vendor to assist you. They can evaluate your current software integrations and make suggestions appropriate to your business.

Work with Large or Non-Office Files

Some businesses work with very large files or file types not well-suited to being managed by Office 365. SharePoint Online allows files that are 250 MB each, but at that size you could quickly reach your SharePoint Online capacity. As stated earlier, you cannot buy additional capacity in Plan P1. Even if you could, working with large files in the cloud might or might not be a good idea, depending on your bandwidth, Internet reliability, and how frequently you need to update or modify the files. Firms that create large media files or create large CAD/CAM files as a part of their business would fall into this category. These types of firms will likely find that managing large files over the Internet is too slow.

Another case arises when you plan to use Office 365 to work with files that are not well-suited for SharePoint Online. For example, you cannot store executable files on SharePoint Online, so software developers cannot store their applications or works in progress by using Office 365. Of course, this is related to file management only for which an on-premises server might still be needed, but in this scenario you could easily use Office 365 for mail, messaging, and other purposes. Many small businesses are taking advantage the best of both online and on-premises services.

For More Information

As you consider which Office 365 plan is right for your business, remember that plans and pricing details are subject to change. To find the latest information, browse to *http://office365.com*. For details about each individual service, read the service descriptions. The easiest way to find them is to search for "Office 365 Service Descriptions." If you already know that Plan P1 is right for you, turn to Chapter 3, "Signing Up for the Office 365 P1 Plan."

Signing Up for the Office 365 P1 Plan

Signing up for Microsoft Office 365 is straightforward and intuitive. Simply provide some basic information, such as your name, address, and email, and get started! While the process is easy, you will need to know some important details. This chapter walks you through the process from signing up for a free trial of Office 365 to purchasing your subscription, and points out key issues along the way.

The Free Trial

Your Office 365 subscription can begin with a free 30-day trial. A trial account offers almost all of the same features as a paid account and is delivered identically. The trial account is provisioned with 10 licenses, which you can increase or decrease when you convert the trial to a paid subscription.

Of course, the problem with trials is that they expire. If you find that your trial is ending and you need to download your email and data, no worries. Microsoft offers a generous grace period at the end of the trial, during which you can continue to use your services. While the grace period can change without notice, 30 days has been the standard policy. After this period, you can log on but cannot access the services. In this way, you can manage passwords and users, or you can buy the service, for example, but not send and receive emails. When you log on to the administration portal, Microsoft notifies you about the number of days left in your trial period, as shown in Figure 3-1. In addition, you will receive email alerts sent to the email address you provide during the sign up process.

Note When you sign up for a trial, add a reminder to your calendar one week before the expiration date. This will prompt you to either make the purchase or download your data.

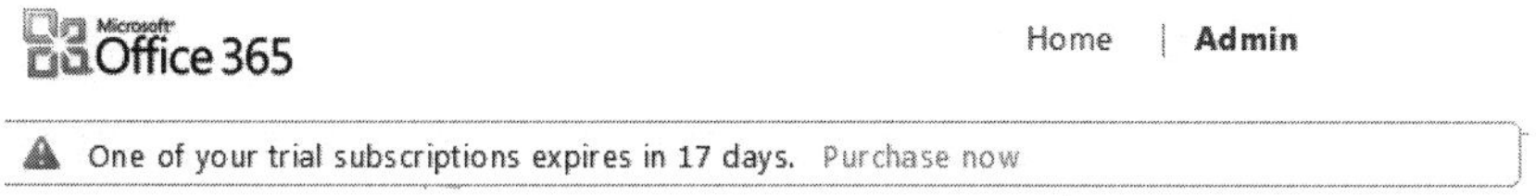

Microsoft Office 365   Home | **Admin**

⚠ One of your trial subscriptions expires in 17 days. Purchase now

FIGURE 3-1 The trial account expiration notice at the top of the Office 365 portal.

Sign Up for the Trial

To sign up for a trial subscription to Office 365, browse to *http://office365.com*. On the main page, click the button to launch the trial sign-up. The specific language and landing page on Office365.com change from time to time. As of this writing, you should see a Free Trial button and a Buy Now button. They initiate, essentially, the same process except that in the Buy Now process you provide a payment method and agree to terms.

Step 1: Complete the Sign Up Page

As shown in Figure 3-2, the first form you encounter is more complex than it appears. Begin by designating your country or region from the drop-down list. Note the warning "Can't Be Changed After Sign-Up" with the hyperlink "Why?" next to it. Click Why? to see the explanation, which is shown in Figure 3-3.

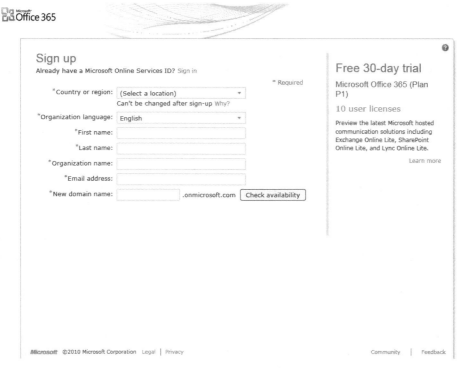

FIGURE 3-2 Office 365 for professionals and small businesses trial sign-up page.

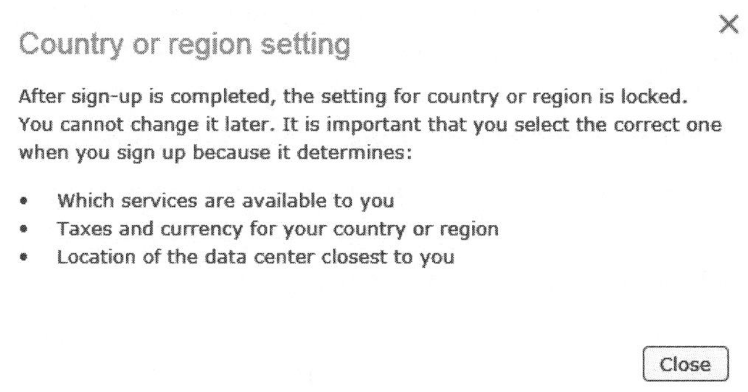

Country or region setting
×

After sign-up is completed, the setting for country or region is locked.
You cannot change it later. It is important that you select the correct one
when you sign up because it determines:

- Which services are available to you
- Taxes and currency for your country or region
- Location of the data center closest to you

Close

FIGURE 3-3 The explanation as to why location cannot be changed.

Country and Organizational Language

When you specify a country or region, Microsoft sets the data center that is best suited to host your data. Microsoft makes this determination for you. You cannot elect to have your account in a data center other than the one Microsoft selects, and once set, it cannot be changed. For most businesses, this is not likely to be an issue. However, if you are in a country that restricts where your business data is stored, be advised that Microsoft does not guarantee that your data will stay in the "home" data center.

Office 365 is designed to work for multinational companies, so it's not a problem to have workers who reside in different countries using the same account. It's up to you to ensure that using the services complies with the rules and regulations of the worker's home country.

The only other impact that might affect you is that the features of Microsoft Lync Online can vary depending on the country you choose. See *http://www.microsoft.com/en-us/office365/licensing-restrictions.aspx* for details about licensing restrictions.

Related to your Country setting, the Organization Language setting determines the default language for the sign-up process and the Office 365 portal and for other websites you will access related to Office 365.

Name and Organization

The First Name, Last Name, and Organization fields are self-explanatory. These are used for billing and identification purposes. If you need to identify yourself to Microsoft to discuss billing or other issues, these are the names it will refer to in validating ownership of the account.

Special Purpose of the Sign-Up Email Address

The email address you provide is far more important than you might think. This address will receive essential notices about billing issues. It is used whenever Microsoft needs to identify you as the owner of this account. If you do not monitor this account, you will not see notifications about billing and service upgrades. Some users have entered an unmonitored account for this address and have had problems with their billing, not realizing it until their account was nearly suspended. If you find yourself in this situation, you do not need to worry that you will be disconnected from your data and your email deleted at the first opportunity. Microsoft makes it easy for you to continue using the services while issues like these are resolved with the 30 day grace period.

The key point is to use an email address that you check regularly.

Your Base Domain and the New Domain Name Setting

The New Domain Name field is vital. Your Office 365 login credentials are unique and can be issued to you immediately. For these reasons, during the sign-up process, Office 365 creates a base domain name for you and also a user account assigned to that base domain name. The entry you make in this field creates a unique, permanent domain name for your Office 365 account. It will look something like the following: yourcompanyname.onmicrosoft.com.

Of course, you probably would prefer to use your own domain name rather than an onmicrosoft.com domain. You can add a custom domain name to the account after you have purchased service. We will cover this process in Chapter 6, "Working with Custom Domains."

What Is a Domain?

A domain is the .com part of an email address or website. For example, if you are sending an email to andyr@fabrikam.com, *fabrikam.com* is the domain. Domains can have other extensions beyond .com, such as .gov, .net, or .org.

The first part of a domain name can be a company name or any phrase you choose, as long as it is still available for registration. You can find many domain name registration services where you can buy a domain name. Typically, a small business will want to purchase a domain name that customers can easily remember and that represents the company or brand. When you own the domain name, you can use it with your website or email services.

Domain names are unique, like phone numbers. When you type in a website address like *www. microsoft.com*, your computer automatically searches out a unique number called an IP address that is associated with the domain. The IP address is, in effect, the Internet's version of a phone number. All of this happens out of sight for the user, using an Internet protocol called DNS (domain name services).

In the New Domain Name field, enter the name you want to use for the part of your email address after the @ symbol. Typically, you'll want to enter a version of your company name in this field. For example, if your company is Fabrikam Books, you would enter FabrikamBooks with no spaces. Domain names cannot have spaces. Do not enter the .com or .net part of the domain name you plan to add later. While entering your company name in this field is common, you're not required to do so. Enter anything you like, but remember that it cannot be changed.

After entering the domain name you want to use, click Check Availability. If your entry is unique, you will see a notification stating that your domain is available. If your domain name is not available, you will see a message that says the domain is not available and to try again. After your domain name is accepted, several new fields will appear, as shown in Figure 3-4.

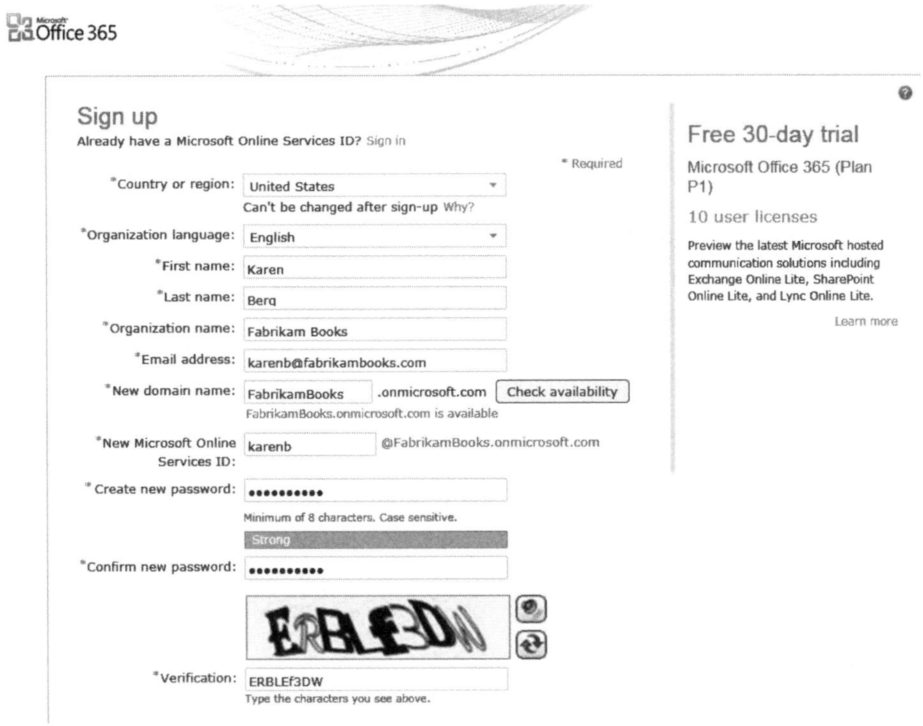

FIGURE 3-4 Completing the Sign Up form.

Your First Account Name

In the New Microsoft Online Services ID field, enter the name of the first account to be created. This account will be a service administrator account. The name you enter will be your logon name and email address for your first Office 365 account. Typically, people enter their first name or first name and last initial.

If you have a small business, employ a consistent pattern for user names. Establish a formula for user name creation with your business, and stick to it. As you add users, you can easily ensure continuity in your address list. This also helps customers identify individual email addresses. If they know Joe's email address at the company is Joe@fabrikam.com, it is likely that the email address for Sanjay, at the same company, is Sanjay@fabrikam.com.

Larger companies often use more than just a first name because it's likely that more than one person will have the same first name.

Create a Password

The Create New Password field requires you to create a password between 8 and 16 characters. The password must contain three of the following: uppercase letters, lowercase letters, numbers, and symbols. The password strength indicator tells you when the password is evaluated as a strong password, which is mandatory. Do not forget this password.

> **Important** Do not forget your initial password; it cannot be recovered. You will have to contact Microsoft to have your password reset if you find yourself unable to log on.

Prove You Are Not a Machine

In the Verification field, enter the characters you see in the graphic above the box. This technique is used to ensure that a human being is completing the form, not an automated system. If you cannot read the characters in the graphic, click the arrow next to the graphic to refresh the characters. If visually impaired, you can click the speaker button and then complete an audio challenge.

Accept the Terms

Next you will be asked if you want to receive offers from Microsoft Partners. By doing so, you can receive useful offers from Office 365 partners. Microsoft has one of the most sophisticated partner networks in the world. Partners in your area can assist you with advanced Office 365 capabilities, such as automating Microsoft Office to work in specialized ways with Microsoft SharePoint Online or providing training for your staff.

Before clicking the "I Accept And Continue" button, take a moment to review the Microsoft Online Services Agreement and Privacy Notice.

Step 2: Sign In

Next, you will see the Signing In screen, as shown in Figure 3-5. While the account is being provisioned, the Continue button remains gray.

FIGURE 3-5 Waiting while the account is provisioned.

When the button becomes enabled, click Continue to log on to Office 365.

Step 3: Ensure Administrator Password Recovery

When you log on to the Office 365 portal for the first time, you are asked to add additional information for your administrator account, as shown in Figure 3-6.

This is a very important step that you should not skip. If you provide a mobile phone number capable of receiving text messages and an alternate email address, you can use the self-service password reset feature built in to Office 365. This feature is available to administrators only, so by providing this information you can ensure that you always have access.

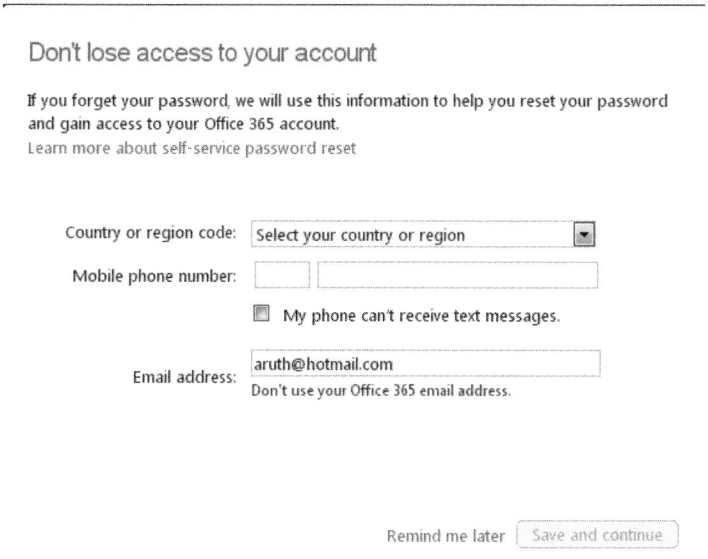

Don't lose access to your account

If you forget your password, we will use this information to help you reset your password and gain access to your Office 365 account.
Learn more about self-service password reset

Country or region code: | Select your country or region | ▾ |

Mobile phone number: [   ] [   ]

☐ My phone can't receive text messages.

Email address: | aruth@hotmail.com |
Don't use your Office 365 email address.

Remind me later   [Save and continue]

FIGURE 3-6 Information needed for password recovery.

Step 4: Use Office 365!

The next page, as shown in Figure 3-7, is the Admin landing page.

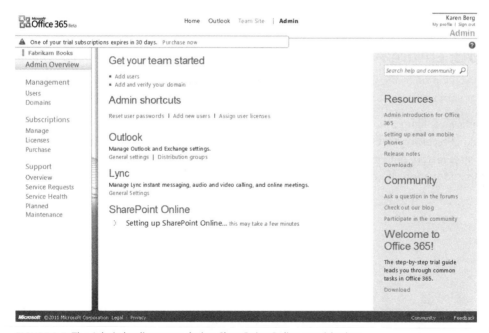

FIGURE 3-7 The Admin landing page during SharePoint Online provisioning.

Notice that Admin is in bold at the top to indicate that you're on the Admin page. On this page, you manage Office 365, including adding users, domains, and configuring your services.

When you first arrive, your account might still be in the provisioning stage. In Figure 3-7, you can see that SharePoint Online is still being set up. This is common when you first log on, but it should resolve in a few minutes.

When the account is completely provisioned, the SharePoint Online section changes to match Figure 3-8.

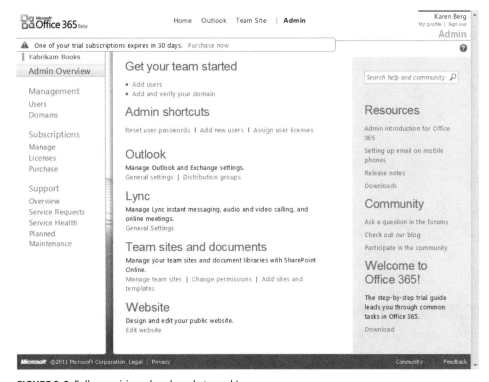

FIGURE 3-8 Fully provisioned and ready to rock!

After a service is provisioned, you can start using it immediately. Just click the Outlook link at the top of the page to start sending and receiving mail from your provisioned email address, using the web-based Microsoft Outlook Web App.

Purchase the Service

You might opt to purchase Office 365 for professionals and small businesses rather than start with a trial. You can also elect to pay for the services at any time during the trial or during the grace period after the trial.

You have more than one entry point into the purchasing process. At the top of the screen shown in Figure 3-8, at the end of the expiration alert message, you can select Purchase Now. This takes you to the screen shown in Figure 3-9.

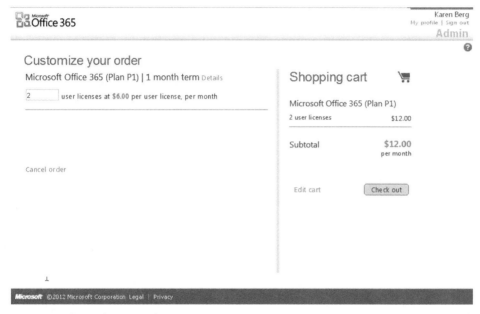

FIGURE 3-9 Customize your order.

Alternatively (also shown in Figure 3-8), if you click Purchase, in the left column under Subscriptions, you will see the screen shown in Figure 3-10.

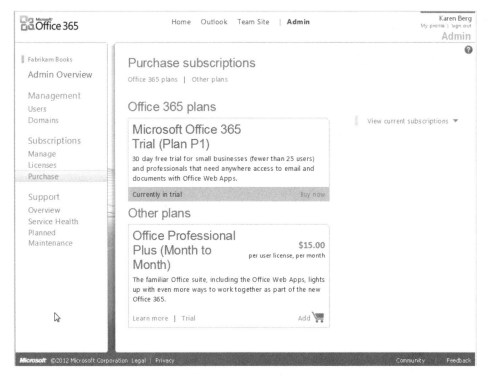

FIGURE 3-10 The Purchase Subscriptions page.

The Purchase Subscriptions page includes Microsoft Office 365 Plan P1 and Office Professional Plus. You might find it in your best interest to purchase Microsoft Office on a subscription basis, rather than paying for the costs out of pocket at all once. My personal preference is to keep up with the latest software for products that I use extensively, and Microsoft Office is certainly in that category.

Note Office Professional Plus is entirely optional. You can use Office 2007 or simply access the services by using your browser. For more on the pros and cons of subscribing to Office Professional Plus, see Chapter 2, "Choosing an Office 365 Plan."

Whichever screen you use, the remainder of the process is a standard shopping cart experience: you provide your billing address, review the service agreements, payment information, and confirm your order. When complete, you will see your default Office 365 Administrator page. The only difference is that now you will not see a warning showing the number of days until your trial expires at the top of the screen. In addition, after the purchase, you can provision a custom domain.

Next Steps

Chapter 4, "The Dual Purpose Office 365 Portal," walks you through how to use the Office 365 Portal to access and manage your services. This sets the stage for validating a custom domain, after which you can create users and deploy desktops. However, at this point, you should not set up your desktops for Office 365 until you have validated a custom domain. Even so, your services are now fully functional, even if not personalized, and you should feel free to explore.

CHAPTER 4

The Dual Purpose Office 365 Portal

Your landing zone upon arrival, the Microsoft Office 365 portal has two main functions: it serves as a home page for normal users, and as an administration portal for administrators. The portal even changes its appearance depending on the role of the person who signs in and the amount of time his account has existed.

When users log on, they see the home page of the portal. Here, they can change their passwords; quickly access Microsoft Outlook Web App, Microsoft SharePoint Online, and other web-based services; download required software to set up their systems; and access online resources about Office 365.

When you log on to Office 365 as an administrator, you see the Admin page of the portal. The Admin page provides configuration settings for all the services, including links to the service administration portals themselves. For example, Microsoft Exchange Online and SharePoint Online have stand-alone administration capabilities that are connected to but separate from the Office 365 administration portal. Lync Online configuration is limited to allowing external sharing, managing conference call service providers, and allowing users to transfer files and use voice and video. Finally, administrators can purchase new seats and manage billing through the portal.

In day-to-day operation, you will access the portal primarily to manage users and reset passwords. When traveling or using a computer other than your own, the portal provides a convenient way to find links for OWA and SharePoint Online.

This chapter will walk you through the use of the portal both for administrators and for end users. As the service administrator, you need to know how to navigate the various options and be aware of some not-so-obvious configuration details.

The Main Menu

The main navigation menu (see Figure 4-1) resides at the top of both versions of the portal (*https:// portal.microsoftonline.com*). From this menu, you can navigate to the various services at any time. The users see Home, Outlook, and Team Site options, whereas administrators see an additional Admin option, as well. The Home page is the landing page where users can find links and resources related to Office 365. The Outlook link takes you to Outlook Web App, not to Outlook installed on your computer. You can click Team Site to reach SharePoint Online. Administrators can reach their dedicated page by clicking Admin.

Home   Outlook   Team Site | Admin

FIGURE 4-1 Office 365 P1 portal top-level menu.

The Home Page

When users log on to the portal, they see the Home page, as shown in Figure 4-2. Clicking the Home link in the main menu at the top of the screen will also bring you here.

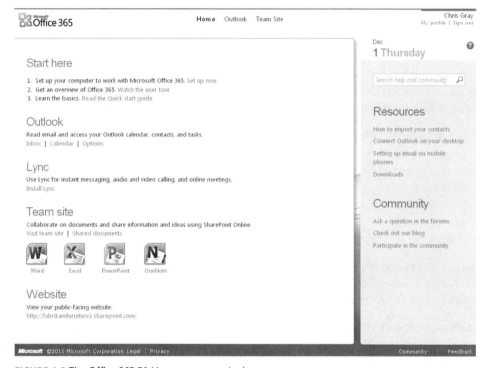

FIGURE 4-2 The Office 365 P1 Home page: user's view.

From the Home page, users can launch or locate the following:

- Outlook Web App

- The Team site

- Your website

- Office Web Apps

- Online help, resources, and community links

- The user's Office 365 profile page, which includes a password reset function

- Software downloads for setting up their computers for Office 365

If you are logged on as an administrator, the page looks slightly different from that of a normal user. As you can see in Figure 4-3, the Start Here tasks are different, and Admin appears in the main menu.

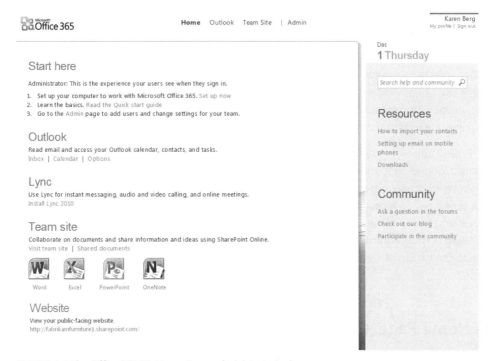

FIGURE 4-3 The Office 365 P1 Home Page: administrator's view.

The Home Page: First Use

The portal is the first place users go upon receiving a new account. As administrator, you should direct a new user to *http://portal.microsoftonline.com* so that he can log on with his new user name and the temporary password provided when you created his account. The user must change his temporary password to a new unique password for personal use before he can use the services. Office 365 then logs him on to the portal and greets him with the normal user view. Creating and managing users is covered in Chapter 5, "Working with User Accounts." The Start Here workflow instructs the user to set up his computer. Clicking Set Up Now in Step 1 allows him to download and install the Office 365 Setup client and Lync 2010. By the way, resist the temptation to set up your desktop until you've read Chapter 6, "Working with Custom Domains," and Chapter 7, "Desktop Setup and Migration," which discuss working with custom domains and preparing your desktop.

After initial setup is complete, users typically do not return to this portal frequently. Email is usually accessed from Outlook, which logs on to Office 365 automatically. The Lync 2010 client will also log on to Lync Online automatically when started. As a user, if you set your SharePoint Team Site in a favorite's link in your browser, you can browse directly to SharePoint Online, as well. You might be prompted to authenticate for SharePoint Online, depending on a number of factors, such as how long it has been since you last logged on with a web browser to Office 365 or SharePoint Online. In addition, when you open a Microsoft Office document that is hosted on SharePoint Online, you do not need to be logged on to the Office 365 Portal. However, you might be prompted by SharePoint Online to authenticate.

Authentication and Office 365

When you start Outlook, it automatically logs on to Exchange Online. Similarly, the Lync 2010 client logs you on to Lync Online. If you then browse to SharePoint Online, you might be asked to authenticate. Because Outlook and Lync already logged you on, why are you being asked to authenticate to SharePoint Online?

When Outlook logs you on to Exchange Online and Lync 2010 logs you on to Lync Online, you are logged on to those services specifically, rather than Office 365, generally. As a result, when your browser opens SharePoint Online, SharePoint Online might ask to see whether you are authorized to access the requested resource, even though you are already logged on to other Office 365 services. SharePoint Online, Exchange Online, and Lync Online are essentially different services connected by a common infrastructure. Despite this, in practice you'll encounter much less authentication than you might expect.

The Home Page: On the Road

The portal is also quite handy when traveling. If your laptop isn't available, you can log on to the portal to start Outlook Web Access or SharePoint Online on a trusted PC. As always, be careful about entering logon credentials on public systems. Using the web browser, you can instant message your colleagues within OWA, review documents hosted on SharePoint Online directly in the browser, send email, create meetings, view other people's calendars, and more. You'd be surprised how much you and your team members can do from just a web browser on any PC when using Office 365.

The Office 365 Portal Profile

Another feature of the portal is the ability to configure an Office 365 profile. This profile is more important than you might initially think because it provides a way for each user to personalize the services. For example, you can add a photo to the portal profile, and it will appear in Lync 2010! There are some other surprises, as well. When you click Profile in the upper-right corner of the screen, you'll see the My Profile page shown in Figure 4-4.

FIGURE 4-4 The Office 365 portal My Profile page.

Let's take a look at the My Profile page from the top down.

Change Password

Next to the My Profile heading is a link to change your password. This important link provides one of the few ways for users to initiate a password change. Users can also change their Office 365 password in Outlook Web App. Keep in mind that to change your password with this method, you must know your current password. Use this feature if you have reason to believe your password has been compromised.

Change Photo

The blue picture icon is a placeholder for a photo of the user. Office 365 makes good use of this photo, so you or your coworkers can add a picture to each profile as part of the user setup. Both the Lync Server 2010 client and SharePoint Online use the photo, and Microsoft has plans to integrate this picture into Exchange Online, as well. In a small business, most of the workers know each other, but a photo can be quite helpful for new hires, and it adds an appealing personal touch to the services (see Figure 4-5).

To add a picture, just click the photo icon and browse to a .jpg, .gif, .bmp, or .png file that is less than 100 KB in size. Click Upload, and then click Save.

Home   Outlook   Team Site

My profile   Change password

Information

First name:	Chris
Last name:	Gray
Country or region:	United States
Address:	111 W Main
City:	Redmond
State:	WA
ZIP code:	98008
Phone number:	425-555-1212
Mobile phone:	214-555-1212
Email address:	Chrisg@fabrikamfurn.net

Change photo

FIGURE 4-5 A profile page with photo.

Information, Display Language, and Contact Preferences

The Information details are display only. The user's office number, address, phone, email, and fax number are shown as they were entered when the user account was created. In this example, if a colleague looks up Chris Gray's contact information in Outlook, Outlook Web App, or Lync Online 2010, she will find the same information listed here. This makes it easy to find someone's office number or mobile phone number when needed.

Use the Display Language drop-down menu to set the language you prefer for the Office 365 portal.

The Contact Preferences settings determine how and if Microsoft can contact you about the services and other offerings.

The Office 365 Admin Portal

When you or another user designated as an administrator log on to the Office 365 portal, you can view the Admin version of the portal, shown in Figure 4-6.

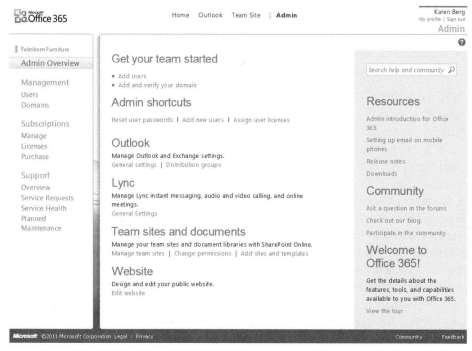

FIGURE 4-6 The Office 365 Plan P1 Admin Overview page.

Don't worry if your page looks different from Figure 4-6; Microsoft changes the websites from time to time. In addition, specific content such as the "Welcome to Office 365" section on the lower right and the "Get your team started" section will change after you've had the services for a while. (See the upcoming sidebar for more information.)

From the Admin page, you can add users, add a custom domain, manage each service, configure your public website, access help, manage licenses, and more.

Microsoft designed the Office 365 small business offering for businesses that do not have IT administrators on staff. For the most part, you do not need much technical expertise to configure and use Office 365. Although each of the services has many features, not all of them are applicable to your business. By the end of this book, you will be comfortable configuring and managing the most popular and useful features of Office 365 for small businesses.

The best way to become familiar with the admin controls is to tour the portal's important links. Start in the left column titled Admin Overview, which has three main sections: Management, Subscriptions, and Support.

Online Services Are Frequently Updated

Within the halls of Microsoft, the rhythm of releasing software and using service packs to provide updates and new features has been part of the culture for decades. This kind of a process works well for large-scale operations like Microsoft's, where each release has to be extensively tested, inspected by security experts, translated into many languages, packaged by installers, and distributed worldwide in a variety of formats. However, it makes it difficult for a specific team to release new features or updates to a product, because any individual update, generally, has to be folded into the release cycle of service packs.

With the advent of Online Services, this old model is completely undone. Now, Microsoft can release updates in a compressed time frame. With the Business Productivity Online Suite (BPOS), the predecessor to Office 365, updates were routinely posted almost on a monthly basis. By the time BPOS was replaced with Office 365, dozens of significant changes had been added to the BPOS service without price increases, and there were no service packs to install. Similarly, Microsoft has continually released new features and capabilities over the life of Office 365. By the time this book is published, Office 365 will have several features that were not available when it first released. For example, Microsoft might change the appearance of specific screens and add new features. During the process of collaborating with Microsoft on this book, the company even made an internal decision to accelerate the release of planned features. This brings more value to customers for the same price and shows that Microsoft is committed to improving its online services more frequently than you might expect. The best place to keep up with the changes is at *http://community.office365.com/en-us/w/office_365_service_updates/ service-updates-for-office-365-for-professionals-and-small-businesses.aspx.*

Management

The Management section covers two important topics: Users and Domains.

When you click the Users link, you go to the page where you can add and manage users, as shown in Figure 4-7.

By adding a user, you give him the authority to log on to the portal. In the process, you can assign him a service license. This license is what you pay for with your service subscription, and assigning the license allows the user to access the services. Note that you can add users from other links in the portal, including the Add Users link under Get Your Team Started and the Add New Users link under Admin Shortcuts. (See Figure 4-6.)

Clicking the Domains link takes you to Domains page (see Figure 4-8) on which you can add your company's domain to Office 365 so that you can use an email address like contoso.com, rather than contoso.onmicrosoft.com.

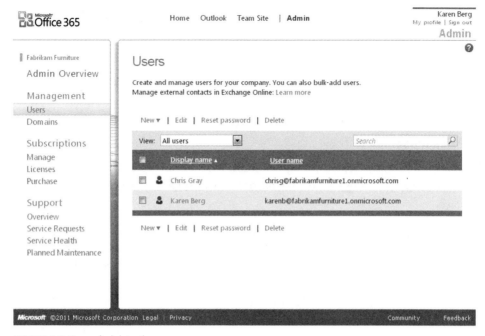

FIGURE 4-7 User administration.

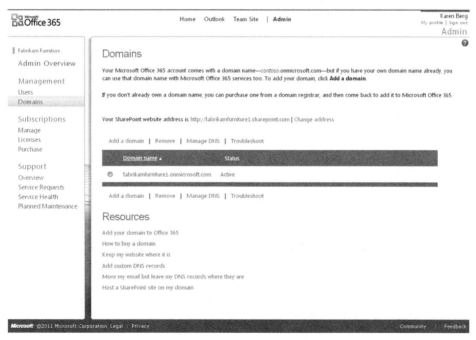

FIGURE 4-8 The Domains page.

Adding a domain to Office 365 is probably the most technically challenging part of configuring your service because it involves DNS (domain name services) settings. DNS controls traffic on the Internet, and making changes to these settings will impact where your Web and email traffic are sent. As a result, it's important to work with some care. To prepare for this, ensure that you know who your DNS provider is and that you can log on to their management console. Chapter 6 goes into detail about working with custom domains.

Subscriptions

This section has three major topics: Manage, Licenses, and Purchase. You will be using each of these sections to add new users, assign licensing if needed, or convert a trial to a paid account. Take a look.

Manage

Clicking the Manage link takes you to a page titled Billing and Subscription Management (Figure 4-9). Here you can see your subscriptions, the number of users, costs, and expiration or renewal dates.

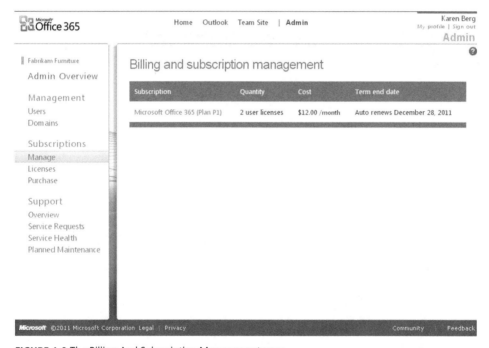

FIGURE 4-9 The Billing And Subscription Management page.

You will always have at least one entry on this page: your subscription to Office 365. If you purchased Office Pro Plus with your service, that will also be listed.

When you click on a subscription, you see Subscription details, such as for Plan P1 shown in Figure 4-10. Note that the screens are different if you are using a trial account or a paid account.

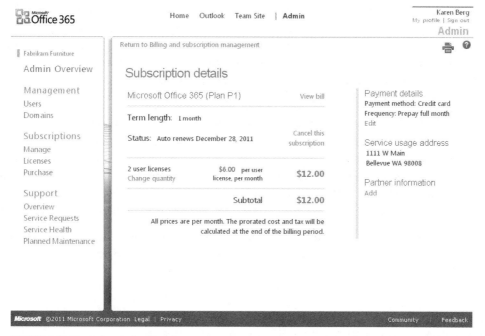

FIGURE 4-10 The Subscription Details page.

Use the Subscription Details page to:

- View your bill.

- Cancel your subscription.

- Change credit cards or billing method.

- Add a Microsoft Partner to your account.

If you click the Add link under the Partner Information heading to the right, you can associate your account with a Microsoft Partner (Figure 4-11).

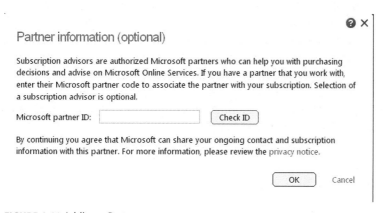

FIGURE 4-11 Adding a Partner.

Why would you want to associate your account with a Microsoft Partner? Microsoft Partners are actively selling Office 365 with ongoing support, training, management, customizations, and other services for their customers. If you have been working with a Microsoft Partner in relationship with Office 365 but no Partner ID is present, ask the Partner for their Microsoft Partner ID, and then add them here. You can find an Office 365 Partner by using *http://pinpoint.microsoft.com*.

Associating your account with a Partner is completely optional. Microsoft expects that most Plan P1 accounts will not be associated with Partners because the technical needs of very small businesses are generally far less complex than businesses of 100 or more employees. Although most small businesses have simple IT requirements, many have complex needs that include custom coding, specialized network devices, security considerations, and more. If this sounds like your company, you might want to engage the services of Microsoft Partner specializing in Office 365. Adding a Partner ID to your account, in and of itself, does not obligate a Partner to provide support or consulting services.

Assigning a Partner to your account has no impact on your costs and does not change the services you receive. You can find an Office 365 Partner by going to *http://pinpoint.microsoft.com*.

Licenses

The Licenses page shows the number of licenses you have in your subscription and how many are assigned. There are no adjustable entries. This page is strictly informational.

Purchase

The Purchase Subscriptions page is where you can convert a trial account to a paid account by using the process described in Chapter 3, "Signing Up for the Office 365 P1 Plan." The Purchase Subscriptions page also lets you add new users and purchase Office Professional Plus.

Support

As noted, the P1 subscription does not come with phone or ticketed support using the administration portal. Even so, you'll find some important links on the Support Overview page, as shown in Figure 4-12.

Although Microsoft does not allow Plan P1 subscribers to directly contact technical support, they do have paid staff who answer support and subscription-billing questions from the community forums. You can access the community site by clicking Get Support From The Microsoft Online Community or browsing to *http://community.office365.com*. In addition, the forums are monitored by a quite a few other individuals in Microsoft, including program managers for the various services, Microsoft consulting staff, MVPs, and other experts. The Help And Community search box is a link to the community forums. You can often find out information about Office 365 in the forums before it finds its way into online help or other official documentation.

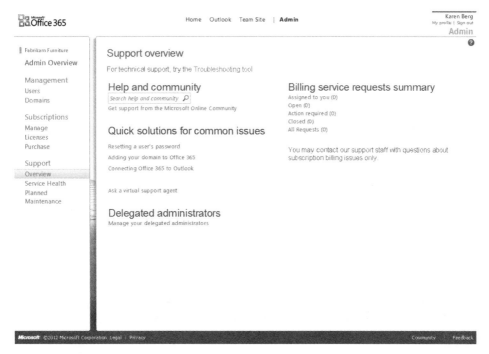

FIGURE 4-12 The Support Overview page.

In practice, some issues can be handled by Microsoft only, such as if you lock out your only administrator account and cannot log on. Microsoft has a self-service password reset ability for administrators, but you have to have a valid alternate email address and mobile phone number with text messaging enabled for this to work. If you don't have an alternate, your only choice is to contact support. Microsoft support will help in these and other circumstances for which support services are required.

Another alternative is the Quick Solutions section, which contains links to a few "how-to" articles that address the most common calls to technical support. One of the more interesting links is the Virtual Agent For Microsoft Office 365; click it to reach the page shown in Figure 4-13.

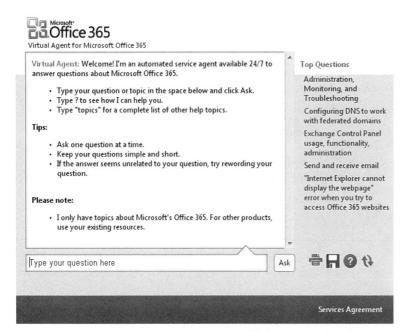

FIGURE 4-13 Virtual Agent for Office 365.

The Virtual Agent is an automated query response system. You ask a question, and it returns an answer with links to selected topics, based on your query. Be advised, however, that the answers provided by the agent are not scoped to issues related specifically to the Plan P1 service. For example, if you ask "How do I create a site in SharePoint Online?", you will get multiple topics in the response, including "Creating and Managing Site Collections," despite the fact that you cannot create site collections with Plan P1. Use the Virtual Agent, but with some awareness that it is a limited tool.

Note One useful feature of the Virtual Agent is that it can provide phone numbers for Microsoft Online Support in any country. Just ask!

The Troubleshooting Tool

Unlike the Virtual Agent, Microsoft's Troubleshooting tool (see Figure 4-14) does differentiate between Plan P1 and the E plans. You are presented with a series of choices on pages 1 through 5, resulting in a list of links and resources related to your problem. You can find this tool at *http://community.office365.com/en-us/p/troubleshooting.aspx*.

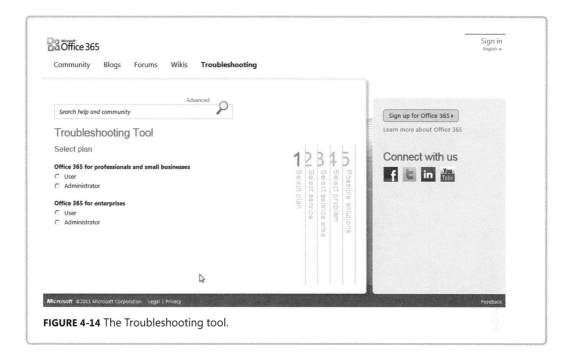

FIGURE 4-14 The Troubleshooting tool.

If you think you'll need more help than the forums and Virtual Agent can provide, another option is connecting with a good Office 365 Partner. If your service is managed by a Microsoft Partner, you can use the Manage Your Delegated Administrators link to authorize the partner as a *delegated administrator*, which allows the partner to log on to your Office 365 account as an administrator. In this way, the partner can remotely add users, reset passwords, configure your SharePoint Online sites, and manage your email settings. Not all partners offer these services. See *http://pinpoint.microsoft.com* to locate a partner in your region.

Finally, the Billing Service Requests Summary section of the Overview page details any open service requests related to billing. As it turns out, you can also actually file a service request by using the Service Requests option on the left of the screen, but it must be related to billing.

Service Requests

Click the Service Request link under Support to ask billing-related questions of the support staff. When you create a service request, the tracking information shown under Billing Service Requests Summary is updated.

When Microsoft replies to your request, the Action Required counter goes up. In this way, you can quickly see whether any open issues need your attention.

Service Health

Click the Service Health link under Support to access the Service Health page (see Figure 4-15). Service Health is one of the most important screens in the Admin portal. Here, you can monitor current and past service issues with Office 365. If you are experiencing problems, you should go here to see whether there is an issue with Office 365 itself.

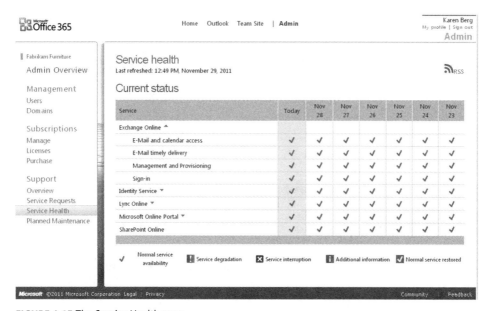

FIGURE 4-15 The Service Health page.

Notice the blue triangle next to most of the services. Click a downward-pointing triangle to expand a listing of details about the related service. In Figure 4-15, the Exchange Online section is expanded to show additional information; you can click its upward pointing triangle to close the detailed list.

If an issue is listed, you can click the icon to reveal further details. Microsoft attempts to report any issues to this page as soon as possible.

In the upper-right corner is an RSS icon. Click this link to subscribe to the service health RSS feed. Using RSS, you can receive notifications of service-related issues by using Outlook, a web browser, or other RSS reader.

Planned Maintenance

Infrequently, service availability is impacted by service upgrades. Click the Planned Maintenance link under Support to access a list of upcoming and historical maintenance events. The Microsoft service license agreement promises a 99.9 percent uptime guarantee, but that does not include scheduled downtime, which Microsoft defines as follows:

...those times when we publish or notify you of periods of Downtime related to network, hardware, or Service maintenance or upgrades at least five (5) days prior to the commencement of such Downtime.[1]

The planned maintenance list constitutes notification for these purposes. You should check this list if you have a problem with the services. In addition, if you are planning on an important webcast or Lync Online session, check to see whether any updates to Lync Online are planned during your event.

Service Administration

In addition to managing your Office 365 environment, such as users and domains, you can manage the services themselves from the main Admin Overview page, as shown earlier in Figure 4-6.

The Admin Overview section contains quick launch links to some common administrative tasks. These include resetting user passwords, adding new users, and assigning user licenses. You'll learn more about these topics in Chapter 5.

The Exchange Online page contains two links: General Settings and Distribution Groups (see Figure 4-16).

Outlook

Manage Outlook and Exchange settings.
General settings | Distribution groups

FIGURE 4-16 Outlook (Exchange Online) administration.

Clicking either link takes you to the page shown in Figure 4-17.

FIGURE 4-17 Outlook General Setting (Exchange Online Adminstration).

---

[1] From the document titled Service Level Agreements for Microsoft Online Services located at *http://www.microsoft volumelicensing.com/DocumentSearch.aspx?Mode=3&DocumentTypeId=37.*

The page looks different from the Office 356 administration portal because you've been switched into the administrator section of Outlook Web App, where you can also manage Exchange Online. The Office 365 administration portal simply provides a link to this location. In other words, to manage your mail settings, you can log on to OWA or to the Office 365 Portal, which will take you to OWA.

Because service administration for mail services happens in OWA and not the Office 365 portal, Exchange Online administration is covered in Chapter 8, "Working with Outlook Web Access." For now, just keep a couple of details in mind about these pages. Not all the features you see are available in Plan P1. For example, Plan P1 does support user roles. Additionally, advanced features are available to you, such as journaling and audit reports, but these are generally beyond the scope of small businesses. Chapter 8 will review the key features you need to know about as well as provide some tips along the way.

> **Note** In Figure 4-17, notice that the mailbox page allows you to add a new mailbox. This is the same as adding a user in Office 365. Here is one area where the Outlook administration page has a feature that is also in the Office 365 portal. I would suggest that you do not use the New mailbox feature to create a mailbox; instead, add it in the Office 365 portal as discussed in Chapter 6.

Lync

When you click the General Settings link under Lync, you are taken to the Lync Online control panel. Unlike SharePoint Online and Exchange Online, Lync Online is administered in the Office 365 portal. The Lync Online control panel has only a few configurable settings. Most options that can be enabled are enabled by default. Lync Online administration is covered in Chapter 12, "Working With Lync Online."

Team Sites and Documents

Under the Team Sites and Documents heading, you can access your Team Site. The Team Site is a pre-built private website on which you and other team members can post notes and documents. The Team Site is very simple to use and works without additional configuration. You can, of course, add functionality, change the layout, theme, and add customizations. Chapter 11, "Working with SharePoint Online," reviews some very useful features of SharePoint Online that you can implement right away.

> **Note** Click Team Site and then add the URL to your favorites. You can then go directly to the SharePoint site without having to log on to the Office 365 Portal.

Website

The final administrative section to discuss is simply called Website. This refers to the public website that is part of Plan P1. The public website capabilities are good for sites that provide information about the business, such as location, contact information, and other static details. Microsoft calls the public website a "basic" website, and you should take that description to heart. For instructions on configuring a public website, see Chapter 11.

Put the Portal to Work

You've seen how the Office 365 portal is used by administrators to configure the services, assist with troubleshooting, and manage licensing. Also, you've seen how users can launch OWA and SharePoint Online, update their profiles, and access downloads for setting up their desktops. In the next chapter, you'll see how to create users who can access the portal and use the services.

CHAPTER 5

Working with User Accounts

Most people don't give user management much thought, but as the Microsoft Office 365 service manager, you have to. User management goes well beyond just enabling new user accounts for coworkers to access the services. In setting up Office 365, you must be strategic about when you create user accounts.

For example, if you validate your domain and direct mail to Office 365 before users are created, no mailboxes are available to receive mail. Or what if someone quits? How do you disable his logon without deleting his mail? If you delete him as a user, his mail is gone! What happens when someone can't log on? The most common user management issue is the all-too-familiar phone call to reset a password. Microsoft has added a password reset function for administrators so that they can reset their password without a service call, but this feature is not available to end users, so you will get their calls. This chapter will help you work through these and other important details of adding and managing users.

Password Best Practices

Throughout this chapter, you will see a process that generates a temporary password for users when new accounts or new passwords are created. Be aware that this temporary password cannot be used to log on to Microsoft Outlook, Outlook Web App, Microsoft Lync 2010, or Microsoft SharePoint Online. The only place you can use the temporary password is the Office 365 portal.

When a user logs in to the portal using the temporary password, she is immediately asked to change the temporary password on the account to a new, personal one that she creates. This ensures that no one but the user knows the password. If the user forgets her password, you must reset it for her, which generates a new temporary password. When this occurs, she cannot log on to the services until she goes to the Office 365 portal, enters the temporary password, and creates a new one.

As the service administrator, when you create accounts, you must communicate the temporary password to users *and* tell them to go to *http://portal.onmicrosoft.com* to create a new password. There they must enter their new password into Outlook and Lync 2010, when prompted.

Finally, remember that passwords do not expire for users who are not administrators. However, administrators (that means you) have passwords that expire every 90 days. As a best practice, put a calendar entry in Outlook to change your password in advance of that date.

Add a New User

To add a user, log on to the Office 365 portal, using administrator credentials to reach the Admin page, which is shown in Figure 5-1.

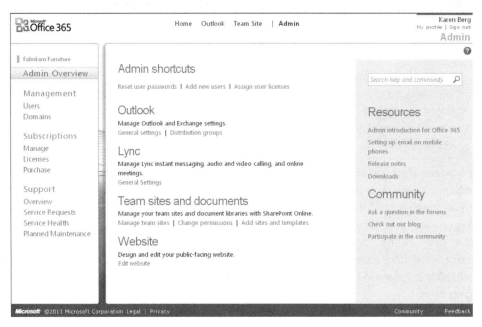

FIGURE 5-1 The Admin page.

The Admin page contains two links that look useful: Users in the left column under Management, and Add New Users listed under Admin shortcuts. Which of these should you use? Clicking the Add New Users link takes you directly to the Add Users page, bypassing the User Management page. After you are familiar with the administrator portal, it's fine to use the shortcut, but for now, click Users to get started.

Before reaching the Users page, some readers will see the Just Checking screen shown in Figure 5-2. This is intended to help you create accounts that have custom domain names rather than onmicrosoft. com names. If you select I Want These Accounts To Have Email Addresses Using A Domain I Already Own, Office 365 takes you out of the task of creating users and into the task of domain validation, which is covered in Chapter 6, "Working with Custom Domains." I suggest that you create users before adding a custom domain because it can take some time and might require you to gather additional information before you can complete the process. You can easily change your users to use email addresses from your custom domain later. For now, if you see the Just Checking screen, choose the onmicrosoft.com addresses option, and then click Next to get on with creating user accounts.

If you do not have a custom domain, clicking Users on the Admin page takes you straight to the Users page shown in Figure 5-3. On the Users page, you can add, edit, and delete users, as well as reset passwords. You can also select multiple users and change them at the same time. Click New, and then click New User to reach the Details page. (You'll learn about the Bulk Add Users option shortly.)

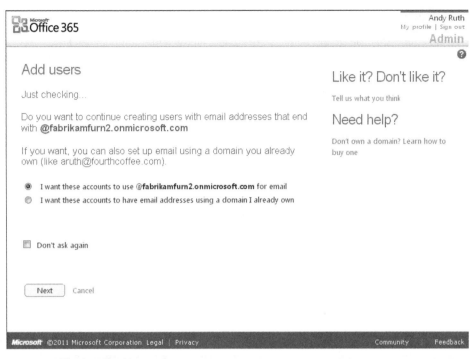

FIGURE 5-2 The Just Checking page.

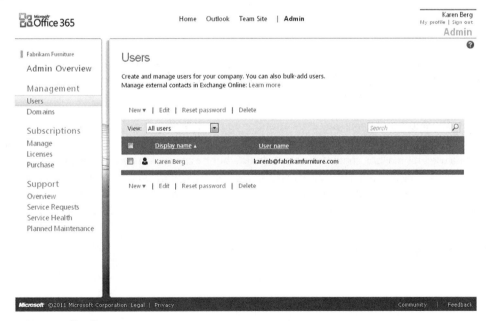

FIGURE 5-3 The Users page.

Step 1: Details

Figure 5-4 illustrates that the Details page has two parts: Name and Additional Details.

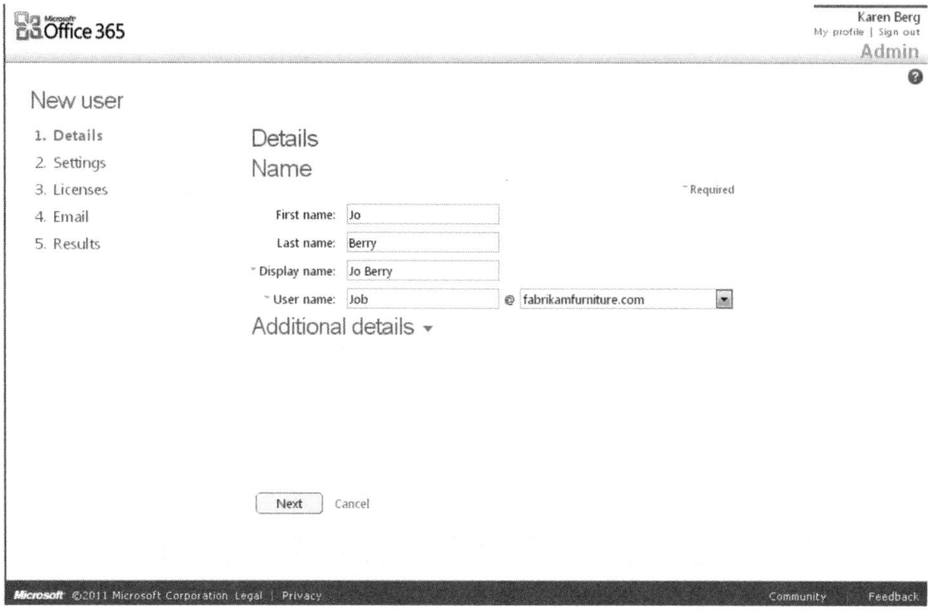

FIGURE 5-4 Adding a new user: Details.

Name

The Name section includes fields for the user's first and last names, as well as the required Display Name and User Name fields. The most important entry is user name, which is the logon name for the Office 365 portal and email address for the user.

When assigning a user name, pay close attention to the domain name. If you have validated a custom domain, you can assign that domain to the user. Keep in mind that if you change the domain name for a user, his mailbox content does not change but he cannot log on with the previous user name. You'll run into this problem only if you add a domain name to Office 365 after you have created users and then change the user names to the new domain. As soon as you do that, Lync Online and Outlook will not log the user on until you update the user's domain in Lync 2010 and Outlook.

Additional Details

To access the second part of the Details page (see Figure 5-5), click the Additional Details blue arrow.

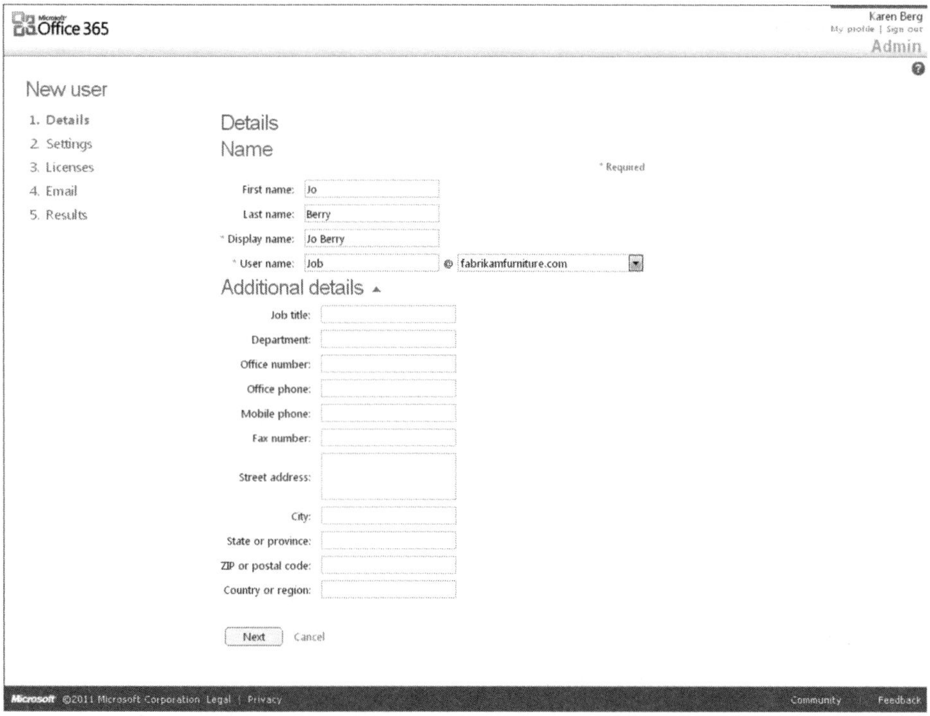

FIGURE 5-5 User Details showing Additional Details.

These details are used in two important ways. First, this information becomes available to others in your organization who use Office 365. Coworkers can view a person's details in Outlook by using the Global Address List (GAL). Chapter 10, "Improving your Business Image and Productivity with Outlook," provides details on how to use the GAL, which can be very useful if you must reach someone by phone but don't know the number. Second, the Mobile phone field has an important and not obvious role. Microsoft implemented a self-service password reset capability that can be initiated from the Office 365 logon screen. The last step of the procedure involves sending a text message to the administrator's account mobile phone listed in this screen. If there is no entry, the reset feature does not work. This process is available only to administrators and is covered later in this chapter. After adding the additional details, click Next.

Step 2: Settings

Figure 5-6 presents the Settings page, which has two parts: Assign Permissions and Set User Location.

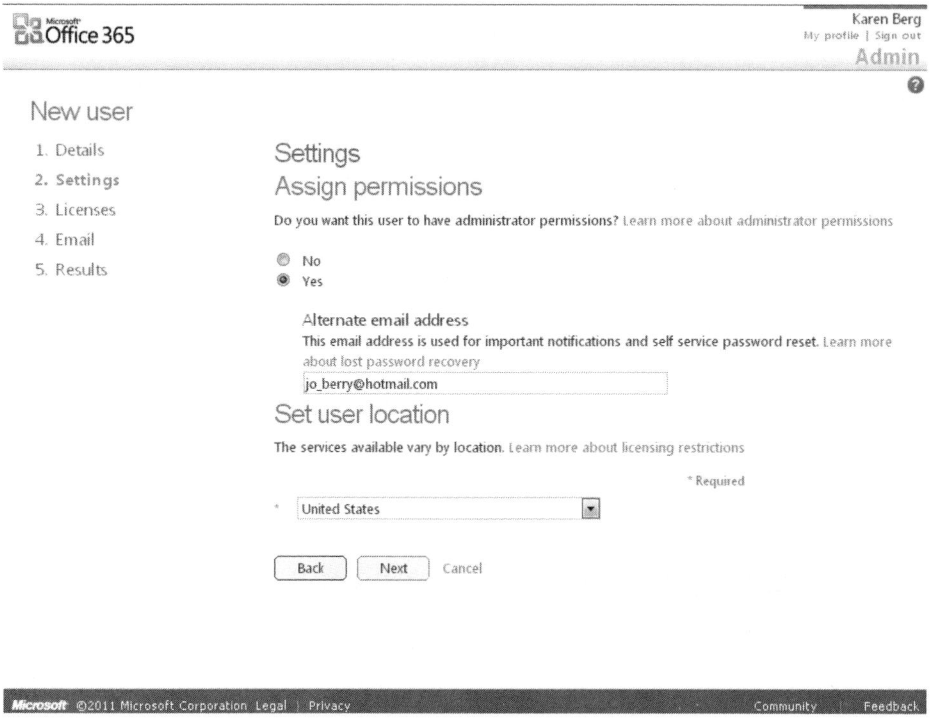

FIGURE 5-6 The New User Settings page.

Assign Permissions

The Permissions setting determines whether the user is a normal user or service administrator. Choose Yes to assign a user administrator privileges. Now the user will see the Admin menu when he logs on to the portal and will have administrator rights in all the services. Only two types of users are in Plan P1: normal users and administrators. The E plan series gives you more granular control, meaning that you can give someone the right to reset his password without also granting him ability to delete or add users. You can change this setting at any time for an existing user. Nothing changes operationally for the user other than having access to administrative features.

The Alternate Email Address field appears only when the user is set as an administrator. This address is used as part of the password reset process, so ensure that it is a valid address and is not the same as your Office 365 account.

Best Practice: Add a Free Second Administrator

When working with Office 365 users, you will need to change user settings from time to time, but what happens when you need to change your own user settings? There are a few settings you cannot make to your own account when logged on. The only way to make these changes is as an administrator, so you must have a second administrator account accessible with which you can make specific edits. Adding a second administrator account is a good idea because it solves the self-edit problem; just as importantly, if you forget your password, you can still log on as an administrator.

But don't you have to pay for the second admin account? No, you don't. You can create the account and assign the administrator role but not assign any licenses. This creates a user who cannot access the services but who can log on to the service and change the password, add users, and otherwise manage settings in the Office 365 portal. Some companies do this so that a consultant or partner can manage Office 365 on their behalf without giving the rights to the service.

Set User Location

Office 365 is a global, Internet-based service. Even for small businesses, it's not uncommon to have users in multiple countries. The rules and regulations that govern privacy, security, and access to personal information by government agencies vary from country to country. In addition, the laws governing voice and video carriers are different. In some cases, Lync Online is not allowed to carry voice data. As a result, Microsoft has to know the location of each user to offer only the services that are permitted for the region.

The User Location setting does not change where a user's information is located. If your company's data is provisioned in the United States data center and you have users in other parts of the world, they will all connect to the United States data center regardless of the Location setting. Set the location for the user, and then click Next to proceed.

Step 3: Assign Licenses

You use the Assign licenses form (see Figure 5-7) to specify which services a user can access. If you purchased Office Professional Plus, that is also listed. You do not have to assign all the licenses to everyone. By selectively assigning licenses, you have the option of giving some employees access to one service while denying access to others. Note that if you do this, you do not "free up" a license for another user. The three services are bundled as a unit, and you can use them all, if you like, but if you use just one, the other two are not available to be reassigned.

FIGURE 5-7 Adding a new user, step 3: assign licenses.

You also can create a user and not assign licenses at all. This technique can be used to create a backup administrator account without buying additional seats for your service.

It's important to know that if you remove a Microsoft Exchange Online license, the mailbox is deleted, which means that the email in that mailbox is gone.

Step 4: Send Results in Email

The Send Results In Email form shown in Figure 5-8 allows you to enter up to five email addresses to receive the Results page that includes the user's temporary password. Don't forget that the user cannot yet log on to her Office 365 account, so you need to use a different email address or other means of communication to give her the temporary password. Click Create to continue.

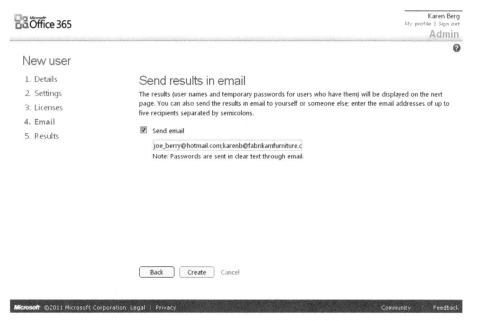

FIGURE 5-8 Setting up to send results in email.

Step 5: Results

The temporary password for the user appears on the Results page, as shown in Figure 5-9. An email containing the password is sent to each address that you provided in the Send Results In Email screen.

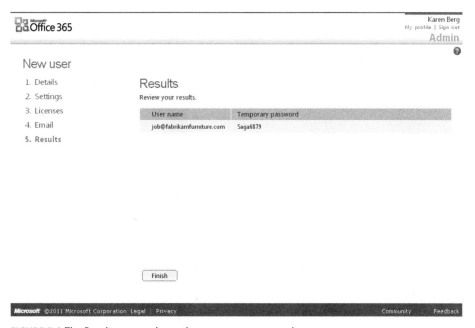

FIGURE 5-9 The Results screen shows the temporary password.

Bulk Add Users

Most small businesses add one user at time. For businesses with more than 10 users, you can save time by using the Bulk Add feature. The process is simple. You just download a spreadsheet from the Admin portal, add all the user information, and upload it into the Bulk Add Wizard. If problems occur with the imported file, the wizard will tell you. When those are corrected, it generates the accounts and temporary passwords. The most common mistake is not providing the correct domain name in the spreadsheet.

To access the Bulk Add Users feature, log on to the Admin portal, and then under Admin Overview, in the left column, click Users. From the Users page (refer to Figure 5-3), select New, and then click Bulk Add Users.

Step 1: Select File

When adding information for multiple users, you must provide their information in a CSV file. To help you, the Select A CSV File page offers you the options of downloading a blank CSV file to use as a template or downloading a sample CSV file (Figure 5-10). A variety of applications, from simple text editors like Notepad to Microsoft Excel, read and write CSV files.

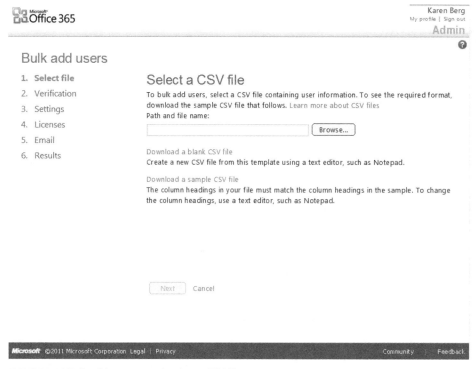

FIGURE 5-10 Bulk add users, step 1: select a CSV file.

Download the sample CSV file, and you'll see a simple spreadsheet with 14 columns: user name, first name, last name, display name, job title, department, office number, office phone, mobile phone, fax, address, city, state or province, and country or region.

Note The Country or Region field, while listed in the file, is not used. You designate the country or region specifically in step 3 of the build wizard, which is applied to all the up-loaded users. As a result, all users you bulk upload in a spreadsheet should be in the same country or region. Alternatively, you can manually correct each entry after the accounts are created.

Complete the spreadsheet, adding your users and their information. The only required fields are Username and Display name. The user name is the Office 365 email address.

Important Office 365 user names are represented as an email address, such as bob@fabrikam.com. The domain used for the user name must match the one in your Office 365 account. You can use the default domain assigned to you when you created your account, such as fabrikam.onmicrosoft.com (bob@fabrikam.onmicrosoft.com), or a custom domain you add to the account (bob@fabrikam.com). If you do not assign a valid domain to the user name, the account will not be created.

Save the spreadsheet in Excel by selecting File, and then click Save As. Type in a file name; ensure that the file type is correctly listed as CSV. In my testing, the file type by default was TXT rather than CSV and needed to be changed. Click Next.

Step 2: Verification

The verification page inspects the file for errors (see Figure 5-11). If any problems occur with the file, this page reports the issues. This page is effective at spelling out what problems are encountered. Correct any issues, and then reload the file, if needed. When no more errors appear, click Next.

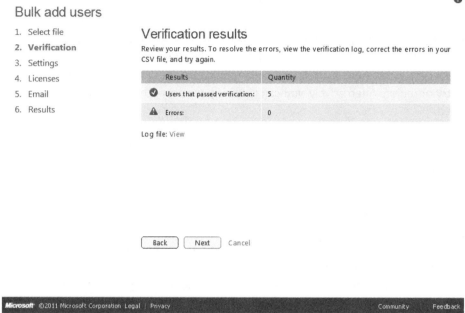

FIGURE 5-11 Bulk add users, Step 2: verification.

Step 3: Settings

As Figure 5-12 demonstrates, the Settings form for a group of users is similar to the Settings screen for adding a single user (refer to Figure 5-6). Instead of optionally setting a user to be an administrator, here you can choose the sign-in status for created users. Generally, you will want the users to sign in, unless you are staging your deployment and want to prevent access until a specific time. Set the location, and then click Next.

Step 4: Licenses

In the Assign Licenses page depicted in Figure 5-13, indicate which licenses to assign to the users. Because you are bulk uploading, remember that the same setting will apply to all users. Click Next.

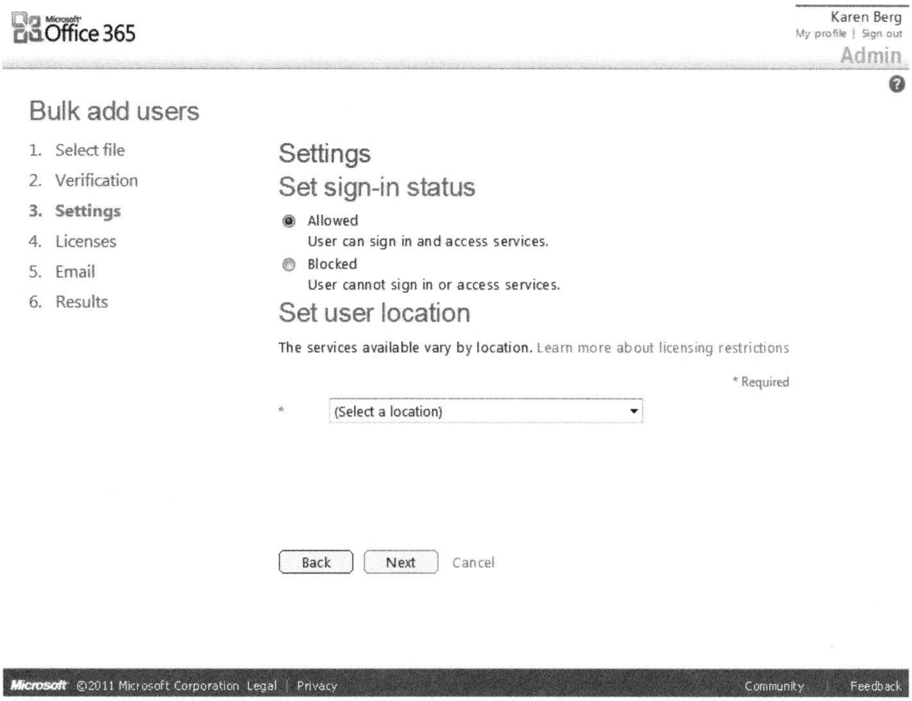

Bulk add users

1. Select file
2. Verification
3. **Settings**
4. Licenses
5. Email
6. Results

Settings
Set sign-in status

◉ Allowed
User can sign in and access services.

◯ Blocked
User cannot sign in or access services.

Set user location

The services available vary by location. Learn more about licensing restrictions

* Required

* [(Select a location) ▾]

[Back] [Next] Cancel

Microsoft ©2011 Microsoft Corporation Legal | Privacy   Community   Feedback

FIGURE 5-12 Bulk add users, step 3: settings.

Bulk add users

1. Select file
2. Verification
3. Settings
4. **Licenses**
5. Email
6. Results

Assign licenses

☑ Microsoft Office 365 Plan P1   6 of 10 licenses available

   ☑ Lync Online (P1)
   ☑ SharePoint Online (P1)
   ☑ Exchange Online (P1)

[Back] [Next] Cancel

Microsoft ©2011 Microsoft Corporation Legal | Privacy   Community   Feedback

FIGURE 5-13 Bulk add users, step 4: licenses.

Step 5: Email

Like the process for adding a single user, you can email yourself the temporary passwords when adding multiple users, as shown in Figure 5-14. On the Results page that follows (Figure 5-15), you can see the unique passwords generated for each user. Click Create.

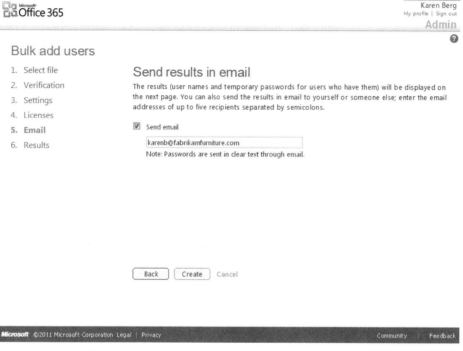

FIGURE 5-14 Bulk add users, step 5: send results in email.

Step 6: Results

The Results page lists the new users and their passwords. If you elected to email the results in step 5, this information is included in the email. In any event, ensure that you have a record of the password. If a user forgets or misplaces a temporary password, you can reset the password for that user to regenerate another temporary password.

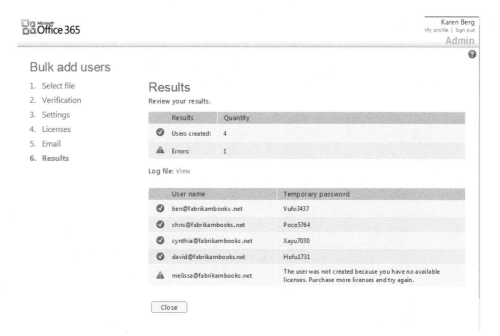

Results

Review your results.

Results	Quantity
✔ Users created:	4
⚠ Errors:	1

Log file: View

User name	Temporary password
✔ ben@fabrikambooks.net	Vufo3437
✔ chris@fabrikambooks.net	Poco5764
✔ cynthia@fabrikambooks.net	Xayu7030
✔ david@fabrikambooks.net	Hofu1731
⚠ melissa@fabrikambooks.net	The user was not created because you have no available licenses. Purchase more licenses and try again.

Close

FIGURE 5-15 Bulk add users, step 6: results.

Problems are also reported, such as the one shown in Figure 5-15, indicating that you do not have enough licenses to create all the users. In this case, the solution is to buy another license. Then you can create the account individually.

After the users are created, you can distribute the logon identities and passwords.

Important Users *must* change their passwords at *https://portal.microsoftonline.com* before they can log on to the services. After changing their password, the user is placed on the Office 365 portal Home page, where they can discover how to start the web-based services and access useful information about Office 365.

Reset Passwords

When a user is unable to log on because of a forgotten password, a password reset is required. For a non-administrative user, the process is simple but requires a service administrator. Administrators have a self-service password reset feature. In either case, the user receives a new temporary password, which he must change before he can use the services.

User Password Reset

To reset a user's password, log on as an Office 365 administrator, and then under Admin Shortcuts, select Reset User Passwords. This takes you to the Users page; select the user, and then at the bottom of the user list, click Reset Password, as shown in Figure 5-16.

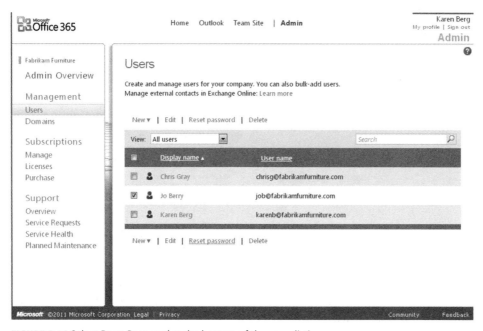

FIGURE 5-16 Select Reset Password at the bottom of the users listing.

From here, the process picks up at step 4 for adding a new user. You select where to send the temporary password (do not use the email address of the locked out account) and view the results.

Administrator Password Reset

An administrator can reset her own password, provided the user settings for her administrator account have correct information for the alternate email address and mobile phone fields.

The alternate email address is located on the user Settings page (refer to Figure 5-6), whereas the mobile phone number is located on the Details page, under Additional Details (refer to Figure 5-5). The mobile phone must be able to receive text messages.

To begin the process, click Forgot Your Password? on the logon page for Office 365, as shown in Figure 5-17.

You are then asked whether you are an Office 365 administrator or end user. If you select end user, you'll see a message that instructs you to contact the services administrator. If you select administrator, you are asked to provide your logon user name and to solve a case-senstive visual challenge, as shown in Figure 5-18.

FIGURE 5-17 The Forgot Your Password? link on the sign-in portal.

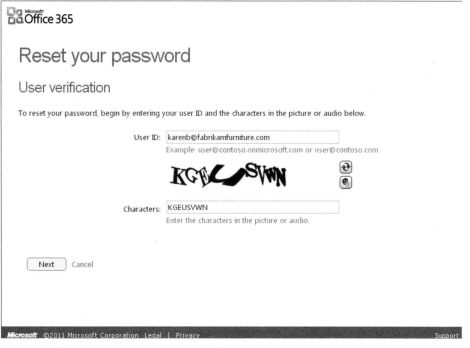

FIGURE 5-18 Resetting your password: user verification.

After successful completion of this page, an email is sent to the alternate email address. You have 10 minutes to reply by clicking on the provided link. When you do, you see the message shown in Figure 5-19, and you are asked enter the security code sent by text to your mobile phone number.

Reset your password

Mobile phone verification

We have sent a code to your mobile phone: *********11.

Enter this security code below.

Security Code:

Next Cancel

FIGURE 5-19 Resetting your password: mobile phone verification.

You have 10 minutes to enter the code before it expires. When you enter the code and click Next, you are taken to the password change screen in which you enter a new password.

Delete a User

Next to the Reset Password link on the Users page (Figure 5-16), you have the option to delete a user. Selecting a user and then clicking Delete brings up the confirmation warning shown in Figure 5-20.

Are you sure that you want to permanently delete the selected users?

When you delete a user, you permanently delete all data for that user. You cannot recover this deleted information.

Yes No

FIGURE 5-20 The Delete Selected User? warning.

When you delete a user, the user's mailbox is deleted from Office 365. Ensure that you have copied any mail you need from the user's system before deleting the user. You cannot add the user back and regain access to the mailbox. Should you need to recover a deleted mailbox, you can post a request on *community.office365.com*, but because support is not included with Plan P1, you have no assurance that the mailbox will be restored.

SharePoint Online documents associated with the user remain intact.

Edit User Information

You can set a user's information from the Users page (refer to Figure 5-16). Simply select the user, and then click Edit.

After selecting to edit a user, you are placed on the Licenses page, as shown in Figure 5-21. You can navigate from here by using the Details, Settings, and More links at the top of the screen. You can use these choices to selectively edit the same information presented when you created the user.

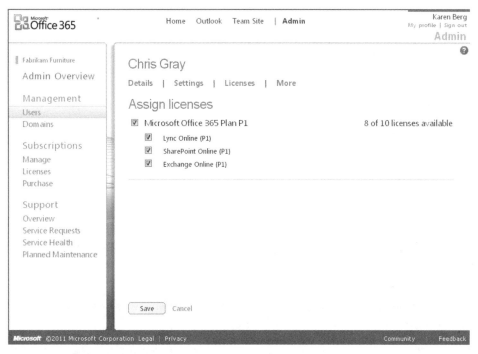

FIGURE 5-21 Editing a user.

 More Info When you click More, you are presented with a page on which you, as an administrator, can edit settings for a particular user's mailbox and Lync Online. Chapter 8, "Working with Outlook Web App," covers the maibox settings, while Chapter 12, "Working with Lync Online," details the Lync Online settings.

Block a User's Sign In

In some situations, you might want to block a user from signing in while still keeping the account. Perhaps you have terminated an employee, or a vendor you used for a project has finished her job. In either case, you probably don't want to delete all the account's email, which would occur if you simply deleted the account.

Choose to edit the user's account, and then click Settings on the edit user menu (beneath the user name in Figure 5-21) to reach the page shown in Figure 5-22.

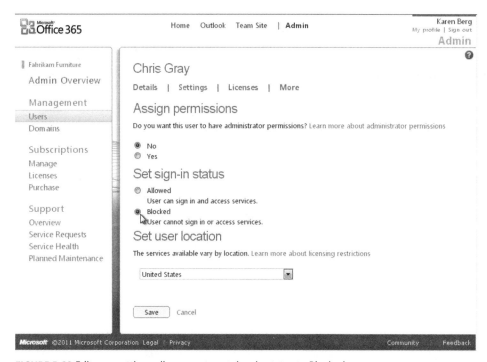

FIGURE 5-22 Edit user settings allows you to set sign-in status to Blocked.

By now, this page should look familiar, but you'll notice that in the center is a new section not available when you created the user: Set Sign-in Status.

By default, the sign-in status is Allowed. When you choose Blocked, the user cannot log on to Office 365. This does not evict a currently logged on user from access to the services, but it keeps him from accessing services at next logon.

When the user next attempts to log on to the Office 365 Portal, he will see the message shown in Figure 5-23.

⊗ Sign-in is blocked

Sign-in with **chris@fabrikambooks.net** is blocked for one
of these reasons:

• Someone entered the wrong password too many times.

• If you signed up for this ID through an organization, you
might not be able to use the account yet.

Reset your password

Sign in using another Microsoft Online Services ID

FIGURE 5-23 The Sign-In Is Blocked message.

In addition to setting the account to blocked, you should also reset the account password. By
doing this, if the account setting becomes unblocked by accident, the user still cannot access the
services.

Bulk Editing

A nice surprise lurks in the Office 365 administration portal. If you select multiple users and click Edit,
you can bulk edit specific settings, as shown in Figure 5-24, including the user's domain.

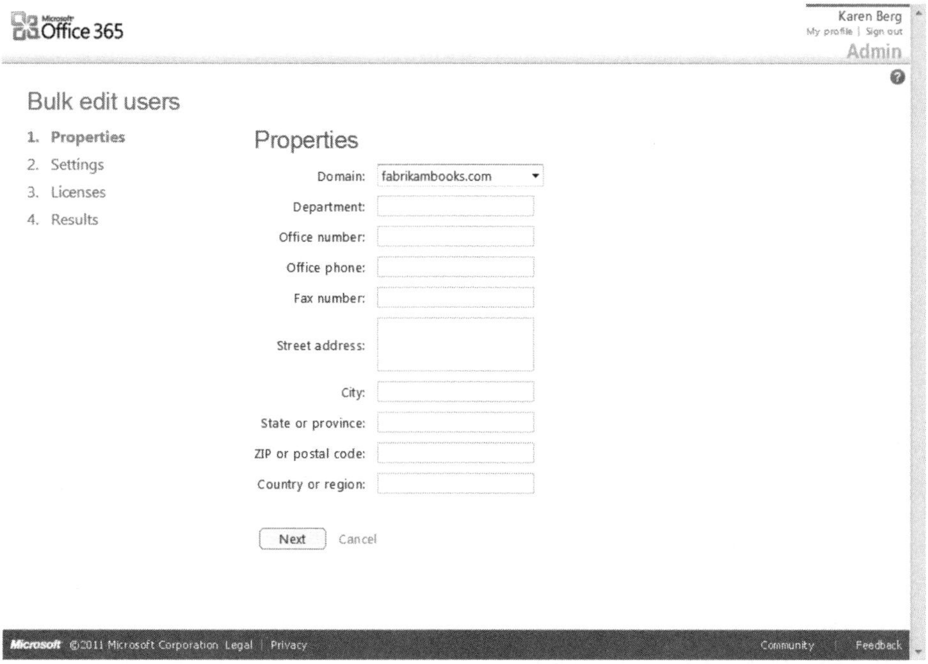

FIGURE 5-24 Bulk Edit mode.

After entering the updates that you want to apply, click Next to cycle the additional pages in the
same sequence as the Add Users capabilities.

This is a very useful feature when you add a new domain, change telephone numbers, address, or
otherwise need to update the information for several users at the same time.

Adding Users Recap

Adding users in Office 365 is straightforward. You can add them one at a time or in bulk. You can even bulk edit users to make multiple changes simultaneously. You should add a second administrator account as soon as possible to have a backup for access to administrative capabilities as well as to have an account with which to log on to make changes to the default administrator account. The second admin account can be a real user or just a placeholder without licenses assigned. Even without licenses, the account can log on and make changes to users in the Office 365 Portal.

As a best practice, add your users first and then delegate your domain. Before you set up your users, change the user logon name to the new domain. This helps you avoid issues related to reconfiguring the client software after you add a custom domain.

CHAPTER 6

Working with Custom Domains

When a domain name represents your company branding, rather than an online service like Hotmail, Yahoo, Google, Comcast, or Microsoft Online, it is a custom domain. An email address like *<your name>@<your business>* projects a professional image and helps to imprint your brand with customers and the public. Every email you send reinforces the message that you have a unique identity and are not just using a public email service. Like your company logo, your custom domain helps set you apart from other businesses.

To use a custom domain with Microsoft Office 365, you must first own the domain name that you want to use. If you do not already have a domain, they are simple and inexpensive to acquire from a domain name registrar. Domain names must be unique, so be prepared to be a little flexible. If someone already owns the rights to your first choice, you might need to try a variation or two. Services and pricing vary widely, but you can buy a domain name, which you must renew annually for about $5–$20.

This chapter will guide you through the process of adding your custom domain to Office 365. You'll be alerted to common problems that can occur, how to avoid them, and a few tricks of the trade to help the process along.

About Domains and DNS

A domain name is like a phone number: just owning one doesn't mean people can call you. You need a phone and connection to the phone company or cell network. In addition, when people dial your number, there has to be a way for that number to reach your phone. The phone company handles routing all the phone calls. When you dial a number, the connection is made automatically, so you aren't aware of the technology or the process of how the call is routed. Unless you get an "all circuits busy" or something goes wrong with dialing, the process is completely transparent. Even so, there is a huge traffic-switching network behind the scenes that provides the ability to call anywhere in the world.

A similar process occurs on the Internet. When you connect to a website or send an email, behind the scenes, your system uses a directory service called *DNS*, or Domain Name Services, to locate the service (website, email, or other Internet entity) you requested. If someone requests access to a service on your domain (by sending an email or accessing a website by using your domain name) your domain must have a listing that shows where these services are available. Often, you aren't aware that these entries exist because the domain name registrar takes care of all this for you. For example, if you buy a domain name, email, and website from GoDaddy, it all just works because the company hosts your DNS services and configures the DNS settings automatically for you. You can modify these DNS settings if you choose to do so, and you even can specify that another provider, such as Microsoft, host the DNS instead of GoDaddy. In this case, GoDaddy is still the domain name registrar, but Microsoft would host the DNS services.

When Registrars Do Not Host DNS

This chapter assumes that your registrar is also your DNS provider. However, some registrars sell domain names and do not host DNS services. In this case, you will have both a domain name registrar and a DNS service provider at two different web addresses. Keep in mind as you read the chapter that in some cases you will need to log on to the domain name registrar (to change the name of your DNS servers), and in other cases you need to log on to your DNS provider (to update DNS settings).

Microsoft's DNS Solutions

Because Office 365 provides website, email, and other services, making changes to your domain's DNS settings is an unavoidable technical reality. Many business owners and managers don't know about DNS and don't have time to learn the details to set up an email account with Office 365 or any other provider. In response, Microsoft implemented a system to make it as simple as possible for most small businesses to add domains to Office 365.

Microsoft's solution for correctly configuring Office 365 for small businesses is to provide DNS hosting for the small business accounts. This ensures that your DNS settings are correctly configured for Office 365. To achieve this, in December 2011, Microsoft released an important update called the Domain Quickstart for Office 365. Included in the update is a wizard to make certain that you have users ready to receive mail, that your website DNS entries are accounted for, and that you actually own the domain. Originally, the update was released only for new accounts in the United States, but by the time you read this chapter, these updates might have been rolled out worldwide or changed again.

You can determine whether you have the updated Domain Quickstart Wizard when you add a new user. If at that time you are asked whether you want the user to have a custom domain name and if you see a screen similar to Figure 6-1, then you have the Domain Quickstart Wizard.

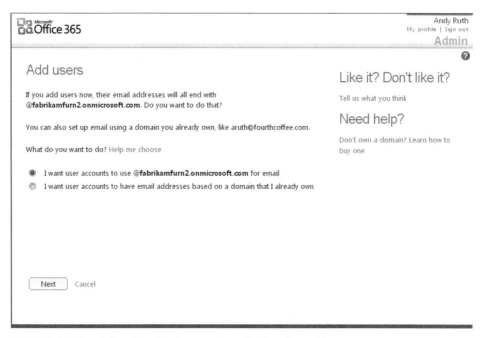

FIGURE 6-1 Updated domain validation experience begins when adding a new user.

The section "Add a Domain by Using the Domain Quickstart Wizard" walks you through using the wizard later in the chapter. If your version of the Office 365 Admin portal predates the Domain Quickstart Wizard, or if you previously used the wizard but now need to add additional domains, you can follow Microsoft's standard method outlined in the section "Add a Domain Without the Domain Quickstart Wizard," later in this chapter.

An Alternate DNS Solution

Some situations do not allow you to redirect your name servers to Microsoft. You should determine whether this applies to you before you go much further. You might be in this situation if:

- You have multiple websites and settings that you do not want to manage on Microsoft DNS system.

- You rely on software that integrates with your existing DNS provider.

- You need DNS entries other than a CNAME or A records. The Microsoft DNS Manager allows only custom A and CNAME records to be added.

- You're unable to delegate to another DNS provider due to your circumstances. In some regions, this ability is restricted by policy or law. For example, .no and .de domains cannot be delegated.

- You simply want more control over your DNS entries than Microsoft provides and are comfortable with your existing provider.

  In other words, if you prefer to keep your DNS services where they are, there's no problem in doing so. The "Add a Domain Without Redirecting DNS" section at the end of this chapter shows you the way. In addition, for an article that details the process for configuring your existing DNS provider with Office 365 settings, you can consult Microsoft's online help at *http://onlinehelp.microsoft.com/en-us/office365-smallbusinesses/hh416759.aspx.*

Timing and DNS Changes

Making changes to DNS entries can be an exercise in patience. You will see messages from Microsoft and possibly your DNS service provider during this process, saying to expect delays of up to 72 hours. In practice, most updates to DNS for Office 365 take effect within a few minutes. The amount of time you must wait depends on many circumstances, most of which are outside of your control. For this reason, you can expect that your domain validation and setup will be completed in a short amount of time, but don't be surprised if it takes longer.

Your First Domain

Your first domain is the "base" onmicrosoft.com domain that you designated during the signup process for Office 365. The *<domain>*.onmicrosoft.com name is permanently assigned to your account and cannot be edited or deleted. You can use this domain for any and all Office 365 purposes. In other words, even though adding a custom domain is common, it is entirely optional.

When to Add Users

Before users can receive mail in Office 365, user accounts that are assigned to the custom domain must already exist. For this reason, you should add users before you validate a domain. To ensure that you have users' accounts ready for receiving mail, the wizard that adds a domain will ask you if you want to add users. In addition, after the domain is added, any existing users can be switched to use the new domain all at one time.

If you have a mail service using your current domain name, that mail service will stop receiving mail after you fully complete the process of adding a domain to Office 365. If you want to transfer mail to Office 365 using your existing logons with the Connected Accounts feature of OWA, you should do this before you transfer mail routing to Office 365. Again, you need user accounts in Office 365 to use this method, which is another reason to create user accounts before adding a domain.

Reuse Your Domain in Office 365

If you previously validated your domain with Office 365 in a different account, perhaps a trial account, or used it with the Business Productivity Online Suite (BPOS), you must remove the domain completely from the previous account before it can be validated. Prior to deleting the domain from the administration console, you must remove any reference to the domain from user logons, conference rooms, distribution lists, and Microsoft Lync Online. For Lync Online, the fastest way to remove custom domains assigned to user names is to remove the Lync Online license assigned to the user in the old account. If you are still unable to delete the domain, you will require Microsoft technical support or the assistance of a partner.

Add a Domain: Common Steps

Whether you add a domain by using the Domain Quickstart Wizard, standard method, or without changing DNS services, you will follow the same general procedure:

1. Identify your DNS provider.

   You will need to know who your DNS provider is and how to log on to the DNS administration console for your domain. Locate this information before you begin. If you do not know who your provider is, try browsing to *http://www.internic.net/whois.html*. Enter your custom domain name on the page, and then click Submit. In the resulting report, look for "Registrar" to see which registrar hosts your domain. You can use this information to track down your domain registrar and contact them, if necessary, about accessing your DNS settings. Additional assistance is available in the Office 365 portal Microsoft online help during the domain validation process.

2. Document your existing DNS settings.

   With access to your DNS settings, be sure to print or otherwise record these settings for your domain. You will need these for future reference when configuring DNS for Office 365, so if something goes awry, you will have a record of how to return your settings to the original state. This is an important step that you should not omit. Include MX records, your current name server settings, as well as all other entries you see.

3. Verify ownership of the domain.

   Imagine if you masqueraded as someone from Microsoft.com or another organization while you sent and received email. That of course would be unacceptable. Fortunately, using Office 365, it is not possible. Microsoft ensures that you are the owner of the domain that you want to move to Office 365 through a process known as "domain validation."

Here's how it works. During the domain validation process (covered later in this chapter) you are given a unique "secret" (looking something like MS=ms234323) to enter into the DNS system. Office 365 then queries DNS for the domain to see whether the designated secret is present. If found, the domain is accepted for use. The underlying assumption is that if you have the authority to edit the DNS entries for the domain, you effectively own the domain. This technique is widely used by many services.

Domain validation is technical but not hard to do. If you follow the instructions and have access to the DNS settings for your custom domain, you can validate the domain without technical assistance. Alternatively, a helpful DNS provider can add these changes for you. If you follow the instructions, domain validation will not affect your current mail or services.

4. Assign users to the new domain.

   After adding the domain, you need to convert the email addresses of any existing users to the new domain. When converted, users must log on using the new email address.

5. Configure DNS for Office 365.

   As described earlier, Microsoft prefers that you assign Microsoft as your DNS provider. Office 365 settings are created for you. You can then add any additional DNS settings that you require in the Office 365 administration console. Alternatively, you can add Office 365 DNS settings to your existing DNS settings at your DNS provider.

Add a Domain by Using the Domain Quickstart Wizard

Microsoft's Domain Quickstart Wizard was designed to assist with the task of moving your first domain to Office 365 and assigning users to the domain. The wizard asks you a few questions and then creates a step-by-step plan for you to follow. You can act on or revise the plan as needed.

The wizard begins with the Add New User page, as shown earlier in Figure 6-1. I prefer to create users *before* adding a domain so that mail can be migrated by using the Connected Accounts feature in Outlook Web App. In addition, domain validation can take a while to execute correctly; creating a user takes only a minute or less.

You can also start the wizard by clicking Add A Domain on the Domains page, as shown in Figure 6-2.

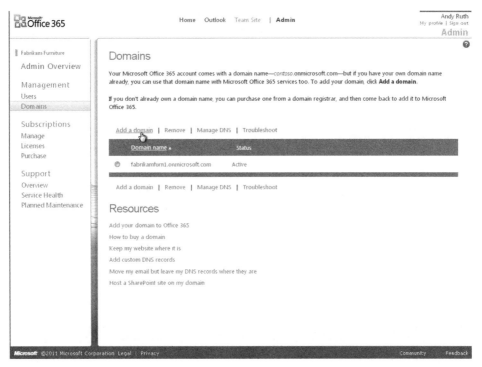

FIGURE 6-2 The Domains page: add a domain.

Important Microsoft regularly updates the administration portal and has made significant changes to the domain validation and DNS transfer process since the services were released. Because Microsoft releases updates regionally for testing and refinement before they are released globally, the process you encounter might be different from the one described. Even so, the basic issues remain the same. You need to validate your domain according to instructions, ensure that your users are assigned to the new domain, and then designate Microsoft as the DNS provider when you are ready to receive mail. During the process, be aware of the impact of these changes on your website entries or on any other services for which you have DNS entries.

Enter your custom domain name in the provided text box (Figure 6-3), click Next, and then answer the questions on the Tell Us About page (Figure 6-4).

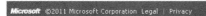

Use your own email address

Change your **@fabrikamfurn1.onmicrosoft.com** email address to use your own domain.

If you already own a domain, like fourthcoffee.com, add it now so you can use Office 365 with an email address that's easy to remember.

fabrikamfurniture.com
Example: fourthcoffee.com

Like it? Don't like it?

Tell us what you think

Need help?

Don't own a domain? Learn how to buy one

Next   Cancel

Microsoft ©2011 Microsoft Corporation Legal | Privacy   Community | Feedback

FIGURE 6-3 Specify the domain to use as your email address.

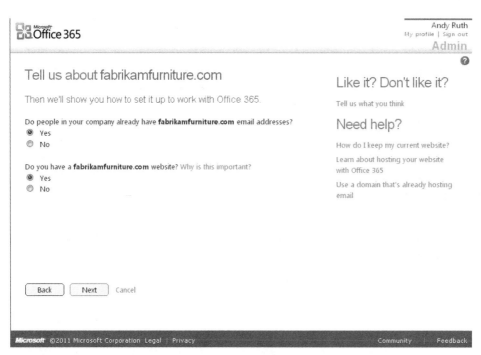

Tell us about fabrikamfurniture.com

Then we'll show you how to set it up to work with Office 365.

Do people in your company already have **fabrikamfurniture.com** email addresses?
- ● Yes
- ○ No

Do you have a **fabrikamfurniture.com** website? Why is this important?
- ● Yes
- ○ No

Like it? Don't like it?

Tell us what you think

Need help?

How do I keep my current website?

Learn about hosting your website with Office 365

Use a domain that's already hosting email

Back   Next   Cancel

Microsoft ©2011 Microsoft Corporation Legal | Privacy   Community | Feedback

FIGURE 6-4 Tell us about your domain.

If you are already using your domain name for email, the transfer is a bit more complex because timing becomes an issue. You want to ensure that you do not have an email interruption during the switch. One way to do this is to use the Connected Accounts feature of Outlook Web App (described in Chapter 8, "Working with Outlook Web App") to read mail from your current service into your Office 365 inboxes before you transfer the domain. Then, when you make the switch, your mail from your previous provider is already in your inbox.

For the purposes of the example, assume that you are already using the custom domain for email and also have a website up and running. Click Next to see the plan, which will be similar to Figure 6-5.

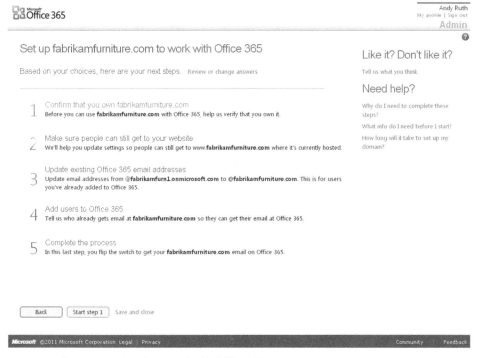

FIGURE 6-5 Set up your domain to work with Office 365.

Confirm That You Own Your Domain (Domain Validation)

To begin the setup process, click Start Step 1; you'll see the Confirm screen shown in Figure 6-6.

Important Although the changes that Microsoft asks you to make for validation will not interfere with your existing services, incorrectly adding, deleting, or changing settings can disrupt your email or web service. Before making any changes, print the DNS listing for your domain for later reference.

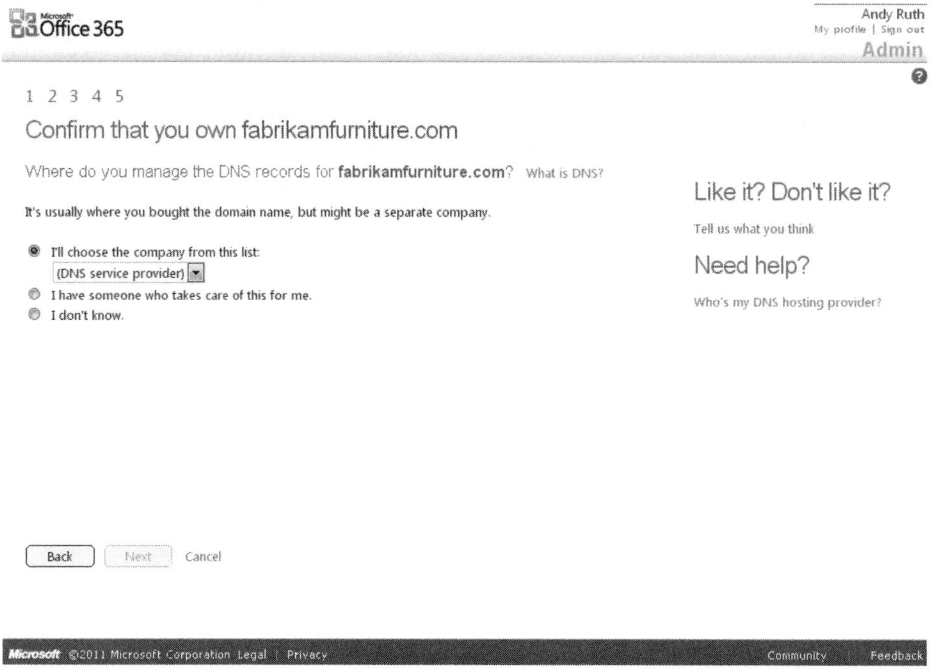

Office 365
Andy Ruth
My profile | Sign out
Admin
1 2 3 4 5
Confirm that you own fabrikamfurniture.com
Where do you manage the DNS records for fabrikamfurniture.com? What is DNS?
It's usually where you bought the domain name, but might be a separate company.
I'll choose the company from this list:
(DNS service provider)
I have someone who takes care of this for me.
I don't know.
Like it? Don't like it?
Tell us what you think
Need help?
Who's my DNS hosting provider?
Back
Next
Cancel
Microsoft ©2011 Microsoft Corporation Legal | Privacy
Community
Feedback

FIGURE 6-6 Identify your DNS registrar.

Microsoft provides specific instructions for several popular registrars, including the following:

- GoDaddy
- eNom
- Melbourne IT
- Network Solutions
- Tucows
- Register.com

If your registrar is in the DNS Service Providers drop-down list, choose it. If not, choose Mine Is Not Listed. If you have a consultant or Microsoft Partner who manages this for you, select I Have Someone Who Takes Care Of This For Me. You'll be provided with a message you can forward that has instructions about how to validate the domain. If you don't know who your provider is, click I Don't Know to go to online help, which provides useful links and instructions about how to identify your DNS provider.

For this example, select Mine Is Not Listed to receive a generic set of instructions applicable to all registrars, as shown in Figure 6-7.

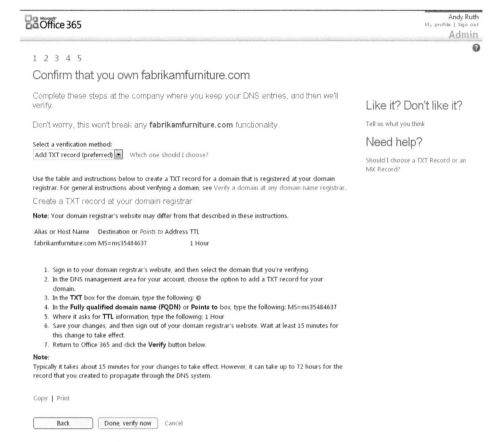

FIGURE 6-7 Domain validation instructions.

This is where tasks take a technical turn. To proceed, you will need to log on to your DNS providers and make the requested changes. Take note of the message "Don't worry; this won't break any fabrikamfurniture.com functionality." At this stage, you are just verifying ownership and nothing more.

Verification Methods

The entries for any DNS system are composed of a series of *resource records*. These types of records comply with industry standards so that DNS works the same way for everyone. Of the many types (see *http://en.wikipedia.org/wiki/List_of_DNS_record_types* if you're interested), the Verify Domain instructions require that you use a TXT (text) or MX (mail exchange) record verification.

Although it shares the same abbreviation as an unformatted text file, a TXT DNS entry is very different: It's a general purpose record that has many uses in DNS. In this case, you can validate your domain by adding a specific TXT entry in your DNS system.

Some providers do not allow TXT records to be added to DNS, so Microsoft added the MX method. MX stands for Mail Exchange; it is the type of record used to designate where mail for your domain should go. For example, if your mail service is provided by your ISP, the MX record will point to your ISP's mail servers. If your mail service is provided by Google, your MX record will point to Google's mail servers. Because changing MX records is common, DNS providers usually allow changing MX records. In this case, you would validate the domain by adding a specific MX record that is not intended to route mail at all but instead is used only for validation of ownership for your domain.

Of the two methods, the TXT method is preferred because there is little chance that an incorrect entry will interfere with any existing services. Use the TXT method if possible. The following discussion assumes you are using a TXT record, but it also applies to an MX record.

Add Verification Entries

There are many domain registrars on the Internet, so it is not possible to provide step-by-step instructions for everyone. If available, be sure to select the instructions specific to your registrar. Regardless of the specific steps, the end result is that you must add a TXT (or MX) record with the provided information. Figure 6-8 provides a close up view of the general instructions and shows an actual example of what you're asked to add.

Create a TXT record at your domain registrar

Note: Your domain registrar's website may differ from that described in these instructions.

Alias or Host Name   Destination or *Points to* Address TTL
fabrikamfurniture.com MS=ms35484637   1 Hour

1. Sign in to your domain registrar's website, and then select the domain that you're verifying.
2. In the DNS management area for your account, choose the option to add a TXT record for your domain.
3. In the **TXT** box for the domain, type the following: @
4. In the **Fully qualified domain name (FQDN)** or **Points to** box, type the following: MS=ms35484637
5. Where it asks for **TTL** information, type the following: 1 Hour
6. Save your changes, and then sign out of your domain registrar's website. Wait at least 15 minutes for this change to take effect.
7. Return to Office 365 and click the **Verify** button below.

FIGURE 6-8 Generic instructions for validation by using the TXT method.

Enter this information into your domain name registrars' system. In the following example, eNom.com is the host for Fabriakmfurniture.com. In practice, I would have asked for the instructions designed specifically for eNom, but for the purposes of the book, generic instructions are sufficient.

Making the needed updates is actually very simple. Here's all I did to achieve the desired result, as shown in Figure 6-9:

1. Log on to eNom.

2. Select the domain, and then under Manage Domains, select Host Records.

3. Select record type TXT (there is already a blank line when you access the page).

4. Enter an @ sign in the Host Name field. This corresponds to step 3 in Figure 6-8.

5. Copy and paste the "secret" code MS=ms35484637 into the address field. Verify that this is correct, and then click Save.

That's it!

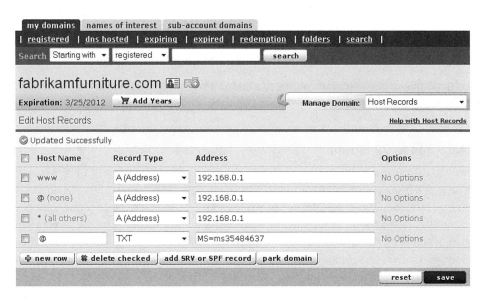

FIGURE 6-9 eNom DNS administration with verification information.

Important Before you make any changes to your DNS settings, print your current configuration. This printout is a backup of your settings and can be very useful when planning your move to Office 365. For example, the entry for www on the first line of Figure 6-9 indicates that a website address is configured and in use. You will need this information later.

Variations from the General Instructions

The general instructions are not likely to map exactly to your provider. In this example, step 4 in Figure 6-8 directs you to add the secret to a box called Fully Qualified Domain Name or Points To. As you can see in Figure 6-9, for eNom (and other providers) there is no such box. Instead, it is named Address.

Also, step 5 of the instructions directs you to update the TTL entry (which stands for Time To Live and controls how long a DNS lookup is valid before it needs to be checked again). The TTL entry is optional and is not configurable in many DNS provider systems.

If you are unsure what to do with the instructions, use the preceding example as a guide. Because DNS is the same everywhere, the forms might change, but in the end, your entry should be similar in appearance to the TXT entry shown in Figure 6-9. Keep in mind that incorrectly entering information in a TXT record will not interfere with your services. Just take care not to change anything else.

Delay Before Validation

At the bottom of Figure 6-7, note the message:

> *Typically it takes about 15 minutes for your changes to take effect. However, it can take up to 72 hours for the record that you created to propagate through the DNS system.*

This is good guidance. There is no harm in trying to validate after 5 minutes, and in many cases, that is sufficient. Taking 72 hours is quite rare but has been known to occur.

15 Minutes to 72 Hours?

Why is the delay so variable? The answer has to do with the inner workings of DNS. When you browse to a website such as bing.com, your system queries a DNS server that looks up the IP address of bing.com. When the DNS server has found the address, on the next query for bing.com, the DNS server checks to see whether it has the result in memory. If so, the server returns the last IP address it found rather than looking up the address. How long a lookup is held by a DNS server depends on settings chosen by the DNS service and is outside of Microsoft's control. Some servers look up every address, every time. Most keep entries in memory for an hour or less. Others hold onto lookups for days. For this reason, the advice given by Microsoft has a very wide range: 15 minutes to 72 hours. In practice, it is usually minutes, not days.

When ready, click Done, Verify Now at the bottom of the screen.

If the validation fails, you will see a message instructing you to wait 72 hours. Verify that you have the correct entries, and then try again after some time. If validation still fails after waiting overnight, it is likely that there is some other issue.

 More Info If you browse to *http://network-tools.com/nslook/Default.asp*, enter your custom domain name, and then select TXT for the query type, you will see a result that shows you whether your TXT entry has been written and is available. If your TXT records appears here and is correctly entered, Office 365 should successfully validate the domain.

When the validation succeeds, you'll see a result similar to that shown in Figure 6-10.

FIGURE 6-10 A successful validation.

Click Next to go to step 2, as shown in Figure 6-11.

Set Up Office 365 DNS for Your Website

This step's title, Make Sure People Can Still Get To Your Website, could be interpreted to mean that something might have just happened to impede access to your current website. That is not the case. Step 2 asks you for your current DNS information about your website. Microsoft will add that to their DNS settings for your account. Then, when you transfer the DNS service to Microsoft, people can still get to your website because the correct DNS entries are present. That transfer doesn't actually happen until step 5.

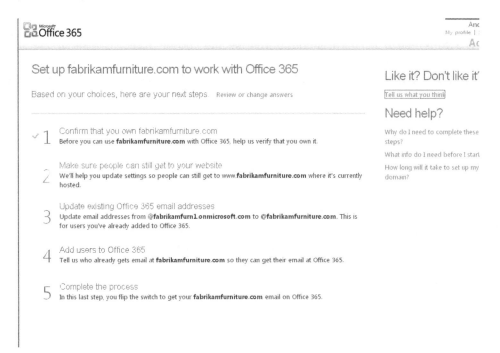

FIGURE 6-11 Ready for step 2.

Click Start Step 2 to see the instructions shown in Figure 6-12.

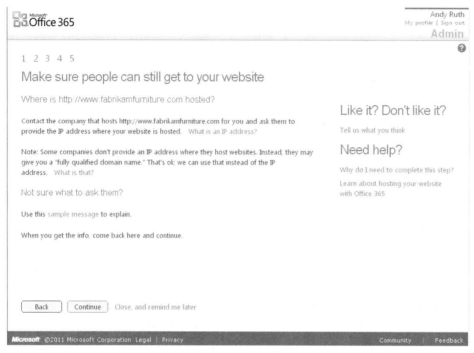

FIGURE 6-12 Obtain the IP address for your website.

This page asks you to find the IP address of your website. This information is in the DNS settings for your domain. You can also discover this by clicking Start, typing **CMD**, and then pressing Enter. In the command window that opens, type **PING** and your website name (as in **ping fabrikamfurniture. com**), and then press Enter. The response will be the IP address associated with your website.

The wizard also provides a prepared message that you can email to your website-hosting provider if you choose to ask them for this information.

When you have the IP address, click Continue, which will bring up the window that you can see in Figure 6-13.

The vast majority of websites will be associated with an IP address. Microsoft also allows you to designate a fully qualified domain name (FQDN), if required. A fully qualified domain name is your website name in full, such as www.contoso.com. The entries in your existing DNS system are your guide to the correct path. In the example, assume an IP address, and then click Next. Enter the IP address for the website, and then click Check Now (see Figure 6-14).

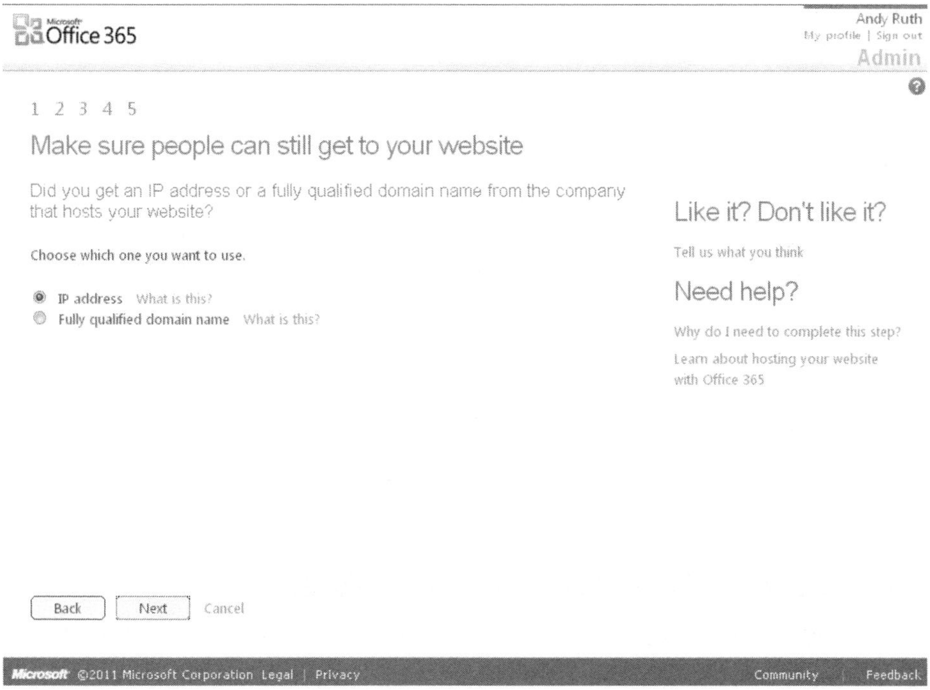

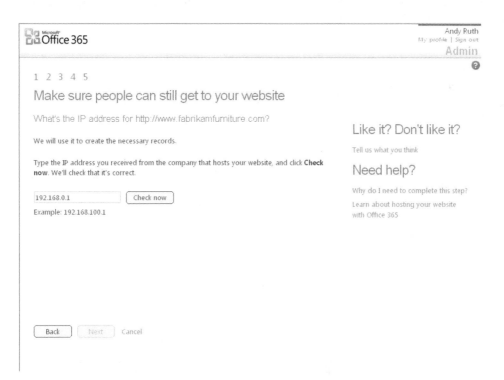

FIGURE 6-13 IP address or FQDN.

FIGURE 6-14 Checking the website IP address.

Office 365 will reply with a confirmation of the address, as shown in Figure 6-15.

✓ Great, this is the right IP address. Click Next to continue.

FIGURE 6-15 The IP address, confirmed.

When you click Next, a message appears (see Figure 6-16), alerting you that the website is ready to work with Office 365 and to continue to the next step.

✓ Great! The fabrikamfurniture.com website is ready to work with Office 365.
Continue to the next step!

FIGURE 6-16 Ready for the next step.

Click Finish to return to the wizard.

Update Existing Office 365 Email Addresses

In Step 3, you can update existing user accounts to use the new domain name, as demonstrated in Figure 6-17. All the users you change must log on using the new email address. Be sure to tell users to do this if you have already given them access to the services. In addition, if you configure Outlook or Lync Online prior to adding the domain, you will need to update both applications to work with the new domain name. Passwords do not change.

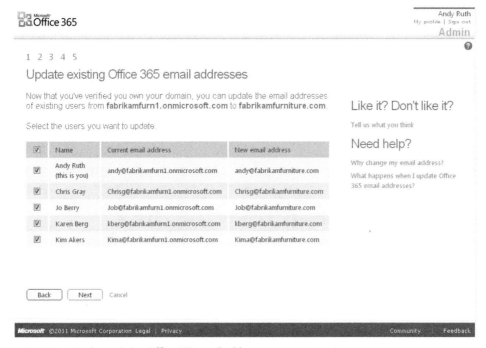

FIGURE 6-17 Update existing Office 365 email addresses.

When you click Next, a confirmation page opens; you're required to sign out if you changed your own email address.

Add Users

When you log off and log on, you can return to the wizard from the top of the Admin screen, as shown in Figure 6-18.

FIGURE 6-18 Resuming the wizard.

When you click step 4 in Figure 6-18, you are again taken to the wizard setup page presented in Figure 6-19.

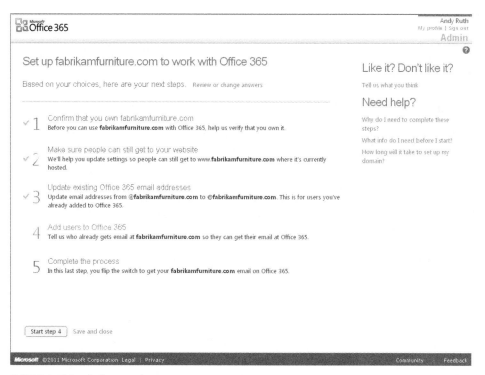

FIGURE 6-19 Ready for step 4.

When you click Add Users to Office 365, you'll have the choice to add new users or skip this step (see Figure 6-20). If your users are already set up, you can skip this step by clicking No, I'm The Only One With A *<Custom Domain Name>* Email Address.

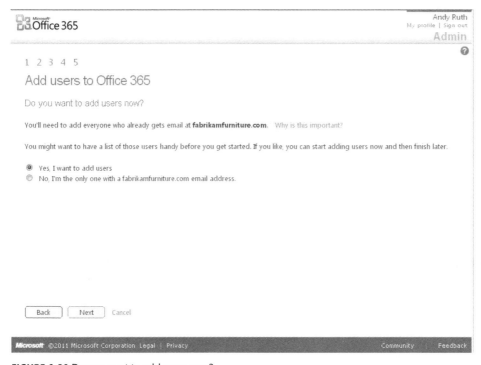

FIGURE 6-20 Do you want to add users now?

The wizard employs a "short form" for adding users, which is shown in Figure 6-21.

Chapter 5, "Working with User Accounts," covers more of the details that you can complete for users, but the short form is sufficient to get you going. As you add users, be sure to make note of the temporary passwords created, because users will need them to log on. Instructions for their first logon will be emailed to the address entered in the form.

The key point is that before you actually transfer the DNS services to Microsoft (the next step), you must have users set up or there will be no mailbox to receive mail.

To proceed with the next step, click Done Adding Users on the summary page that is displayed after you add the last user.

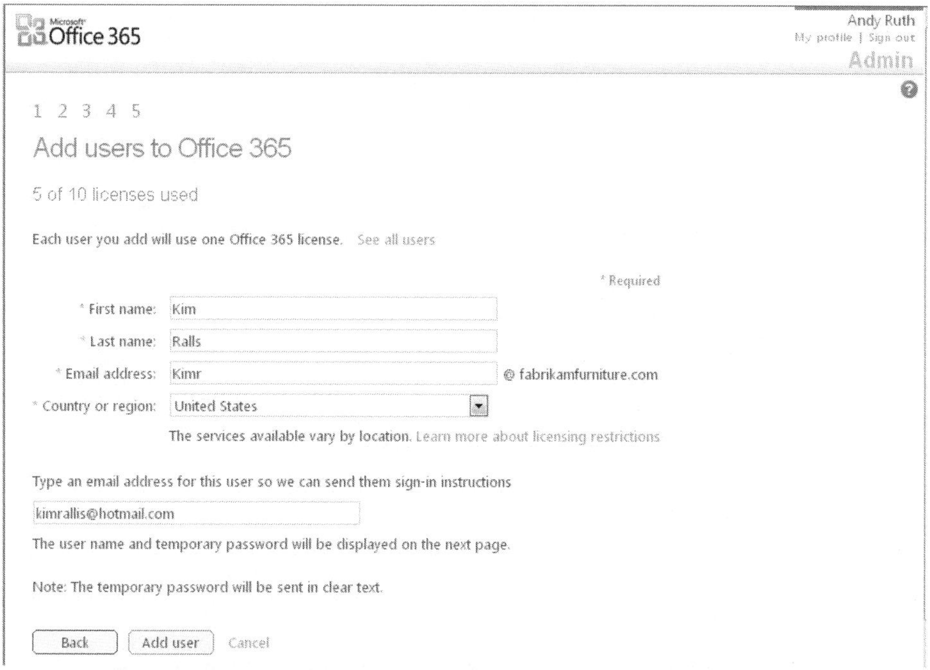

FIGURE 6-21 Do you want to add users now?

Complete the Process

When you click step 5, Complete The Process, the page shown in Figure 6-22 appears.

You can return to adding users, if you need to, or click Yes, Let's Continue. If you choose Yes, Let's Continue, a pop-up message appears reminding you to be sure to have all the users added before you "flip the switch." To see the page shown in Figure 6-23, confirm that you are ready to proceed.

Andy Ruth
My profile | Sign out
Admin

1 2 3 4 5

Complete the process

Ready to flip the switch?

When you complete this step, email sent to addresses ending with **@fabrikamfurniture.com** will start coming to Office 365. After that, you won't see new email in your old email system anymore.

Before you continue, make sure you have added everyone who already has an email address ending with **@fabrikamfurniture.com**.

Still have users to add? Add users now

Like it? Don't like it?

Tell us what you think

Need help?

What happens to my email when I switch my domain to Office 365?

[Back]   [Yes, let's continue]   Cancel

FIGURE 6-22 Complete the process.

Office 365
Andy Ruth
My profile | Sign out
Admin

1 2 3 4 5

Complete the process

Where did you buy **fabrikamfurniture.com**?

To finish adding your domain, you'll update DNS records at your domain registrar. Typically, this is the place where you bought your domain.

Choose your domain registrar to see directions for updating the necessary records.

(DNS hosting service) ▾
(DNS hosting service)
Mine is not listed
Enom
Go Daddy
Melbourne IT
Network Solutions
Register.com
Tucows

Like it? Don't like it?

Tell us what you think

Need help?

Who's my domain registrar?

Why do I need to change my name server records?

[Back]   [Done, go check]   Cancel

FIGURE 6-23 Where did you buy your domain?

You're now getting down to the finish line. In the end, you have to return to your domain registrar and update your domain's settings to use Microsoft DNS services. Like the Domain Validation Wizard, specific instructions are provided for some registrars, as well as a generic set of instructions, as shown in Figure 6-24.

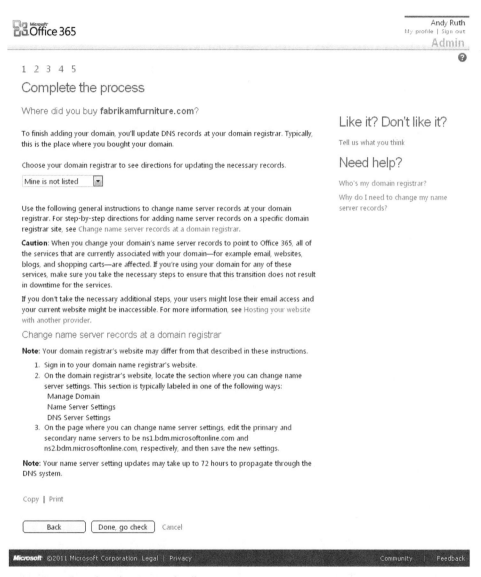

FIGURE 6-24 Complete the process details.

This long detail can be summarized as follows: at your domain registrar's site, update your domain settings to use the DNS servers located at *ns1.bdm.microsoftonline.com* (primary server) and *ns2.bdm.microsoftonline.com* (secondary server). When you do this, the DNS entries you created by going through the domain wizard (which occurred in the background) are the ones that now drive access to your email and to Internet services such as your website.

Before proceeding, take a look at the DNS settings Microsoft has created for you, and compare them to your existing DNS configuration.

To View Your Office 365 DNS Settings

At the bottom of the screen, click Cancel, as shown in Figure 6-24. Next, click Save and Close, and then answer Yes to the prompt "Skip domain setup for now?" This returns you to the main Admin page.

On the left side of the Admin screen, under Admin Overview, click Domains. You'll see the window depicted in Figure 6-25, but now your custom domain is added. Select the custom domain, and then click Manage DNS.

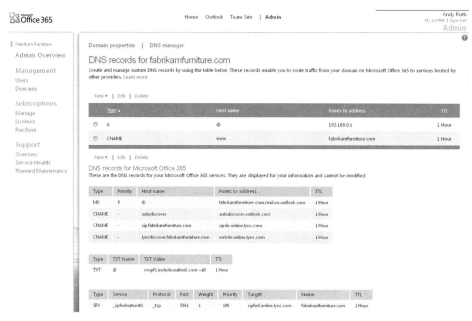

FIGURE 6-25 DNS records for a custom domain.

The entries in this page will be in effect when your DNS settings are set to use Microsoft's name servers. Most of the entries are those required for Office 365. At the top of the page, you'll see the entries that were added for the website in step 2 of the wizard. Examine the entries in your existing DNS provider's setup to see what might not be accounted for in Microsoft's DNS setup. For most businesses, the website and email services are all that are present.

If needed, you can use this page to add entries to Microsoft's DNS settings.

Important You can add only CNAME and A records. If your business requires entries other than these, see the section "An Alternative DNS Solution" earlier in this chapter.

Assign Microsoft as the DNS Provider

Log on to your DNS provider's administration screen and locate where your name servers are specified. In our example, Fabrikamfurniture is hosted at eNom. By selecting the domain and then DNS Server Settings as shown in Figure 6-26, you can change the name server entries.

Important Before you make any changes to your DNS server settings, be sure to record the existing settings. If you need to switch back quickly because of some issue that might have been overlooked, you will need to know the original settings.

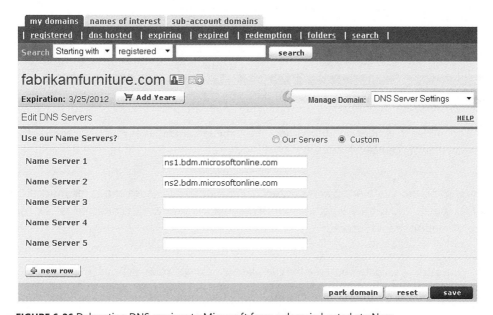

FIGURE 6-26 Delegating DNS services to Microsoft from a domain hosted at eNom.

After you save the settings, mail will start to flow to Exchange Online as soon as the DNS entries are updated on the Internet. This can take from 15 minutes to a couple days, depending on how the DNS servers involved are configured. When I changed the settings at eNom for this example, a pop-up stated that the update would take 24 hours. It actually took about 30 minutes.

When completed, return to the wizard at Microsoft to verify the changes. You might need to click through the pages in step 5 again to return to the Complete The Process page (refer to Figure 6-24). At the bottom of the page, click Done, Go Check.

If the check does not verify, you will see the message shown in Figure 6-27.

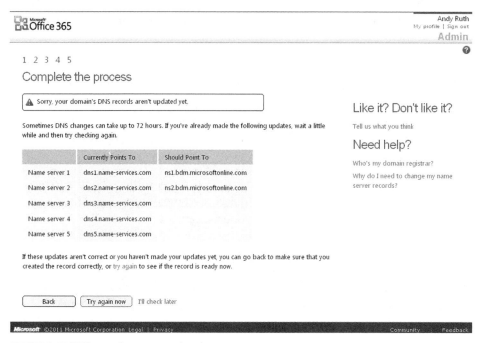

FIGURE 6-27 DNS records are not updated yet.

It's a good idea to double- and triple-check the name server entries at your DNS registrar to ensure that they are completely correct.

> **Note** If you browse to *http://network-tools.com/nslook/Default.asp* and enter your custom domain name, you can see whether your DNS servers are showing as directed to Microsoft. If so, validation should succeed.

After the settings validate, you'll see the completion message shown in Figure 6-28.

Because you are delegating DNS to Microsoft, your DNS entries are certain to be correct for email, Lync Online, and Microsoft SharePoint Online. It might take some time for your DNS provider changes to take effect. The only possible issues relate to addresses you add for your website and to the amount of time it takes for DNS to "catch up" with the changes you've made.

You can test that email is flowing by sending mail to your Office 365 email address. If the mail is received, you've confirmed that email is being routed correctly. If not, check to see whether the mail is still being sent to your previous email provider. If the mail is being routed there, you should just wait for a while for the DNS system to catch up with the changes.

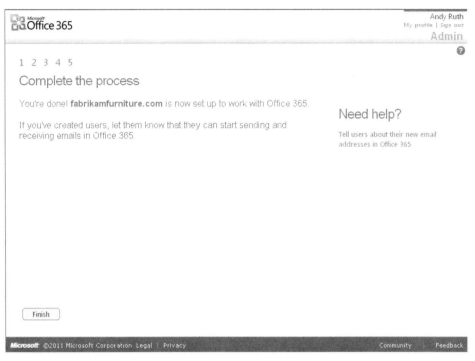

FIGURE 6-28 DNS has been changed to Microsoft.

Verify that your website is available by browsing to your website. If it's not available, verify the entries in your DNS configuration for the domain by clicking the domain and selecting Manage DNS.

Add a Domain Without the Domain Quickstart Wizard

If your version of the Office 365 Admin portal does not offer the Domain Quickstart Wizard, or if you previously used the wizard and need to add additional domains, you can always fall back on the original method that Microsoft provided with the Office 365 Plan P1.

This method is a bit more manual than using the Domain Quickstart Wizard but has the same outcome. One of the differences between the Domain Quickstart Wizard process and this process is that the wizard procedure will ask you about your website DNS settings, if any, and configure DNS accordingly. Without the wizard, you need to add those settings manually to Microsoft DNS setup before completing the finish step. As a result, the actual workflow is:

1. Specify your domain.

2. Verify the domain.

3. Prepare your accounts for changing name servers.

4. Update Microsoft DNS entries for your website.

5. Change name servers.

6. Finish.

Specify Domain

You start the process from the Domains page in the Office 365 Admin portal (see Figure 6-2). Clicking Add A Domain takes you to the first step and to the Specify Domain page, as shown in Figure 6-29.

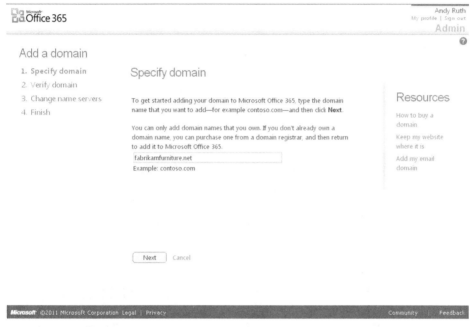

FIGURE 6-29 The Specify Domain page.

Type your domain name in the text box, and then click Next.

Verify Domain

Figure 6-30 presents the Verify Domain page, which asks you to select your domain name registrar from the pull-down list. If your registrar is not listed, select General Instructions.

Microsoft
Office 365

Andy Ruth
My profile | Sign out
Admin

Add a domain

1. Specify domain
2. **Verify domain**
3. Change name servers
4. Finish

Verify domain

Before we can add your domain name to Microsoft Office 365, we must verify that you are the owner of the domain. To begin the verification process, you add a specific record to the DNS records at your domain registrar. We then look for the record to verify ownership.

Each DNS provider supports different features, so we provide two ways that you can verify ownership: by creating a TXT record or an MX record.

Note: The new DNS record does not affect how your domain works. Learn more

See instructions for performing this step with:
(Select)

Verify   Cancel

Resources

Where do I add the DNS record?

Should I use a TXT record or an MX record?

Microsoft ©2011 Microsoft Corporation Legal | Privacy   Community | Feedback

FIGURE 6-30 The Verify Domain page.

After you make a selection, you will see information similar to that shown in Figure 6-7. Office 365 instructs you to enter a specific "secret" in your existing DNS provider's setup for your domain by using the MX record or TXT record. After you have added the information to your existing DNS service provider's forms, click Verify. Office 365 then checks whether you entered the secret as directed.

More Info For important details about how to verify your domain, refer to the section "Confirm That You Own Your Domain (Domain Validation)" for an example of the verification process; other than cosmetic differences in the screens, that section's real-world example of the validation process is identical to the steps you should follow.

When you are ready, click Verify; Office 365 will validate the entries you made and, when confirmed, will accept the domain for use with the services.

You're probably not expecting this, but after validating the domain, click Cancel. You will come back to this step in a bit. First, you have some business to attend to.

Prepare Your Accounts

For the best experience, stop after validating the custom domain. If you continue with the workflow by editing the name server records, as directed by the Office 365 portal, mail for your custom domain will start being routed to Office 365 before your user accounts are set up to receive it. You need to prepare those accounts now by assigning the custom domain to your users' email addresses. If you have not created users yet, now is a good time do so. Figure 6-31 shows the user management Properties page. To reach this page from the Admin portal, click Users, select the user, click Edit, select the domain name from the pull-down list, and then click Save.

 Note You can select all the users at the same time, and click Edit to enter Bulk Edit Mode, which enables you to set all the accounts to the custom domain at the same time.

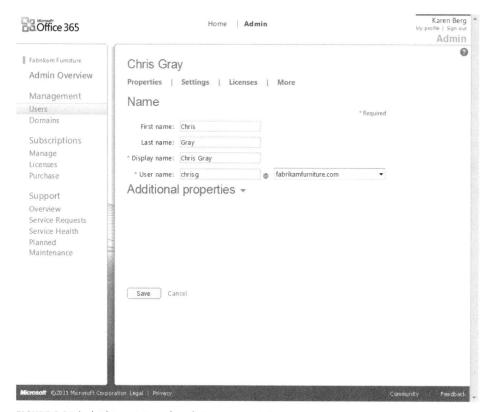

FIGURE 6-31 Assigning a custom domain to a user name.

As previously mentioned, when you change the email address of the user, she must log on with the new address. This will affect Outlook and Lync 2010 if you have already set them up with the old address.

Update Office 365 DNS for Your Website and Other Services

As soon as you validate your domain, Microsoft creates the correct Office 365 DNS entries for the domain immediately. *They are not in use yet* (that doesn't happen until you make a final change at your current registrar), so there's nothing to worry about in terms of disrupting existing services. Because DNS on Office 365 is set up but not in use, you have a window of opportunity to do some additional preparations before you fully delegate the domain. Basically, you're pausing between step 2 (Figure 6-30) and step 3 (Validate and Change Name Server, respectively). At this stage, you can view the entries Microsoft created for your domain. From the Domains page, select your verified domain, and then click Manage DNS, as shown in Figure 6-32.

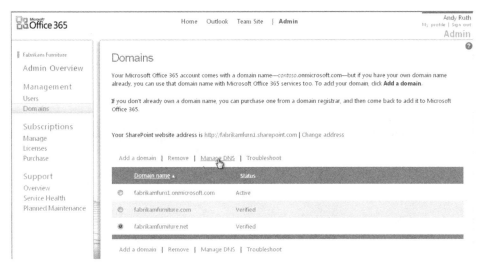

FIGURE 6-32 Selecting to manage DNS.

The DNS Manager displays the DNS entries created for you by the validation process. Figure 6-33 shows the default settings from an actual validation.

FIGURE 6-33 DNS records created by Microsoft for a custom domain.

If you have a website using your custom domain (such as www.fabrikamfurniture.com), your current DNS provider has the proper settings to support your site. You need to identify those entries and re-create them in the Microsoft DNS system *before* assigning Microsoft to host your name services. You can create the record after transferring DNS to Microsoft if you can abide with the potential for disruption in access to your website while you make the changes. Remember, due to the nature of DNS, there can be delays from minutes to hours between the time you make a change and the time they are available.

For example, Figure 6-34 shows the DNS settings for Fabrikamfurniture.net as provided by eNom.com.

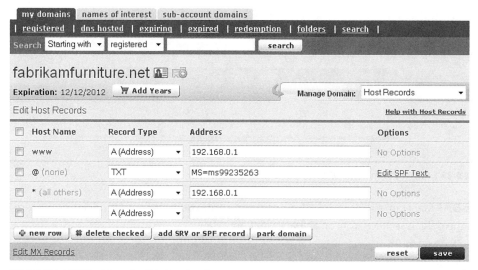

FIGURE 6-34 DNS settings for Fabrikamfurniture.net.

The first line directs all traffic for www.fabrikamfurniture.net to the IP address of 192.168.0.1 (an invalid Internet IP address used for illustration purposes). This line does not exist in the Office 365 DNS settings, so it needs to be added.

In addition, on the next line, you'll see an @ sign going to the same IP address. This permits fabrikamfurniture.net to be used as the website address (no www). This line also needs to be added to the Office 365 DNS setup.

To add these entries to Office 365, click New, select A (Address), and then add the entries from your existing DNS system, as illustrated in Figure 6-35.

×

Add a DNS record

Use this form to create an A record.

Host name or Alias: | www

IP Address: | 192.168.0.1

TTL: | 1 Hour ▾

[Save] [Cancel]

FIGURE 6-35 Adding a DNS record to enable an existing website.

When complete, the custom DNS settings in the Office 365 DNS manager will look similar to Figure 6-36.

Domain properties | DNS manager

DNS records for fabrikamfurniture.net

Create and manage custom DNS records by using the table below. These records enable you to route traffic from your domain on Microsoft Office 365 to services hosted by other providers. Learn more

New ▾ | Edit | Delete

Type ▲	Host name	Points to address	TTL
A	www	192.168.0.1	1 Hour
A	@	192.168.0.1	1 Hour

FIGURE 6-36 Custom entries for a website.

Now, when switching to the DNS settings hosted by Microsoft, access to your existing website will be uninterrupted. If you choose to switch to the public website of SharePoint Online, the DNS settings will be updated automatically.

Change Name Servers

You assigned users to your new domain and you updated the Office 365 DNS entries with any custom records that you require. However, before proceeding, I suggest that you recheck your new Office 365 DNS setting against your existing provider's DNS settings to ensure that everything is accounted for properly. When satisfied, you're ready to "throw the switch" by directing DNS services for your domain to Microsoft's DNS servers. But where should you direct them?

To find out, you need to use a little sleight of hand. Even though you haven't completed setting the domain (the name servers have not been changed), you'll ask Office 365 Portal to troubleshoot the DNS setup. The resulting page will show you the entries that you're after. To begin, go to the Domain page, and then select Troubleshoot (see Figure 6-37).

Troubleshoot domains

Check your status

To troubleshoot the status of your domain, select the statement that best applies:

- ○ I have not changed the settings at my provider yet.
- ○ I changed the settings at my provider less than 72 hours ago.
- ● I changed the settings at my provider more than 72 hours ago.

[Next]   Cancel

Microsoft ©2011 Microsoft Corporation Legal | Privacy   Community   Feedback

FIGURE 6-37 Troubleshoot domains to return to wizard.

Even though it might not be true, select I Changed The Settings At My Provider More Than 72 Hours Ago; the Troubleshoot Domains page appears, as shown in Figure 6-38. If you select any other option, the troubleshooting does not actually start. Instead, you see a message that says, in effect, "wait awhile and try again."

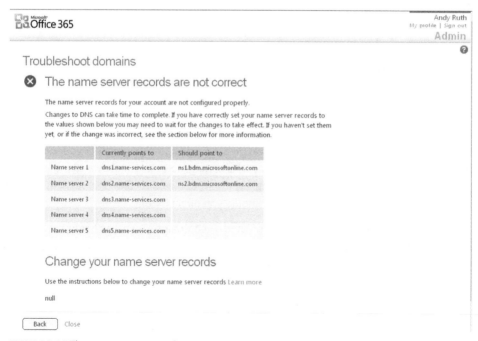

FIGURE 6-38 The name server records are not correct.

The Should Point To column tells you that your name servers should be set to *ns1.bdm.microsoftonline.com* (primary server) and *ns2.bdm.microsoftonline.com* (secondary server). To delegate name services hosting to Microsoft, you must set up your domain so that it refers to *NS1.bdm.microsoftonline.com* and *NS1.bdm.microsoftonline.com* as name servers. Figure 6-26 shows the eNom entries for changing DNS servers. Refer to the section "Assign Microsoft as the DNS Provider" for additional details. After you update the DNS provider settings for your domain, return to the Office 365 portal and select Troubleshooting The Domain again (or click Back if you did not close the window).

When the name server entries are verified by the troubleshooter, the window presented in Figure 6-39 appears. This might take some time before it can be detected.

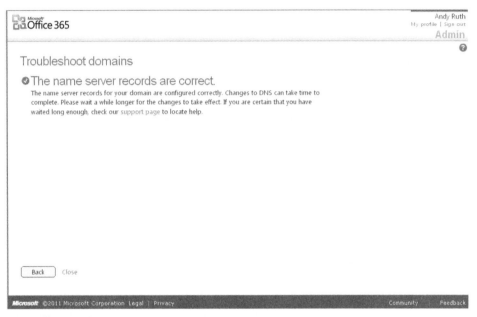

FIGURE 6-39 The name server records are correct.

Add a Domain Without Redirecting DNS

In some circumstances, Microsoft cannot host your DNS services. For example, some countries do not permit re-delegation. In other cases, you might need DNS entries for your domain that are not allowed in the Microsoft DNS system. Finally, you might simply be more comfortable keeping DNS services where they are. To configure this, follow the instructions in the section "Add a Domain Without the Domain Quickstart Wizard," up to and including verifying the domain. Then, instead of transferring DNS services to Microsoft, view the DNS settings for your domain in the DNS Manager (Figure 6-25) and add the entries to your existing DNS service. When you add the MX records, your mail will be routed to Office 365. Using this method ensures that access to your existing website will continue and that any other DNS entries you rely on will remain present.

On the downside, if Microsoft adds services that require new DNS entries, you have to manually make the entries when you keep control of DNS. This occurred in December 2011 when Microsoft released Lync Mobile for Windows 7 phones. For those with DNS hosted at Microsoft, the update worked seamlessly. Those hosted elsewhere had to manually update their DNS.

> **Important** When you host your own DNS, the DNS troubleshooter in Office 365 will always report that DNS is not properly configured. In addition, if you plan to use SharePoint Online for a public website, you must make the changes to DNS yourself. For these and other considerations, see the section "Limitations in Office 365 Services when Office 365 doesn't host your DNS," at *http://onlinehelp.microsoft.com/en-us/office365-smallbusinesses/hh416759.aspx*.

Multiple Domains

Small businesses commonly have multiple lines of business. You can add domain names for each for your businesses, but be aware that the Domain Quickstart Wizard you used (if available) for your first domain does not appear for additional domains. Follow the guidance in the section "Add a Domain Without Using the Domain Quickstart Wizard" to add additional domains.

After adding another domain, you can assign users to log on using the new domain or add the domain as an alternate email address in their inbox properties. You will learn how to add multiple domains to a user account in Chapter 8.

SharePoint Online and Custom Domains

You can use your custom domain with the public website that comes with SharePoint Online. If Microsoft hosts your DNS settings, DNS will automatically be updated. If you host your own DNS settings, you need to update your DNS settings with the entries for SharePoint Online.

To change the URL for SharePoint Online, in the Office 365 administration portal, on the Domains page, click Change Address as shown in Figure 6-40.

Domains

Your Microsoft Office 365 account comes with a domain name—*contoso*.onmicrosoft.com—but if you have your own domain name already, you can use that domain name with Microsoft Office 365 services too. To add your domain, click **Add a domain**.

If you don't already own a domain name, you can purchase one from a domain registrar, and then come back to add it to Microsoft Office 365.

Your SharePoint website address is http://fabrikamfurn1.sharepoint.com | Change address

FIGURE 6-40 Changing the address of your SharePoint Online public website.

You can then select from a list of validated domains as illustrated in Figure 6-41.

FIGURE 6-41 Selecting a new address for the SharePoint Online public website.

Office 365 next displays a message indicating that changes might require 24 hours to take effect. In practice, the delay is usually much less than this, often minutes. When Office 365 has finished making the changes to its DNS system for your domain, the domain name shown in Figure 6-42 changes to show the new domain name.

If you host your own DNS settings, you need to update your DNS entries to direct traffic to SharePoint Online. After you've assigned the custom domain, select the domain from the Domains page, and then click DNS Manager.

FIGURE 6-42 The DNS Manager with new entries for SharePoint Online.

The entries you need to add for SharePoint Online are the last CNAME entry with host name www, and the A record with the host name of @.

As usual, with DNS, allow time for any changes you make to take effect.

Final Thoughts

Adding a custom domain to Office 365 is a key step in the deployment process. Microsoft added the Domain Quickstart Wizard to the service to assist you through the process. The key feature of DNS for Plan P1 is that Microsoft hosts the DNS services for your domain. This ensures that your DNS settings are correct and remain updated as new services become available. Even so, you can continue to host DNS at your existing service provider if you need or prefer to. Many small businesses have multiple lines of business. You can add multiple domains without a problem and assign them individual users or have users with multiple email addresses. Finally, you can use the public website of SharePoint Online as your public website if you choose.

Now that you have users created and your domain set up and ready to go, you are ready to set up your desktops for your users.

CHAPTER 7

Desktop Setup and Migration

You've created your users and configured your custom domain. Without any further action, you can access the browser-based features of Microsoft Office 365, such as Microsoft Outlook Web App and the Microsoft SharePoint Online Team Site—just head for the Office 365 portal Home page (see Figure 7-1) and click Outlook or Team Site. These web-based access points to Office 365 services are useful, but most businesses also want to set up Microsoft Office and Lync 2010 for use with Office 365. To achieve this, you must download and install some software from the administration portal.

To get the most out of Office 365 for you and your coworkers, resist the temptation to dive in right away. Before you begin, take some time to review your existing setup and think through how you want to treat your existing mail. Investing the time now to configure your desktop to use Office 365 will reap benefits later.

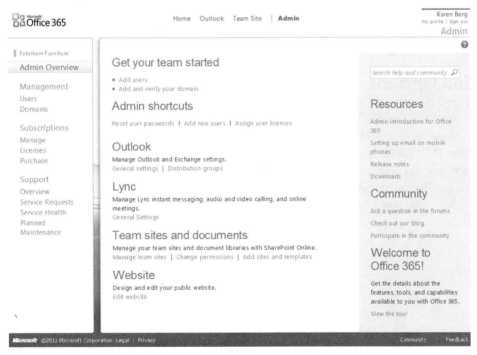

FIGURE 7-1 The Office 365 Plan P1 Home page, as shown to administrators.

Cleaning House

Many small businesses have gigabytes of mail history, much of which is not relevant to their current business. If you plan to move your mail into Office 365, now is a good time to clean up your inbox. Take some time to remove the mail in the junk folder, empty the trash, and delete those embarrassingly old emails that you've been meaning to get around to. No need to clog up your pristine Office 365 mailbox with unnecessary mail that needlessly increases the migration time and then slows down searches.

Document Your Existing Setup

Take a look at your settings in Outlook for your existing mailbox. Are you using contacts, rules, signatures, or other customizations? Have you created folders in your mailbox to help organize your mail? These kinds of settings are specific to your inbox, so when you add your new Office 365 inbox, they will not be carried over. Most people have only a few custom settings, so it doesn't take much time to reconfigure them in Outlook for Office 365. If you have a complex setup, you can export and import rules and other settings.

Frequently, small businesses use Outlook contacts as an important part of their operation. If so, consider how you want to move the contacts. The process can be as simple as dragging the contacts from one inbox to another, but it might also involve exporting the contacts into a file and then importing them into your Office 365 inbox. See "Export from Outlook," later in this chapter.

Migration Options

Before you set up Outlook for Office 365, determine how you want to manage your existing mail. Some companies choose to simply add their Office 365 inbox to their existing setup and have all new mail arrive in Office 365, and their old mail just stays in their old service. Others choose to migrate their mail, calendar, and other information to Office 365. You have lots of choices. To help you decide which is right for your business, the following sections outline the most common scenarios and provide implementation tips.

Special Circumstances

The migration methods presented in this chapter will work with most versions of Outlook as well as other mail clients, but you do need to keep a couple special circumstances in mind. One such occurs if you use Outlook 2007 and your current mailbox is hosted on an Microsoft Exchange Server (locally or in the cloud). Office 365 is also an Exchange mailbox, and Outlook 2007 does not allow you to have more than one Exchange mailbox in the same profile. In this case, you can export your existing mailbox to a PST (and import it into your Office 365 inbox or attach it as described later), upgrade to Outlook 2010, or use a migration service. All of these work very well to move not only your mail but also your Calendar and other information into Office 365.

If you have Outlook Express on the same system as Outlook, you can directly import mail and other settings by following the instructions in the KB article "How to upgrade from Outlook Express to Outlook 2010, to Outlook 2007, to Outlook 2003, or to Outlook 2002," at *http://support.microsoft.com/kb/291602*. Note that you do not want to import your email account configuration, just the contents.

If you use an email client other than Outlook, you will need to refer to its documentation for specific import and export information. Because Outlook is the most common email client in the world, most other email clients have the ability to transfer information into and out of Outlook. Look for details about how to export the files into a CSV (comma-separated value) or PST file format.

Use a Partner or Service

You can migrate your content yourself, or you can get some help. You can find Office 365 Partners and consultants available who can manage your migration. Browse to *http://pinpoint.microsoft.com* and search for Office 365 to find someone in your area.

In addition, inexpensive online services such as Migration Wiz (*http://migrationwiz.com*) can move your mail and related content (depending on your service provider) to Office 365 for a flat, affordable fee.

Move Mail with PST Files

Outlook 2007 and Outlook 2010 have the ability to host multiple inboxes at the same time. If you simply add your Office 365 inbox to Outlook and you already have an inbox, you now have two mailboxes. When you set up your account this way, you can easily access your old mail and use Office 365 at the same time.

With two mailboxes, your previous mail is available to you in Outlook but not in Office 365. To add your old mail to your Office 365 inbox, just drag your previous mail into your Office 365 inbox. It really is that simple. You can do the same with contacts, your calendar, tasks, and other items associated with an Outlook inbox. This is perhaps the most commonly used method for migrating small businesses to Office 365 because it is easy to do and works well.

Because Outlook has both inboxes, a special problem arises when you move your domain name from your previous service provider to Office 365. When you make the DNS changes, Outlook will be unable to log on to the old service. The resulting errors shown in Outlook are more or less cosmetic, because you don't use the previous mail service anymore (and if you do, both Office 365 and your previous provider will have different domains, so this won't be an issue). Even so, it can be annoying to have Outlook showing errors.

To solve this problem, first export the contents of your inbox to a PST file. When exporting the inbox to a PST, you effectively copy the contents of the inbox, including contacts, calendars, mail, and tasks, to a portable file that is now separated from the original service. With Outlook, you can work with a PST file in a variety of ways. You can import the contents into your Office 365 mailbox, or you can simply open it in Outlook where you can work with the mail and other contents as if it were your old inbox (see Figure 7-18). In either case, you can then safely delete your old inbox. Outlook will no longer try to contact your old mail service, which stops any error message you might be receiving. Both methods are covered in this chapter.

What Is a PST File?

Outlook has the ability to store mail, tasks, calendars, contacts, and other information in a *PST*, or *personal storage*, file. In general, most Outlook users don't know about or need to know about their PST files, but when you start to move your mail around, these files can become important. You easily create PST files from your existing mail and add contents from a PST to a new mailbox. In effect, this lets you simply add your existing mail into Outlook without having to move all the mail from one server to another. Outlook's flexibility in working with PST files is one of the keys to moving to Office 365 when you have existing mail to bring forward.

Export from Outlook

Via a PST file, Outlook makes it easy to export the mail, contacts, calendar, and other settings from one account (or computer) and then import to another. This might sound technical, but it is really quite simple. In Outlook 2010, for example, follow these steps:

1. Click the File tab.

2. Click Options.

3. Click Advanced.

4. Under Export, click Export.

5. Click Export To A File, and then click Next.

6. Click Outlook Data File (.pst), and then click Next.

7. Select the account to export, as shown in Figure 7-2, and ensure that the Include Subfolders option is selected. This will export all the settings, including mail, calendar, tasks, contacts, and notes. Click Next.

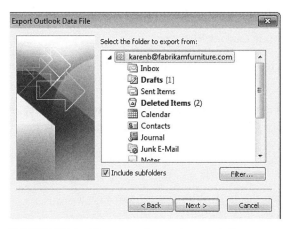

FIGURE 7-2 Select the account name to export all.

8. Click Browse to select where you want to save the Outlook Data File (.pst), enter a file name, click OK, and then click Finish.

When prompted, consider protecting your exported file with a password, because this file might contain valuable information.

> **Note** Using the PST file technique, you can export your entire previous profile or only specific pieces, such as contacts, mail, tasks, or any other information. This gives you the ability to be very precise in deciding what information you want to export.

Now you have a file that you can attach or import to your new profile when the time comes. See "Import Mail, Contacts, and Other Settings from a PST" and "Attach the PST to Your Outlook Profile as a Local Folder," later in this chapter.

Use Connected Accounts

A second option for moving your mail into Office 365 is to use Outlook Web App's Connected Accounts feature. With Connected Accounts, you can configure your Office 365 mailbox to regularly copy mail from an external service into Office 365. When set up, Office 365 will periodically read the external mailbox to bring in new mail, but *only* mail. Connected Accounts does not read or import calendars, contacts, or other information from the external service. In addition, the mail from the external service is co-mingled with your Office 365 mail. For example, email read from a Hotmail account addressed to joe@hotmail.com is mixed in with messages addressed to joe@contoso.com by default, but you can create a rule to sort mail from Connected Accounts into its own folder.

Connected Accounts is a great way to go, particularly when moving your custom domain to Office 365. However, if you choose to use Connected Accounts, it is imperative that you import your mail from the previous provider *before* you validate your custom domain in Office 365. The following is an example workflow for migrating mail by using this method:

1. Configure Connected Accounts in Outlook Web App.

2. Wait until email is fully imported (this might take some time, depending on the volume of mail).

3. Set up Office 365 to use your domain name. Your existing mail service will stop receiving mail. All mail will now be received by Office 365 and be available through OWA.

4. Set up your desktop, including Outlook. Your mail from your previous mail service will be in your inbox.

5. Optionally, archive your old mailbox in Outlook. (Export it to a PST.)

6. Remove the old inbox from Outlook.

7. Remove the Connected Accounts settings from OWA.

For a more detailed explanation of the Connected Accounts feature, as well as instructions for creating rules in OWA, see Chapter 8, "Working with Outlook Web App."

Export Calendar Settings

Calendars are an important part of most businesses. When you import mail to Office 365, in some cases—such as when you are using a POP email service—your calendar information is not migrated. Fortunately, most calendar systems support exchange information in the ICS (Internet calendar sharing) format, also known as iCal. For example, you can export your Google calendar as follows:

1. Log on to Google Calendar.

2. Choose the calendar that you want to export, and then click the down arrow in the My Calendars box.

3. From the menu, select Calendar Settings.

4. Under Private Address, right-click the iCAL button, and then select Save As, Save Target As, or your browser's equivalent language for saving to file.

5. Save the link to a file on your desktop or other easy to find location.

To export your calendar from Hotmail:

1. Log on to Hotmail, and then select Calendar.

2. Select Share, and then select My Calendar.

3. Select Send People A View-Only Link To Your Calendar.

4. Under Links That Show Event Details, click ICS: Import Into Another Calendar Application.

FIGURE 7-3 The ICS link for a Hotmail calendar.

5. Highlight the link as shown in Figure 7-3, and then press Ctrl+C to copy the link to your clipboard.

6. Start your browser, and then paste in the link as a URL, but change "webcals" to "http."

7. Download the ICS file to a convenient location for use later.

Other online services, including Hotmail, support exporting calendar information in this way. When exported, you can import the ICS file into Outlook by using the import wizard. For details, see "Import Calendar Information by Using an iCAL File," later in this chapter.

Set Up Your Desktop for Office 365

Now that you have your migration plans in order, you're almost ready to set up your desktop. However, before you do, take a moment to review the Office 365 system requirements to ensure that you have everything you need. To check the formal list of requirements, access the online help by clicking the ? (Help) icon at the upper-right of the Admin portal, and then select Getting Started, followed by Software Requirements For Office 365. The resulting help page (*http://onlinehelp.microsoft.com/en-us/office365-smallbusinesses/ff652564.aspx*) details operating systems, browsers, and requirements for each service.

In general, if your system can run Microsoft Office 2007 or Microsoft Office 2010, you can use Office 365. However, as you know by now, Office 365 does not support Outlook 2003, so you must upgrade Office 2003 *before y*ou configure your desktop for Office 365. The upgrade process will keep your existing settings and give you more options to manage your existing mail. If you have a Mac, refer to the service description paper titled "Office 365 Support for Apple Mac and iOS devices" at *http://www.microsoft.com/download/en/details.aspx?id=13602*. In general, Office 365 works well with Apple systems, but there are significant details to consider.

> **More Info** If you're interested in "roadmap" information, the Office 365 team blog at *http://community.office365.com/en-us/b/default.aspx* has traditionally been the best place to get the official news when features are updated.

Download Steps

After you review your Outlook setup, you can begin setting up your desktop with confidence. The required software is located on the Downloads page shown in Figure 7-4. To access this page, on the Office 365 Home page, in the Start Here section, click Set Up Now. It's also available there from the Downloads link under Resources.

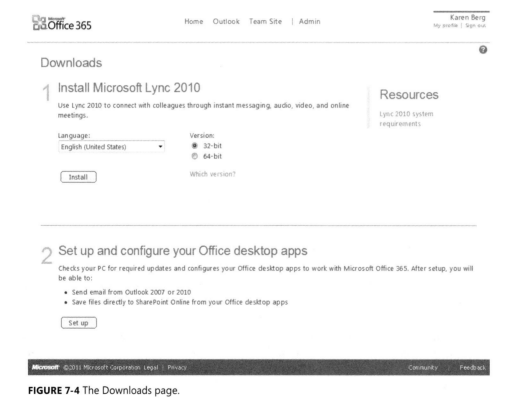

FIGURE 7-4 The Downloads page.

You need to install Lync 2010 and then the Office 365 setup application, in that order. The setup application applies specific updates and configuration settings to your system to ensure that it works with Office 365. Before you begin, take a moment to consult the Lync 2010 System Requirements link in the Resources column. The link takes you to an online help document that explains that Lync 2010 works with Windows 7, Windows Vista with Service Pack 2, or Windows XP with Service Pack 3. Apple Mac users should receive the Lync Server 2011 client when they select to install Lync. To make the best use of Lync Online, also consider using a webcam and voice headset with your computer.

Why Is Software Sometimes Called a Client?

In this and other books, you will see software installed in your system, like Lync 2010 or Outlook, called a *client*. Just as when you (the client) consume the services of an accountant (the provider), Lync 2010 consumes the services of Lync Online. Outlook consumes the services of Exchange Online. This is commonly referred to as the client/server model. The software on your computer, the client software, uses the services provided by the server. Any software on your system that connects to a service provider, including your web browser, is technically a client.

Install Lync 2010

It's simple to install Lync 2010. Just select the language and the proper version for your computer (see the sidebar "64 or 32 Bits?" if you need help determining this), and then click Install. The Lync 2010 client will download. Follow the prompts to complete the installation. On the last screen, clear the Start Lync check box, as shown in Figure 7-5, and then click Close. It is best if you don't start Lync 2010 before running the Office 365 setup program.

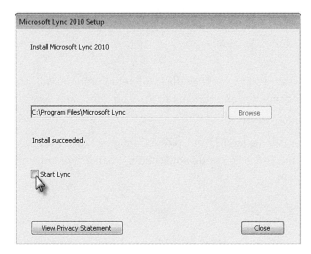

FIGURE 7-5 Clearing the Start Lync check box.

If Lync 2010 does launch, you must close it before you can run the Office 365 setup program. The easiest way to close the Lync 2010 client (you have a few choices) is to click the status under your name. This displays a menu of status options, as shown in Figure 7-7, with Sign Out and Exit at the bottom. Click Exit to close Lync 2010.

Run Office 365 Setup

You're now ready to install the Office 365 setup software. The Office 365 setup program will inspect your system, add specific updates to your computer, and configure Microsoft Office and Lync 2010 to work with Office 365.

On the Downloads page (see Figure 7-4), under step 2, Set Up And Configure Your Office Desktop Apps, click Set Up to download and start the Office 365 setup application. When prompted, enter your logon credentials, and then click Sign In.

FIGURE 7-7 Opening the menu to access the Exit command.

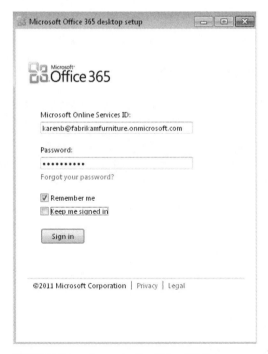

FIGURE 7-8 Logging on to the Office 365 Setup program.

After you successfully log on, you will see the screen shown in Figure 7-9. The setup program is ready to configure Outlook, Internet Explorer, or Microsoft Lync. If you don't want the setup program to configure a particular application for Office 365, clear the appropriate check box. This option is provided for companies that might already have Lync or other applications installed and don't want the setup utility to interfere with the existing configuration.

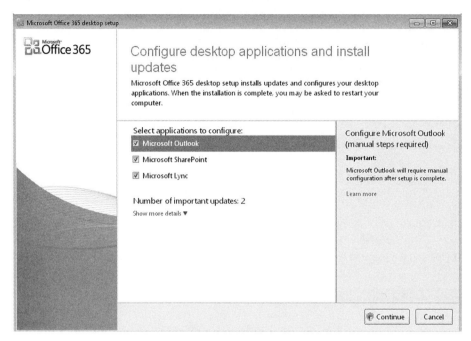

FIGURE 7-9 The Configure Desktop Applications And Install Updates screen.

Note the important message on the left: Microsoft Outlook Will Require Manual Configuration After The Setup Is Complete. As you will see, this is neither as ominous nor as manual as it sounds.

After you click Continue and accept the service agreements, the setup utility will run. The final screen summarizes the updates that were applied and repeat the message about the manual configuration requirement for Outlook (see Figure 7-10).

After you click Finish, you're ready to complete the setup by starting your applications.

Complete the Lync 2010 Setup

Now that the Office 365 setup program has run, Lync 2010 is configured to run with Office 365. You can now start Lync 2010 and log on to Lync Online.

1.   From the Start menu, open Microsoft Lync 2010.

2.   Enter your Office 365 user name for the sign-in address *and* user name, and then enter your Office 365 password (see Figure 7-11).

3.   Click Sign In.

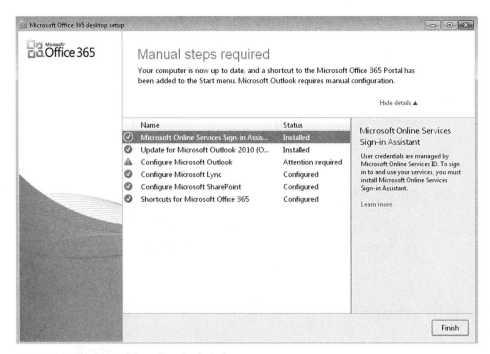

FIGURE 7-10 The Manual Steps Required window.

FIGURE 7-11 Signing in to Lync Online.

Lync 2010 logs on, and an introduction to Lync 2010 opens, as shown in Figure 7-12.

FIGURE 7-12 The Lync 2010 first launch tutorial.

Note The Lync 2010 introduction application contains useful information about how to configure and use Lync 2010. Not all the features contained in the tutorial are available with Lync Online.

Close the Lync 2010 introduction after it completes.

Set Up Outlook

The "manual" configuration of Outlook referred to in the Office 365 setup utility would be better described as "almost completely automated." The basic process using Outlook 2010 is as follows:

> **More Info** You can find step-by-step instructions for Outlook 2010, Outlook 2007, and Outlook for Mac 2011 in the article "Connect Outlook to This Account," at *http://help.outlook. com/en-us/140/ms.exch.ecp.useoutlookanywhere.aspx.*

1. Start Outlook.

    If you have installed but not yet configured Outlook, a setup wizard appears, as shown in Figure 7-13. If you've already been using Outlook, the setup wizard does not appear. To create a new account for Office 365 within Outlook, click the File tab, and then above the Account Settings button, click Add Account.

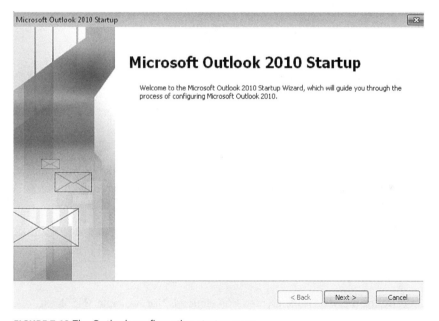

FIGURE 7-13 The Outlook configuration startup page.

2. Click Next.

3. For Would You Like To Configure An Email Account?, select Yes, and then click Next.

4. In the Auto Account Setup form, in the respective fields, add your name as you would like it to appear, your Office 365 email address, and your password (as illustrated in Figure 7-14), and then click Next.

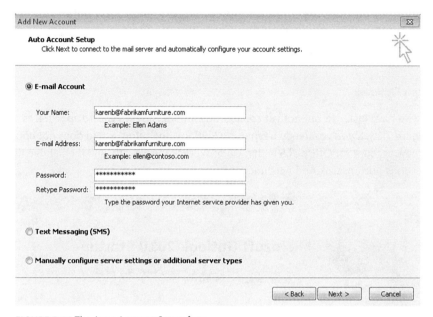

FIGURE 7-14 The Auto Account Setup form.

To use a custom domain, you must configure Office 365 and the user accounts that use the custom domain before entering it here. These details are covered in Chapter 6, "Working with Custom Domains."

5. Outlook 2010 will connect to Office 365 and acquire settings needed to set up your account (see Figure 7-15).

6. When it is complete, click Finish, as depicted in Figure 7-16.

If you receive the message An Encrypted Connection Is Not Available, Click Next To Attempt An Unencrypted Connection, an error occurred during the setup process. There is no point in trying the unencrypted connections as offered, because Office 365 requires an encrypted connection. In this case, click Back and re-enter your credentials, taking care to enter the correct details.

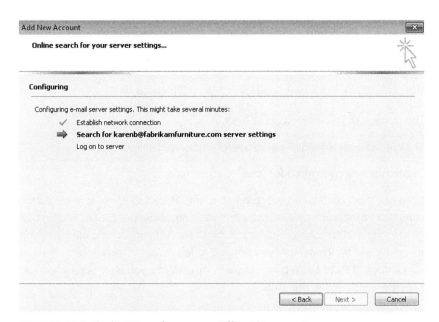

FIGURE 7-15 Outlook 2010 configures your Office 365 account.

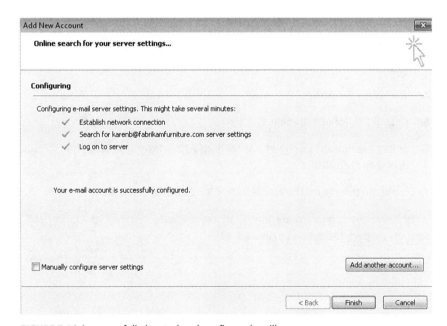

FIGURE 7-16 A successfully located and configured mailbox.

Congratulations! You are now set up to send and receive mail by using Office 365 and Outlook!

Troubleshooting Outlook Setup

The Add New Account Wizard works smoothly when:

- You can reach the Microsoft data centers on the Internet.

- The credentials you entered are correct.

- The user account is assigned a license for Exchange Online.

- DNS is properly configured for your logon domain.

You can test these conditions by logging on to the Office 365 Portal at *http://portal.microsoft online.com*. Start by logging on with the same credentials you used when adding Office 365 to Outlook with the Add New Account Wizard. If you are authenticated, that proves you can reach the data center and the credentials you entered to log on are correct. Next, on the top menu bar, click Outlook. If Outlook Web Access starts successfully, you have verified that an Exchange Online license is assigned to the user.

To test your DNS setup configuration:

1. Log on to the Office 365 Portal by using administrator credentials.

2. Under Admin Overview, click Domains.

3. Select the domain you are using for your Outlook setup (fabrikamfurniture.com in the example).

4. Click View Properties.

5. Click Troubleshoot Domain.

6. Select the option I Changed The Settings At My Provider More Than 72 Hours Ago, and then click Next.

You should see this result: The Name Server Records Are Correct.

If all of the above conditions are true, Outlook will "auto-discover" the Office 365 account and set it up properly, as shown in Figure 7-17.

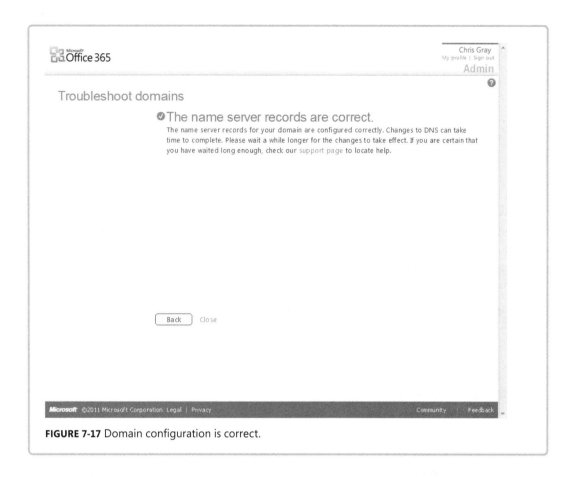

FIGURE 7-17 Domain configuration is correct.

Import Mail, Contacts, and Other Settings from a PST

Your desktop is now set up for using Office 365. If you exported your prior mail, contacts, calendar, and other data mailbox to a PST file, now is the time to bring it into Outlook and Office 365. To make that information available in your new setup, you can merge the contents into your new mailbox, attach the PST to your Outlook profile as a local folder, or combine the two techniques for a custom setup.

Merge the Contents into Your New Mailbox

The easiest and most common approach is to merge the contents of your PST file into your new mailbox. The result is that all your old mail is imported into Office 365, using the same folder structure and with the same content as before. Choose this option when you want to import your contacts, calendar settings, tasks, mail, and other details from your previous email account into your new Outlook account. The content will automatically be copied into your Office 365 online mailbox.

To import a PST using Outlook 2010:

1. Start Outlook.

2. Select File | Options | Advanced | Export.

3. Select Import From Another Program Or File, and then click Next.

4. Select Outlook Data File (.PST), and then click Next.

5. Browse to the PST file, choose how you want to manage duplicates, and then click Next.

Attach the PST to Your Outlook Profile as a Local Folder

Attaching the PST as a local folder is a surprisingly useful and simple technique. Use this approach when you want contents of the PST to be separate from your Office 365 mailbox or you want to drag information from the PST into your Office 365 inbox. Dragging is preferable to an import (as described before) when you want to visually inspect and select content to move to Office 365.

Figure 7-18 shows a PST called Previous Mail attached to Outlook.

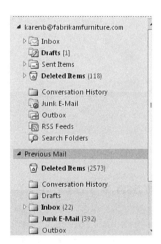

FIGURE 7-18 Previous Mail is an attached PST.

As you can see, the PST looks like a regular Outlook mailbox. You can work with the contents in the PST, reply to mail, and search its contents, which are indexed by Outlook.

To add the PST to Outlook 2010:

1. Start Outlook.

2. Select File | Open | Open Outlook Data File (PST).

3. Browse to the PST file, and then click OK.

That's all there is to it!

Selective Importing and Filtering

If you have requirements that are not met by simply merging or attaching the PST file, you can mix and match between the two. Examples include:

- Instead of importing all content, select a single folder.

- Keep the mail from your PST in one location by attaching it as a file, but merge the calendar entries and contacts from the PST into your main Inbox, using the import wizard.

- Merge mail from a specific user, date range, or other criteria.

These and other advanced filtering options are available in the importing wizard in Outlook 2010. Figure 7-19 shows the Filter window that appears when you click the Filter button in the Import Outlook Data File Wizard page.

You can use the form shown in Figure 7-19 to filter by word, From, To, and Time (how old the mail is). The More Choices and Advanced tabs give you many more capabilities. In short, you have tools available to do refined importing from your PST file, if you require it.

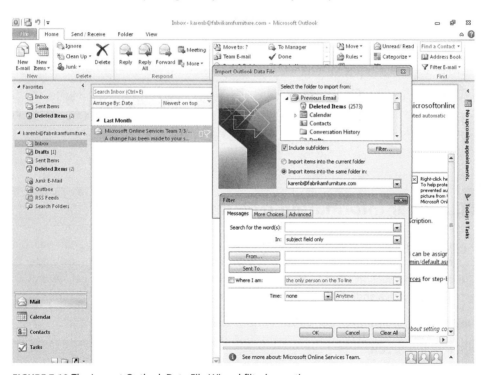

FIGURE 7-19 The Import Outlook Data File Wizard filtering options.

Import Contacts and Other Data by Using a CSV File

For those using a system like Google Mail or Hotmail, you can export contacts and other data, such as tasks, to a CSV (comma-separated value) file. You can import this information by using the same wizard used to import the PST files.

For example, to export and import contacts from Hotmail, perform the following:

1. Log on to Hotmail, select Options (upper right), and then click Export Contacts.

2. Enter the answer to the visual puzzle, and then click Export.

3. Enter a file name, and then save it to an easy-to-find location.

4. Start Outlook 2010.

5. Select File | Options | Advanced | Export.

6. Select Import From Another Program Or File, and then click Next.

7. Select Comma Separated Values (Windows), and then click Next.

8. Browse to the file, choose how to handle duplicates, and then click Next.

9. Select the Contacts folder, and then click Next.

10. Optionally, click Map Custom Fields to review the mapping of fields located in the CSV compared to fields that are used in the Outlook contacts system. Make any appropriate changes, as required.

11. Click Finish.

Import Calendar Information by Using an iCAL File

When you need calendar information merged into your Office 365 system and it is not available in a PST file, you can import an iCAL file like those referenced in "Export Calendar Settings" under "Migration Options." In that section, you saw how to create an iCAL file from Google. Other systems also support this common calendar file format.

To import an iCAL file into Outlook 2010, perform the following:

1. Start Outlook 2010.

2. Select File | Options | Advanced-Export.

3. Select Import An iCalendar (.ics) Or vCalendar File (.vcs), and then click Next.

4. Browse to the .ics file to import.

5. Choose between opening the file contents as a new calendar in Outlook and importing entries into your existing calendar, as illustrated in Figure 7-20.

FIGURE 7-20 Choose to Open As New or Import the calendar.

If you select Open As New, you will manage the calendar individually from your main calendar and can view the entries side by side. This is preferred for situations in which you are viewing calendars that belong to other people or that are managed by other systems. In most cases, during setup of Office 365, you will want to select Import to add the calendar entries into your main calendar.

Next Steps

You're now set up to use Office 365! The remaining chapters focus on how to configure and use the services rather than setup and deployment topics. First you'll learn how to use Outlook Web App for not only accessing mail, but as a way to configure your email services. Then you'll learn how to work with Outlook and Office 365, work with mobile devices, SharePoint Online, and Lync Online. By the end of the book, you'll have a solid understanding of how the services work and how they work together.

CHAPTER 8

Working with Outlook Web App

By using the Microsoft Office 365 web-based email application, Microsoft Outlook Web App (OWA), you can manage your email and calendar when you don't have access to the Outlook application, but it also does a great deal more.

Both Outlook and OWA show the the contents of your Office 365 Exchange Online account, and, in many ways, they look and operate alike. For example, if you find a misplaced message in your Outlook junk mail folder, you can right-click the message and mark it as safe. This updates a safe list that is also available in OWA and shows up in both programs. In addition, folders you create in your OWA Inbox appear in Outlook.

Even though OWA and Outlook display the same information in many cases, they are different applications with different features, configurations, and capabilties. For example, Outlook signatures are not applied to mail you send from OWA. OWA has its own signature capability, meaning that if you use both services, you need to configure a separate signature in each. Plus, Outlook has many more features and capabilites for managing mail. Even so, because OWA is actually part of Microsoft Exchange Online, OWA has several unique features. For example, in OWA you can force a remote wipe of your cell phone in case it is lost or stolen, create public groups, and connect accounts to periodically bring mail from other services to your Office 365 inbox. When you are the service administrator, you can also administer Exchange Online in OWA and make adjustments to other people's email settings.

You can access OWA from almost any modern browser through the Office 365 Portal. Use the Outlook link on the top menu or the Inbox, Calendar, and Options links listed under Outlook in the body of the page, as shown in Figure 8-1.

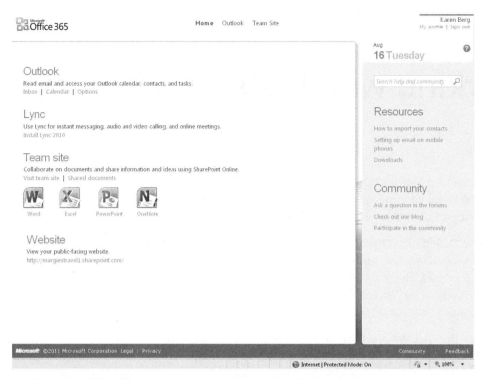

FIGURE 8-1 The Office 365 end user portal showing links to OWA (Outlook).

Using OWA is straightfoward, and Microsoft has many online demonstrations for learning how to do the basics. Rather than focus on the those, this chapter highlights how to personalize and use OWA's exclusive features. In addition, you'll learn about the important choices that service administrators can make for their users through OWA.

Note From within OWA, add its URL to your favorites and quick launch bars so that you don't need to return to the portal every time you want to access the program. To add to your favorites, press Ctrl+D. To add to your quick launch bar, just place your cursor in the address bar and drag the URL to the quick launch bar.

More Info You can find some good instructions regarding the general use of OWA at *http://help.outlook.com*; just keep in mind that not all the features detailed are available in Plan P1. Be sure that the help tip you are viewing displays the notice *Applies to: Office 365 for professionals and small businesses* at the top.

Personalization

You can use many of the settings in OWA to customize its look and behavior to suit your preferences. Taking some time to personalize the portal helps it better suit your needs and work the way you do. You have many ways to add a personal touch, from the way the portal looks to customizing signatures for mail. The personalization process begins the moment you first access OWA.

Set the Language and Time Zone

The first time you access OWA, you see a simple configuration screen, as shown in Figure 8-2.

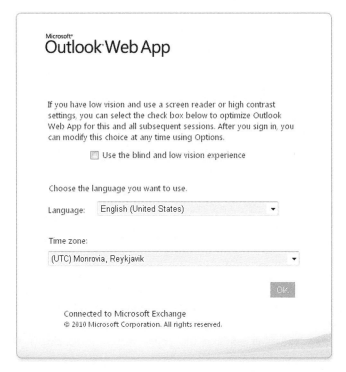

FIGURE 8-2 First access to OWA.

After you set the language and time zone options, you are presented with the main page, from which you can perform almost any email activity you need in day-to-day use.

Set Up Conversation View

Like Outlook 2010, OWA allows you to view your inbox, sorted by Date, From, To, Attachments, and other common email headings. It also has the capability to view your email by conversation. Rather than seeing every mail in sequence as it comes in, Conversation view groups together all mail related to a specific conversation.

Figure 8-3 shows the normal view of an inbox sorted by incoming date. Each message is shown individually. This is a great view for instantly identifying what mail is new, but it does not show which messages are part of the same conversation.

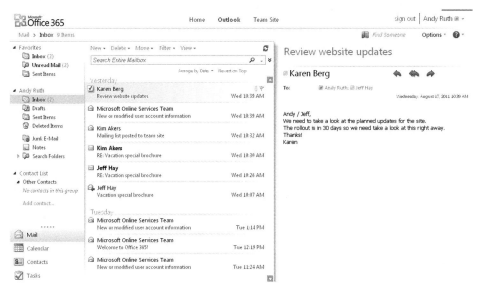

FIGURE 8-3 The default Inbox view.

To switch to Conversation view, just under the search box, click Arrange By, and then choose Conversation from the drop-down list, as shown in Figure 8-4. The thread titled Vacation Special Brochure is expanded in the screen shot to show the email related to that conversation. The reading pane on the right shows all the messages in the conversation.

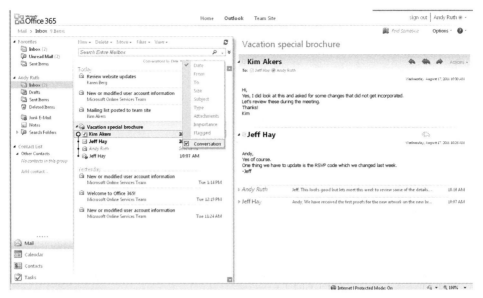

FIGURE 8-4 Enabling Conversation view.

When collapsed, you see just one entry with a triangle next to the subject, indicating that the conversation can be expanded, as shown in Figure 8-5.

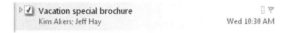

▷ ✓ **Vacation special brochure**
  Kim Akers; Jeff Hay   Wed 10:30 AM

FIGURE 8-5 Conversation view collapsed.

Many consider Conversation view a significant help in organizing increasing amounts of incoming information.

Add Instant Messaging Contacts to OWA

OWA is integrated with Lync Online in a number of ways. For example, you can see the online availability of your colleagues through the use of "presence" indicators. In Figure 8-6, the green indicator shows that both Andy and Kim are currently online and available. This feature is also enabled in Outlook.

sign out | Andy Ruth ◉ ▾

Find Someone   Options ▾   ❓ ▾

Mailing list posted to team site

◢ ◉ **Kim Akers**   ◀ ◀◀ ➤   Actions ▾

To: ◉ Andy Ruth

Wednesday, August 17, 2011 10:32 AM

Andy,
I posted the mailing lists from the Access database to the team site.
Can you take a look? It may need a refresh.
Kim

FIGURE 8-6 The Presence indicator in OWA.

In some cases, rather than replying by mail, it can be faster to start an instant messaging session. Because Andy can see that Kim is online, even if he is on the road and using a computer at a convention, he can right-click Kim's name and start a web-based instant messaging session, as shown in Figure 8-7.

FIGURE 8-7 Starting an IM session from an email in OWA.

What if you want to IM colleagues when you're not viewing an email from them? Just add names to your IM Contact list (the menu option shown in Figure 8-7). You can also add IM contacts on the left side of the OWA screen by clicking Add Contact, located under the Contact List. After you've added a contact, every time you open OWA, you get a view of who is online and their availability. In addition, these contacts will be added to Lync 2010 when you use your regular PC.

You can start an IM session with anyone in your contact list right in your web browser. Contacts are shown at the lower left in Figure 8-8.

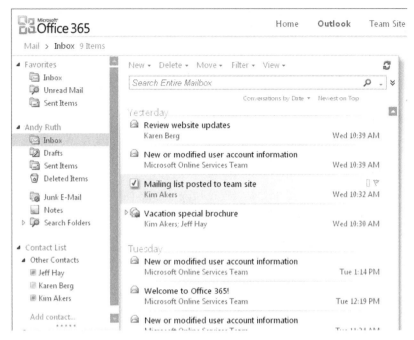

FIGURE 8-8 OWA showing contacts and presence.

Select a Theme

Just for fun, you can select a theme for OWA. Themes are strictly cosmetic and have no impact on Outlook or other settings. When you click the Options menu, you can see several choices, including Select A Theme (Figure 8-9).

FIGURE 8-9 The Options menu.

You can see additional themes by clicking the arrows next to the theme icons. Personally, I like the Finger Paints theme shown in Figure 8-10, but that's just me. You'll want to look for one that suits you. Unfortunately, you cannot customize the themes or add your own.

FIGURE 8-10 The Finger Paints theme.

Create a Signature

As mentioned earlier, signatures you create in OWA are not copied into Outlook, and vice versa. As a result, you will want to set up a signature in OWA for your outbound mail. To do so, click the Options menu, and then select See All Options, as shown in Figure 8-9. The resulting My Account screen has many uses, including links to features on the left and links to useful how-to articles on the right (see Figure 8-11).

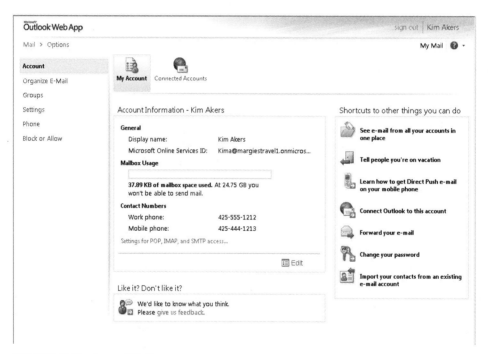

FIGURE 8-11 The Account Options screen.

Next, click Settings to open the Settings Options window, as depicted in Figure 8-12, where you can enter your signature. Enter a new signature or copy the signature you use in Outlook, and then click Save.

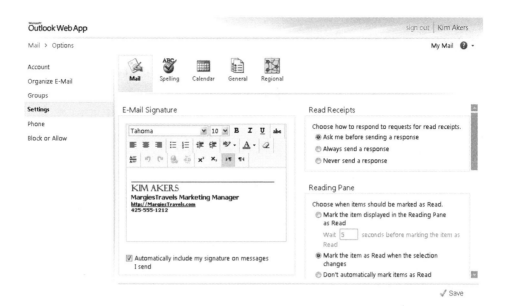

FIGURE 8-12 Creating a signature in OWA.

Configure Message Format, Read Receipts, and Other Settings

In addition to signatures, the Settings page has numerous configurations, including Message Format, Read Receipts, Reading Pane, and Conversations. In addition, you can enable display of the BCC field in this screen.

The default settings for these options work well for most people, so you don't usually need to make adjustments. Even so, you should read over each section so that you'll know what choices are available and make adjustments to suit your preferences. Settings that you adjust here will not be applied to Outlook.

Create a Rule to Send a Text Message to Your Phone

Using rules in OWA, you can accomplish some very useful automation, such as marking a message as important, moving to a folder, or playing a sound when a message arrives that matches your specified selection criteria. Although many are common to both applications, the rules you have available to you in Outlook are much richer than those in OWA. Still, OWA supports one trick that is easy to set up and extremely useful: you can create a rule that will send a text message. Using a text message is a great way to ensure you are alerted when specific events occur. For example, I have set up one that notifies me when one of my websites is offline for any reason. You could set alerts for stock price events, receipt of orders, messages marked as important, or messages from specific individuals.

Note You can set up the same texting capability in Outlook 2007 and Outlook 2010; however, you must first configure an SMS account within Outlook. This is not necessary in OWA with Office 365. In addition, the OWA rule is not dependent on Outlook. The rule will fire anytime a message is received that fits your criteria.

When you click the Phones menu option on the left side of Outlook Web App and then click Text Messaging, you will see the setup window shown in Figure 8-13.

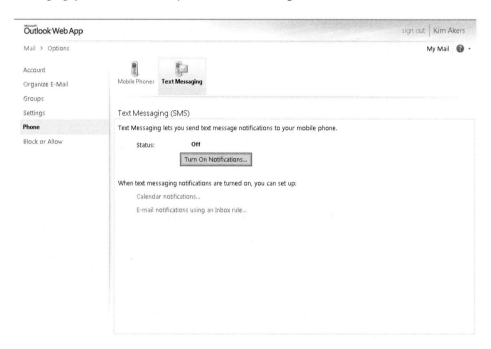

FIGURE 8-13 Configuring text messaging in OWA.

Click Turn On Notifications, and then select your locale and mobile operator from the resulting window (see Figure 8-14).

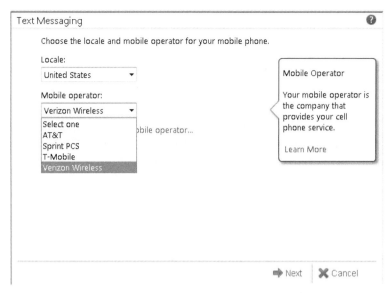

FIGURE 8-14 Select the locale and mobile operator for your cell phone.

The locale and mobile operator will vary depending on your location. If the mobile operator is not listed, this feature is not available to you at this time, but there is a possible workaround. Many cell phone companies provide a means to send a text message to a cell phone number by using a specially formed email address. For example, you can send a text message to a cell phone on the Verizon Wireless network by emailing the *<phonenumber>*@vtext.com, such as 4255551212@vtext. com. When Verizon's email system sees this address, it converts the email to a text message and sends it to the phone. Each cell phone carrier has its own format for this service, so you need to research the proper email address before configuring this. Using this special email address, you can set up a rule to forward the email as text message.

External Contacts

Many small businesses rely heavily on Outlook Contacts to communicate with customers and business associates. When you add a contact to Outlook, you can easily locate the contact's email address, phone, and other information, but that information will not be visible to others in your organization, unless you email them the contact card.

Outlook Contact Cards

Outlook can make use of contact cards in several helpful ways, but many people don't realize that you can email a contact card to other people. The receiver can quickly add the information to her contact list by double-clicking the attachment (and because Outlook uses a universal format for the card, called vCard, the receiver does not need to be using Outlook). This makes it easy to provide contact information to business associates and coworkers, as needed. You can also send others your contact card for easy inclusion into their contact system. This is an often overlooked and generally appreciated gesture, similar to exchanging business cards in a meeting.

By adding yourself to your Contacts in Outlook and then double-clicking your card, you can customize the details, including adding a picture and more information about you or your company. You can then insert your card into any email or include it in every email as your signature. If you do use an image with your card, consider a photo so that people recognize that they are talking to you. Use a low-resolution version suitable for email. In this way, your business associates are sure to have your current email, business address, phone, fax, cell, or any other information you want to include.

For more information about using contacts as business cards, see *http://office.microsoft.com/en-us/outlook-help/create-and-share-contacts-as-electronic-business-cards-HA010356440.aspx?CTT=1.*

Rather than emailing contact cards, you can share contacts with all members of your organization by adding them as an external contact to Office 365. When added to External Contacts, the contact's name and email address are listed with your Office 365 users and groups in the Global Address List (GAL). An external contact has a globe next to the name, so you can quickly identify that the contact is not an internal user, as shown in Figure 8-15.

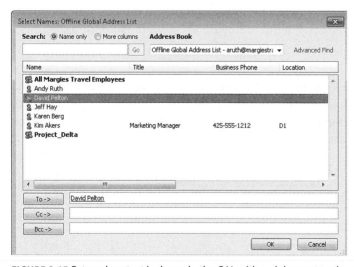

FIGURE 8-15 External contact is shown in the GAL with a globe next to the name.

External contacts are included as part of your company-wide address book (the GAL) and can be added to distribution lists.

Create an External Contact

To create an external contact, at the top of the OWA screen, click Manage Myself, and then select My Organization, as shown in Figure 8-16. You cannot see this option unless you are logged on as a service administrator.

FIGURE 8-16 To create an external contact, click Manage Myself, and then My Organization.

After selecting My Organization, you'll notice a small but important change. Instead of saying Outlook Web App in the upper left, it now says Exchange Server 2010, as shown in Figure 8-17.

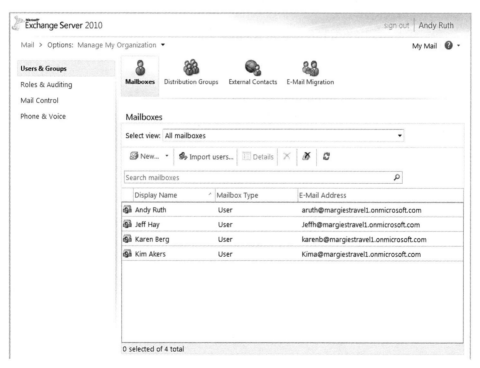

FIGURE 8-17 The Exchange administration console for Office 365.

Adding external contacts is one of the few cases where you need to access the Exchange Administration console. It's very easy to click into the administration pages through OWA, and notice that the pages look and act like OWA in many ways. For all practical purposes, you can think of OWA as a way to work with your email and, if you're an administrator, to manage Exchange Online.

Next, click External Contacts, and then complete the New External Contact form shown in Figure 8-18.

The display name is the name shown in your address book that goes on the To line when sending email. By adding additional information, such the contact's company or relationship to your business (vendor, agent, attorney, accountant, and so on), you can quickly provide details about the contact to users without having them open the contact's card for information.

When you click Save, Exchange saves the contact, and it becomes available to users.

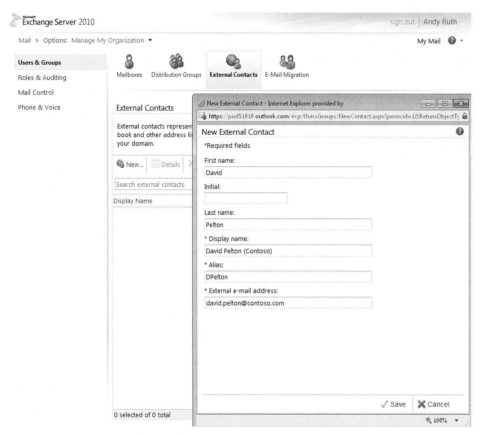

FIGURE 8-18 A New External Contact form.

Add Details to the External Contact

Adding the contact is just the first step. When you select the contact and then click Details, new options become available, as shown in Figure 8-19.

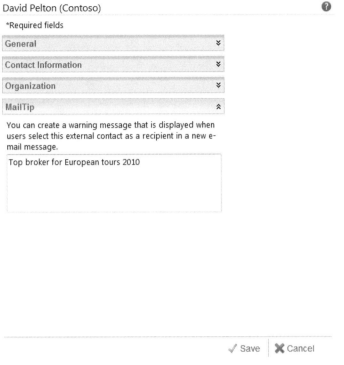

FIGURE 8-19 External contact details.

These new options include the following:

- **Contact Information**   Use this section to add the contact's address, phone, number, and any notes that you want associated with the contact.

- **Organization**   In some cases, the external contact might have a manager in your organization. You can represent that relationship by using the Organization section. Users can then see who manages the contact.

- **MailTip**   Add a MailTip to alert users to details about the contact that will be shown *before* you send a message. A MailTip ensures that anyone sending mail to David will see the tip shown in Figure 8-20 and will know that he is a significant business partner *before* the mail is sent. MailTips can be used to flag competitors, potential customers, individuals you might be involved with legally, or other useful details.

 Note MailTips cannot be seen using Outlook 2007.

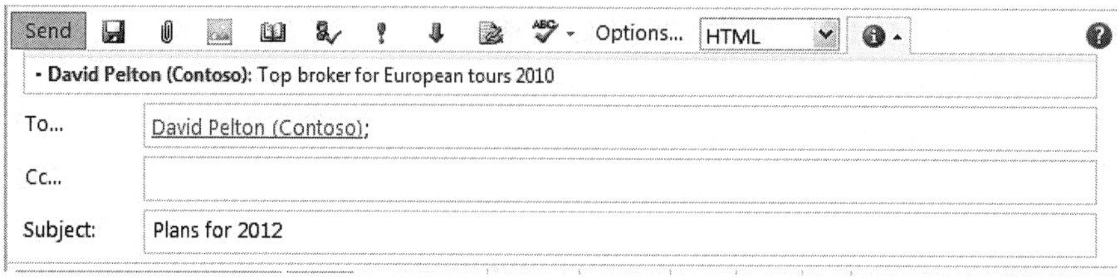

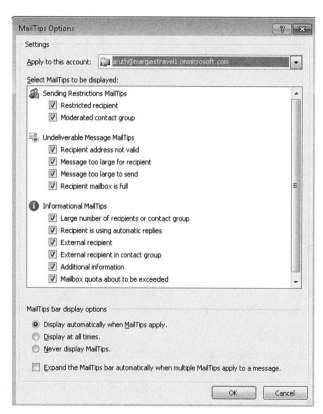

FIGURE 8-20 A MailTip displayed in OWA.

MailTips and Office 365

MailTips are one of the most popular features of Office 365. Several MailTips are built in. They automatically alert you when your mailbox is almost full, if you are sending to a large distribution list, and display other concerns, as shown in Figure 8-21. Access the MailTips screen in Outlook 2010 by clicking File | Options | Mail, and then MailTips.

FIGURE 8-21 The MailTips automatically provided by Office 365.

The built-in MailTips are useful, but the real power lies in adding customized MailTips. Users can add MailTips to distribution groups that they create. Service administrators can add a MailTip to just about anything, including External Contacts, Distribution Groups, Users, and Conference Rooms (Resource Records).

You might use a MailTip to say, "This is an unmonitored mailbox" or "In Litigation with this vendor, do not email without authorization." Keep in mind that MailTips are not shown in Outlook 2007.

Add and Administer a Distribution Group

A *distribution group* (sometimes called a *distribution list*) is a list of email addresses that you treat as one address. When you send an email to the group address, that message is delivered to all members of the group. For example, a group called support@contoso.com could contain the support staff and vendors who provide support for your organization. When someone emails support@contoso.com, all members of the group are notified. You can create distribution groups for in-house contacts (all employees, support staff, a specific project team), external contacts (all customers, all vendors, on-call consultants), or a combination (seminar registration, newsletter). In the next section, you use OWA to set up an example distribution group (public group) for all employees.

List Terminology

OWA, Outlook 2007, and Outlook 2010 all provide the ability to give a list of email addresses a name and then use that name as an email address. Although this book uses the term "distribution group" for such a list, each application uses a slightly different name and gives it a unique flavor. To decipher these, consult this list:

- **Public group**   A distribution group created in OWA. The group is public because the group's name is available in the company address book (GAL). All users of Office 365 in your organization can use this group for emailing, as shown in Figure 8-22. Note that the group's visibility in the GAL can be disabled.

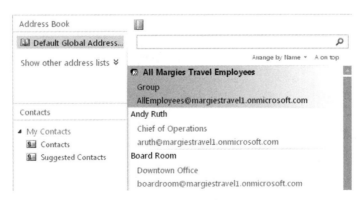

FIGURE 8-22 A public group in the OWA default GAL.

- **Contact group**   A distribution group created in Outlook 2010. This name is *not* visible to others unless you send it to someone in an email. Recipients can add the contact group to their contacts, but it does not appear to others in your organization when they look at the company address book in Outlook or OWA. In effect, it is a private list.

- **Distribution list**   The term used for a contact group in Outlook 2007.

- **Distribution group**   The term used in Office 365 when administrators access the settings for a public group.

   In short (relatively speaking), when you create these groups in Outlook, they are private and are called contact groups (Outlook 2010) or distribution lists (Outlook 2007). User-created groups in OWA are called public groups and are shared. To administer this group, the service administrator accesses the Distribution Group features in Exchange Online. Refer to Figure 8-17, and note the Distribution Groups icon.

Create an All Employees Public Group

Normal users and administrators can create public groups and add members to the group, but only administrators can prohibit users from leaving a group or enable a group to receive mail from outside the organization. For purposes of example, suppose that you are logged on as the service administrator.

The process of creating a public distribution group has two main steps: first, create the group, and second, open the group to modify the details. This general procedure of "create and then modify" is common to many items in OWA.

To create a public group, click Groups in the left menu in OWA, as shown in Figure 8-23.

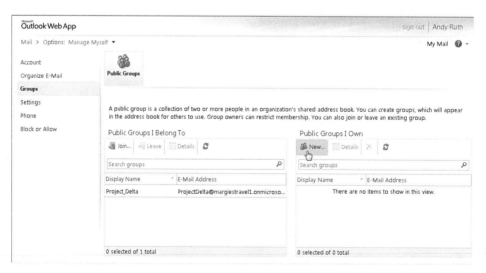

FIGURE 8-23 Creating a public group in OWA.

In the Public Groups screen, under Public Groups I Own, click New. The New Group form appears, featuring four sections: General, Ownership, Membership, and Membership Approval.

1. Fill in the fields under General, as shown in Figure 8-24. All the fields marked with an asterisk (*) are required. The Alias and E-Mail Address fields cannot contain spaces.

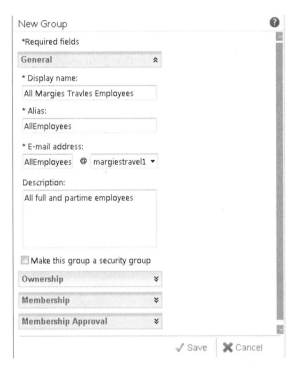

FIGURE 8-24 The General section of the New Group form.

a. **Display Name**   Displays on the To line and in the shared address book.

b. **Alias**   Used to generate the email address.

c. **E-mail address**   In almost all cases, the same as the alias. If you have multiple domain names available, assign the domain by clicking the pull-down list.

d. **Description**   Optional description to inform users of the group's purpose. This description is shown when users click Details on a selected group in OWA.

e. **Make This Group A Security Group**   Select this when you want to use the membership of this group for other purposes, such as allowing access to specific content in SharePoint Online. If the purpose of this group is strictly for mail, leave this cleared. You can convert a group to a security group later, if you decide to.

2. Expand the Ownership section, and add another owner if needed.

The service administrator can always take ownership of a group if necessary. It's a good practice to have more than one explicit owner to manage and moderate a group.

3. Expand the Membership section, and then click Add to add members to the list.

   As the group owner, you can add group members (note that you do not need to add yourself). To create a list for all employees, add all regular employees to the list.

4. Expand the Membership Approval section, and then choose the terms under which users can join or leave your group.

   By default, public groups are set so that all your users can join the group and leave the group. The settings shown in Figure 8-25 are typical for a group that includes all employees. The membership is assigned by the group owners, and users cannot remove themselves.

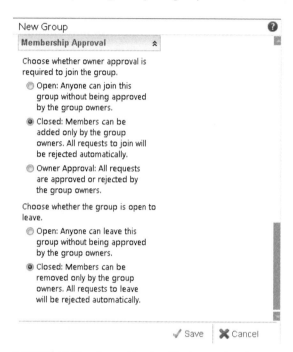

FIGURE 8-25 New Group Membership Approval options.

5. Click Save.

   The group is created at this point, but you are not quite finished. Some important settings become available to you only after a group is created.

6. Under Public Groups I Own, click the group name, and then click Details. This opens the public group form again, but now you see additional choices. Compare Figure 8-24 with Figure 8-26.

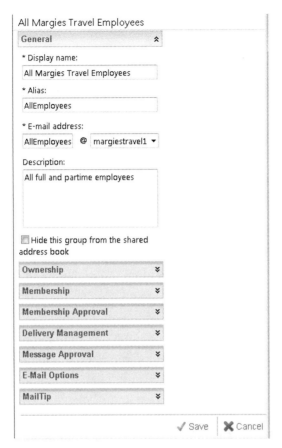

FIGURE 8-26 New sections are available after you create a public group.

Compared to Figure 8-24, four additional sections have been added: Delivery Management, Message Approval, Email Options, and MailTips. Also, a new option called Hide This Group From The Shared Address Book is listed under the General section. Use this setting to hide groups from searches of the public address book.

7. Expand the Delivery Management section, and then designate the individuals who are authorized to send email to this group.

By default, all internal users can send email to the list. By adding Andy and Karen, as shown in Figure 8-27, mail from any other user will be rejected.

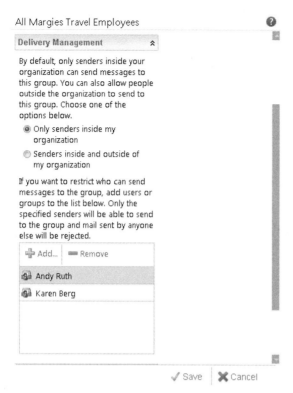

FIGURE 8-27 Delivery Management options.

8. Click Save. You've now completed the All Employees list.

Use Distribution Groups with External Email Addresses

Frequently, a business needs to add one or more users to a distribution group who are not a part of the organization. To add a user with an external email address to a distribution group, first create an external contact for the user, as described previously in the External Contacts section of this chapter. Then add the contact to a distribution group just as you would add a user. Next you need to enable the group to allow external mail.

Allow All External Users to Send Mail to the Group

By default, a public group is set to receive incoming mail only from members of your organization. This prevents people outside of your organization from sending to the group. Even if you explicitly add an external contact to the group, that contact will receive mail from the group but cannot send mail to the group.

To allow your external contact to send email to a group, in the Delivery Management section of the Public Groups screen, click the Senders Inside And Outside Of My Organization radio button (see Figure 8-27). This setting opens the list to receive mail from the world. Figure 8-28 shows a suggestion box distribution list set to accept all mail.

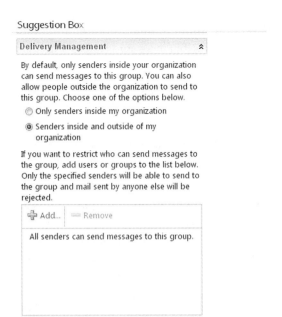

FIGURE 8-28 A distribution group set to accept all mail.

This is perfect for a group like suggestions@contoso.com or applications@contoso.com, where you want unknown others to send mail to members of the group. But when you want to allow only specific external users to send to the group, you must designate which users are permitted.

Restrict Senders to the Group

Allowing anyone from anywhere to send mail to the group can be very useful but is too permissive for groups that require a specific membership. To restrict who can send to the group, just add approved names to the form (Figure 8-28). To add an external name, the user must first be added as an external contact.

Get Creative (Groups Within Groups)

You can add distribution groups to other distribution groups. Although this might be overly complicated for many businesses, it can be quite useful in certain cases. For example, suppose that you wanted to receive email externally from anyone and wanted incoming mail to the group to be distributed to everyone in your organization. To configure this, you would need to manually add all the members of your organization to the Membership section of the group, one at time.

As an easier alternative, you can create your group, set it to receive mail from all external users, and then add the All Employees distribution group rather than individual email addresses. Using this as an example, you can get creative about how to receive and distribute incoming mail by using distribution groups.

When *Not* to Use Distribution Groups

Office 365 works great for many common business scenarios, but there are a couple of uses that I would not recommend.

Public Email Discussion Groups

Public email discussion groups (also called email discussion lists) are very popular on the Internet. Some organizations host these groups to facilitate their business interests. For example, it wouldn't be uncommon for a nonprofit organization with the goal of raising money for a certain cause to host an email discussion group of people sympathetic to that cause.

Office 365 has the basic capabilities needed to host such a list. You can add external contacts to a discussion group, and Office 365 will receive and deliver mail for all the users. But email discussion groups require more than just the ability to deliver mail. For example, email discussion groups generally allow users to automatically subscribe and unsubscribe from the list. On most lists, recipients can find instructions on how to unsubscribe at the end of every message. In addition, servers that host these groups (called list servers) are often specifically designed for this purpose so that you can manage mail loops, bounces, email flooding, and other issues that can occur when you provide a mail delivery service to a group of unrelated individuals or organizations.

Office 365 would work well for this purpose only if a group is small and doesn't change much. For example, I would not hesitate to create a list of this sort for a special interest group of 10–20 people. Otherwise, given the manual administration of email addresses and other mail list–related issues, you probably would be better served by a service designed for this purpose. A quick search for "host your own email discussion group" will reveal many good options.

Email as a Business

Office 365 is well designed to provide email services *for* your business, but it is not designed to provide email services *as* a business. In other words, if your business is providing a server that uses email extensively, such as the distribution of newsletters to tens of thousands of users or other commercially focused, large email loads, it would be advisable to purchase services designed for this use. Office 365 has built-in email delivery throttles on messages per second and limits regarding how many emails can be sent from a single address each day. These limits are placed on the service to prevent overuse of resources by individual accounts, thereby protecting performance for all users. These limits are not encountered in general use but would likely be an issue in a commercial delivery service.

The current limits are published at *http://help.outlook.com/en-us/140/dd630704.aspx*.

Join a Public Group

Users can add themselves to a group or request to be added, depending on your Membership Approval settings, by clicking Join on the Public Groups page as shown in Figure 8-29. Users cannot join a group by sending a "subscribe" email to the group address.

Public Groups I Belong To

FIGURE 8-29 Joining a public group.

Connected Accounts: Add an Existing Mail Service to Office 365

OWA has a unique and very useful feature called Connected Accounts, which is discussed in Chapter 7, "Desktop Setup and Migration." You can use Connected Accounts to add mail to your Inbox from Google Mail, Hotmail, or other email services. After connecting a mailbox, OWA continues to read the mail from the external service every hour; when you log on to OWA, it adds new messages to your Inbox from that account. All users in your Office 365 organization have access to this feature. To access the Connected Accounts feature, log on to OWA, click Options, and then select All Options. Then, click Connected Accounts, as shown in Figure 8-30.

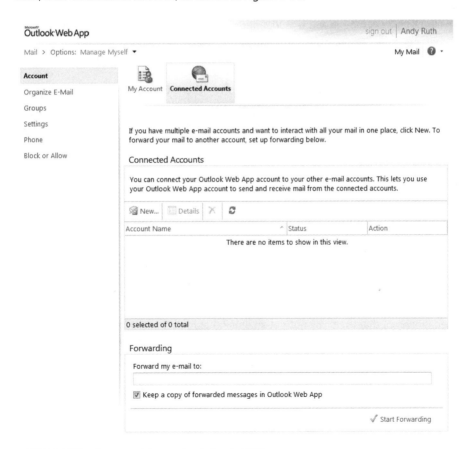

FIGURE 8-30 The Connected Accounts window in OWA.

To add a connected account, just click New and type in the email address and password. If possible, Office 365 connects to the account and starts to import the existing mail. If the connection fails, be sure that you are entering the correct information. Most providers use industry standard settings, but some don't. In those cases, you will need to provide additional information, such as the protocol type and port numbers. The service provider for your connected account will have this information available.

For example, to add a Google Mail as a connected account, you need to enable POP access on Google Mail. Log on to your Google Mail account, and select Settings | Forwarding and then POP/IMAP. Under POP, select Enable POP For All Mail (Even Mail That's Already Been Downloaded) to copy all your mail copied to Office 365. You can also instruct Google Mail to keep the mail even after it has been downloaded. If you have a large mailbox, it can take quite a while (potentially more than a day) for several gigabytes of mail to be copied.

After the initial transfer, you can create a rule that identifies mail coming into the connected account and moves it to a specified folder. You can find a good help file topic about connected accounts with a short video showing how to set it up, including creating a sorting rule, at *http://help.outlook.com/en-us/140/cc511377.aspx*.

Keep in mind that even though this feature imports mail from your connected account, it does not bring over contacts, calendars, or other information.

Send Email from Your Connected Account Address

You can send mail from your connected email account address even though you're using OWA (or Outlook) in Office 365. Simply click From, as shown in Figure 8-31, and then select the connected account address.

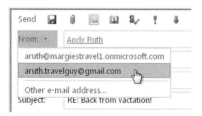

FIGURE 8-31 Sending from the connected account.

Be advised, however, that users will not get an email that looks exactly as if you have replied from that connected account service. Instead, they will receive a message that says it was received "on behalf" of the service, as shown in Figure 8-32.

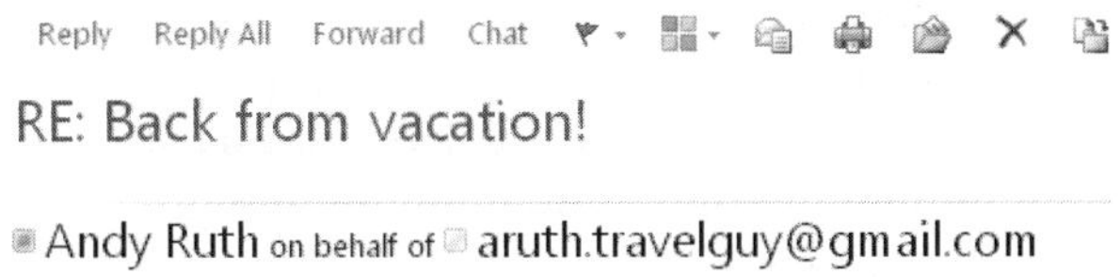

Reply   Reply All   Forward   Chat   ▼ ▾   ▦ ▾   ⬚   🖶   📩   ✕   ⬚

RE: Back from vacation!

⬚ Andy Ruth on behalf of ⬚ aruth.travelguy@gmail.com

FIGURE 8-32 Mail sent on behalf of the connected account.

The "on behalf of" message is necessary so that mail coming from Office 365 does not look like it originated from another service. This message cannot be turned off or customized.

Frequency of Reading Mail from Connected Account

When you first set up your connected account, depending on the service and the volume of mail in your mailbox, it can take several hours for the mail to fully replicate into Office 365. The length of time depends on the service provider and the amount of mail you have saved in that mailbox. In addition, new messages to your connected account are brought over approximately every hour. You can get mail on demand by logging on to OWA.

If you need to see mail that you receive in your connected account in real time, using a connected account is not the way to go. In this case, consider adding the account to Outlook. You will then have an inbox in Outlook for your Office 365 mail as well as your external account. When you open Outlook or click Send/Receive, Outlook will refresh both inboxes, retrieving all available mail. This is a good way to go when you plan to keep using your external account and need real-time access to new mail.

If you instead wish to consolidate all your mail and use only one account, after the mail is in your Office 365 inbox, you can disable the connected account. Simply select the account in OWA, and click Delete. At that time, mail will stop being imported from the external service.

Add and Administer a Conference Room

Many small businesses have resources that need to be scheduled for use. Using Office 365, service administrators can create a resource mailbox designed for this purpose. This mailbox is called a *room mailbox* and does not require an Office 365 license. Even though this feature is called a room mailbox, you can use it for any resource that requires scheduling—delivery vans, digital projectors, or large format printers.

Anyone can see whether the resource is available simply by adding the resource's email address to a meeting request, just as you would add a user. Because the room mailbox is listed with your users, contacts, and groups in the company's email directory in Outlook and OWA, adding the address is a simple task of pointing and clicking. You can then view the free/busy schedule of all the users and the selected resource on one screen, as shown in Figure 8-33. This makes selecting an available time for everyone much easier. Optionally, when you send the meeting request, the resource will automatically accept it and block the time, showing the reserved time as busy for others who view the calendar.

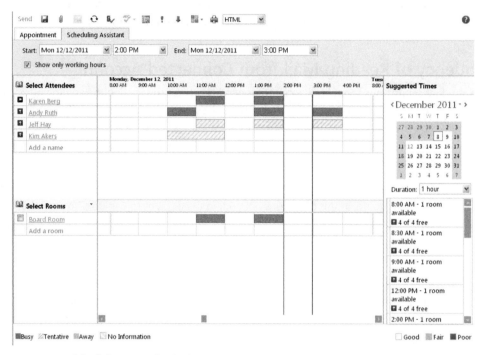

FIGURE 8-33 Scheduling a meeting in OWA.

To add a room mailbox, perform the following:

1. Log on to OWA by using your administrator credentials.

2. Click Options, and then click See All Options to go to the Account Options window, as shown earlier in Figure 8-11.

3. Hover over My Account, and then click My Organization, as shown in Figure 8-16.

4. On the Exchange 2010 administration console, click the downward-facing triangle next to New, and then click Room Mailbox as shown in Figure 8-34.

FIGURE 8-34 Creating a new Room Mailbox.

If you click New instead of the triangle, you will not see the Room Mailbox menu option.

5. Complete the form as shown in Figure 8-35, and then click Save.

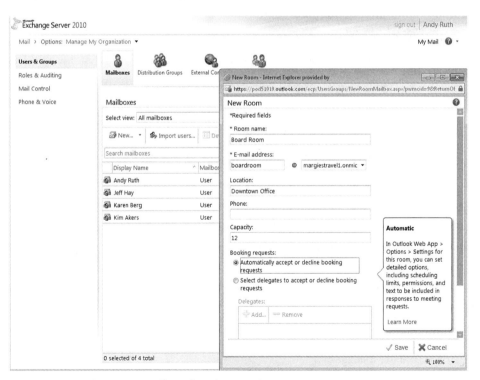

FIGURE 8-35 Creating a room mailbox (shared resource).

After creating the room, select the room and click Details to add a MailTip or to review your settings. MailTips can be particularly useful when rooms or resources have information that you want to communicate to others before they send a meeting request. For example, "digital projector not working," "teleconferencing equipped," or "CC: Andy when reserving this room." You can set maximum occupancy for a room, as well.

Customize a Room Mailbox

You can adjust the following settings for a room mailbox:

- Automatically accept meeting requests.

- Disable reminders.

- Set maximum number of days in advance that a resource can be booked.

- Set maximum time (in minutes) to allow for a meeting request.

- Allow scheduling only during working hours.

- Allow repeating meetings.

- Allow conflicts.

- Set scheduling Permissions:

  - Specify who can automatically schedule the resource.

  - Identify users who can submit a request that must be approved before scheduling.

  - Identify users who can automatically schedule the resource and automatically submit a request for approval if the resource is unavailable.

- Allow additional text to be sent in response to requests.

To access these settings, you use the "working on behalf" feature of OWA that is available only to administrators.

1. Log on to OWA with your administrator credentials.

2. Click Options, and then click See All Options to go to the Account Options window, as shown in Figure 8-11.

3. Hover over My Account, as shown in Figure 8-16. On the Select What To Manage menu, click Another User.

4. From the list of users, groups, rooms, and contacts, select the room (or resource) account you want to manage.

5. On the menu on the left of the screen, as shown in Figure 8-36, click Settings.

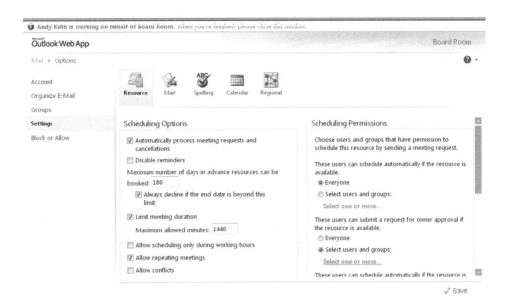

FIGURE 8-36 Customizing a resource by using "working on behalf."

6. Make the changes you want, and then click Save.

> ## Use OWA to Configure Other Users' Mailboxes
>
> In addition to managing settings, service administrators can use the Select Others option under the Select What To Manage menu (Figure 8-16) to manage settings for any Office 365 user. When you access the user's account in this way, you can configure all the settings the user can access in the OWA options pages. This enables you to inspect, troubleshoot, and configure a user's settings from a browser without having to know their password. Note that you cannot read another user's mail by using this feature.

Wipe Your Cell Phone

Another valuable OWA feature is the ability for users to remotely wipe their cell phones. This is a feature that isn't critical until a company phone is lost or stolen, and suddenly you will be glad you have Office 365. To access this option, log on to OWA, select All Options from the Options menu, and then click Phone on the menu at the left of the screen.

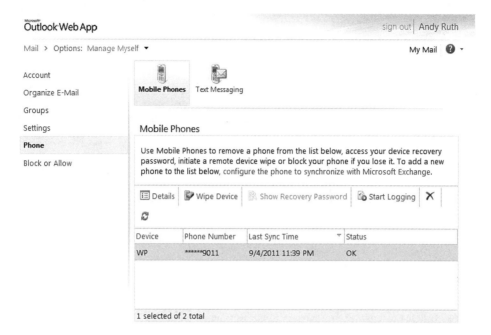

FIGURE 8-37 Wiping a mobile phone.

In the Mobile Phones screen (see Figure 8-37), select the phone and then select Wipe Device. You will be told that the device will be wiped and asked to confirm the action. Keep in mind that when you wipe a phone, all the data on the phone is permanently erased. When approved, the status for the phone will change from OK to Wipe Pending. The next time the phone connects to the service, it will be wiped.

If a user has lost the phone but cannot access OWA to initiate wipe, use the administrator's option to manage another user's account (as detailed in the sidebar "Use OWA to Configure Others Users' Mailboxes") to access this menu on the user's behalf and initiate the wipe.

Enable and Configure the Personal Archive

A personal archive is a separate cloud-based mailbox that contains mail that is past a designated age. The archive mailbox appears as a separate mailbox in OWA and Outlook. You can drag mail into the archive and set policies that control both when to move mail into the archive and how long it should be retained.

Suppose that you don't have a cloud-based archive. Where is your old mail stored? Outlook is configured to ask you periodically if you want to archive your old mail. Mail archived by Outlook is stored in a PST file on your PC. If the PST files are lost or corrupt, your history goes with it. Another problem with PST files surfaces when you need to search your email history for legal or business reasons. This can be challenging when dealing with PST files over the course of years.

The Office 365 personal archive addresses both of these issues. Because your archive is in the cloud, you don't have to be concerned about backups or losing the data. In addition, the archives inbox can be searched like any other mailbox, making discovery much easier. Finally, you can use policy to automatically move mail from an inbox to the archive so that it is self-maintained. This policy can be applied to everyone in your business so that everyone is archiving email in a consistent way. If mail needs to be recovered from archive, the policy makes it easy because it has defined how that mail was archived. In the event of legal action, an enforced archive policy makes discovery easier.

Outlook Auto-Archive vs. Personal Archive

Although auto-archive and personal archive sound similar, they are very different features. Outlook's auto-archive feature is built into Outlook, so Outlook has to run for the feature to work. You have probably seen the auto-archive from Outlook before. Outlook's auto-archive is easy to use and automatically moves older messages to a local PST file. However, because those PST files are stored on your PC (and everyone else in your business has theirs stored on their PCs), they are easily lost. The personal archive, on the other hand, is a cloud mailbox, and policy rules are stored in Office 365. Mail is archived according to the policy, even if you never open Outlook. In addition, the personal archive is backed up by Microsoft, so you don't have to worry about securing PST files.

When using the personal archive, keep in mind that the Office 365 archiving policy to move old mail into the personal archive does not move mail in Outlook's local archive. Mail must be in your Inbox or one of its subfolders to be automatically moved to the cloud-based archive. Now that you have Office 365, you should turn off auto-archive in Outlook 2010 by clicking File | Options | Advanced | Auto-Archive, and then clearing the check box next to Run Auto Archive Every __ Days.

 Important Your Exchange Online inbox has a 25 GB limit that is shared with your personal archive. The size of your archive plus your inbox cannot exceed 25 GB.

To enable the personal archive for a mailbox, perform the following:

1. Log on to OWA by using your administrator credentials.

2. Click Options, and then click See All Options to go to the Account Options window, as shown in Figure 8-11.

3. Hover over My Account, and then click Manage My Organization, as shown in Figure 8-16.

4. Select the user from the list of users (see Figure 8-17), and then click Details.

5. Expand the Mailbox Features section.

6. Select Archive, and then click Enable.

7. Enter a name for the archive or accept the default, and then click Save.

8. Click Save again.

Now, when you view your Inbox in OWA or Outlook, you will see an Archive mailbox along with your normal inbox, as shown in Figure 8-38.

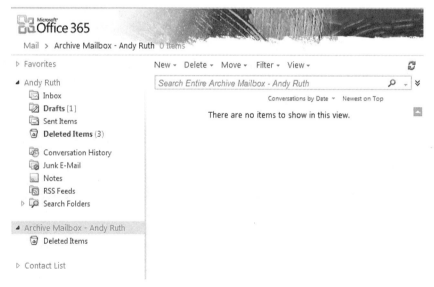

FIGURE 8-38 An archive mailbox in OWA.

The archive mailbox will be empty until the policy service inspects and moves mail to the archive. You can also move mail to the archive manually (by dragging it) or by using rules.

Enable and Apply Archive Policy

Although you can't really tell by looking, a default archive policy has been applied to users, which instructs Office 365 to move mail that is more than two years old to the archive. Alternatively, you can choose to archive after one year or not to archive at all. To enable one of these alternative policies, perform the following:

1. Log on to OWA by using your Office 365 credentials.

2. Click Options, and then click See All Options to go to the Account Options window, as shown in Figure 8-11.

3. On the left menu, click Organize Email, click Retention Policies, and then click Add.

4. Select the two archive policies, as shown in Figure 8-39, click Add, and then click Save.

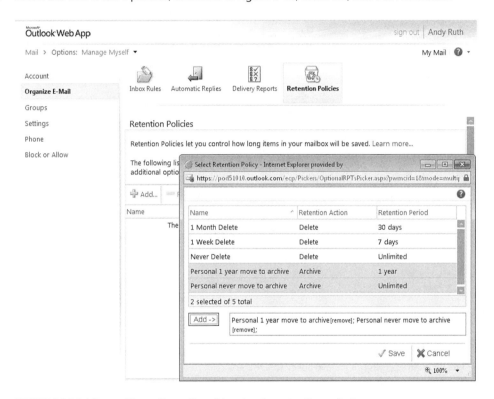

FIGURE 8-39 Adding archive policy options (also showing retention policy).

Now when you right-click a folder or mail item in OWA, you see two new menu options: Archive Policy and Retention Policy. Figure 8-40 shows the right-click menu for the Inbox, with the Archive Policy menu selected. The green check mark adjacent to Use Folder Policy means that the default settings are in place. Recall that the default archive setting is to move mail that is two years old or more to the archive. Selecting a different archive policy for the inbox automatically applies the new policy to all mail in the Inbox. The exception to this rule is that folder policy is not applied to any individual mail item with a different policy applied.

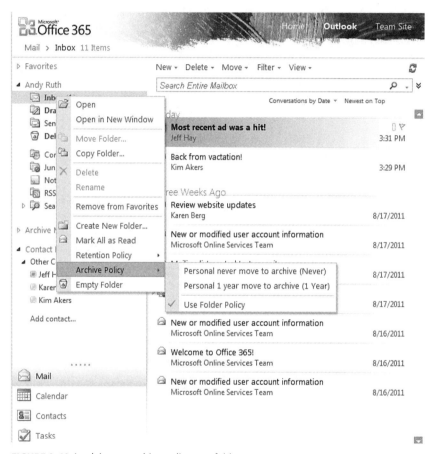

FIGURE 8-40 Applying an archive policy to a folder.

Note You can add custom archive policies by using advanced techniques involving a scripting language called Windows PowerShell. PowerShell commands for Office 365 are beyond the scope of this book. If you need a more advanced archiving policy, consider using a consultant or Microsoft Partner to assist with the setup. As an alternative, in Outlook (not OWA), you can create rules to move or copy mail to the archive folder to fit criteria that you designate. One of the options is to move mail that is received on, before, after, or between specific dates. You can also set the rule to copy the message rather than move the message. This gives you a lot of flexibility in deciding exactly what kinds of messages should be moved or copied to the archive and when. You can also import a PST into your personal archive, providing a convenient way of moving existing archives into the cloud. You import mail to the archive the same way you would to your Inbox. Instructions about how to create and import PST files are provided in Chapter 7, "Desktop Setup and Migration."

Enable and Apply Retention Policy

A retention policy controls how long an item is in your inbox before it is deleted. For most small businesses, retention policies are better handled by using rules or Auto-Archive in Outlook. This provides much greater flexibility in determining which mail you want to delete, archive, or keep in your inbox.

The retention policies available in Plan P1 are shown in the first three rows and have Delete listed as the Retention Action. The following policies are available: delete mail after a month, a week, or never delete. By default, when you enable the personal archive, the retention policy on your mailbox is set to Never Delete.

If you want Office 365 to automatically delete messages that are one week old or one month old, you can enable the policies by selecting them from Retention Policies options (Figure 8-39). Then, when you right-click a folder or email items (as shown in Figure 8-40), you can select Retention Policy and apply the desired policy to the item.

As with archive policy, retention policies can be customized by using advanced techniques that are beyond the scope of this book. For more information about archive and retention policy, see *http://help.outlook.com/en-us/140/cc950504.aspx*.

Outlook 2010 and the Personal Archive

With some versions of Outlook 2010, you can apply retention and archive policies to folders and mail in the same way that you can in OWA. The specific details about which versions of Outlook 2010 are supported for this are a bit fuzzy, but it appears that volume-licensed editions of Outlook 2010 are supported as well as stand-alone retail versions of Outlook 2010 (*http://office.microsoft.com/client/helppreview14.aspx?AssetId=HA102576659&lcid=1033&NS=O UTLOOK&Version=14&CTT=3*). This means that if you bought Microsoft Office 2010 as part of any retail package, such as Home Office and Professional, the policy capabilities are not shown in Outlook.

Figure 8-41 shows the personal archive mailbox just beneath the normal Inbox. So even though your version of Outlook might not allow you to right-click and apply policy, the personal archive is still available for searching, manually adding content, importing PSTs, and using rules to move mail to your cloud archive.

FIGURE 8-41 A personal archive Inbox in Outlook 2010.

For More Information

Microsoft has done a good job of providing how-to videos for using OWA. You can find these in the help documents at *http://help.outlook.com/en-us/140/gg605090.aspx*. In particular, the article "Set Up Your Email Account on Your Mobile Phone" gives you a preview of some of the topics covered in our next chapter on mobile devices.

CHAPTER 9

Working with Mobile Devices

One the best features of Microsoft Office 365 is the ability to connect to it by using a mobile device. Using your email-enabled phone, for example, you can keep in touch with the flow of information related to your business, which can both save time and improve your professionalism.

Here's a common example: you're on the campus of a large company to talk to a manager about a potential business opportunity. When you check in at the receptionist desk, you realize you don't know the number of the conference room where you are to meet. This one is easy. Just look at your phone! Because your phone is synchronized with your Calendar, using Office 365, you'll see an alert that the meeting is starting in five minutes. The alert displays the conference room number right next to the meeting start time. You wind up in the correct conference room, right on time.

Today's most popular phones all work well with Office 365, from Microsoft phones to the iPhone, Droid, and BlackBerry. Most mobiles devices provide the ability to connect to an Microsoft Exchange server, which allows your phone to synchronize email, calendar, contacts, and tasks with Office 365. You can also use your mobile device to view and (depending on your phone's capability) edit Office documents from Microsoft SharePoint Online.

Putting on your administrator hat for a minute, if company employees are using Office 365 with their mobile devices, you might want to ensure that those devices are secure, using PINs and passwords. OWith Office 365, you can designate which users can synchronize email to their phone and to enforce specific policies on those phones, such as requiring a PIN or strong password. In addition, you can configure new phones so that they are "quarantined" until approved.

In Chapter 8, "Working with Outlook Web App," you saw how to set up Office 365 to wipe your cell phone if it is lost or stolen, and to send a text message when a specific email arrives. In this chapter, you'll delve deeper into connecting Office 365 with your mobile device, from setting up email to working with SharePoint. In addition, you'll learn how to implement phone policies via the Admin portal.

Windows Phones

Microsoft's latest phone is called Windows Phone 7.5; it has built-in support for Office 365. Behind the scenes, Microsoft uses an auto-discover technology that makes adding your Office 365 account as simple as typing in the account's email address and password. In addition, you can add a Hotmail or other account to the phone and manage them both at the same time. You can view your personal and business calendars simultaneously in Office 365, as shown in Figure 9-1.

FIGURE 9-1 Windows 7.5 Phone Calendar integrated with Office 365.

Contacts that you add to Office 365 (as described in Chapter 8) are automatically downloaded to the phone. When a contact calls you, his name appears, telling you at a glance who is calling.

Windows Mobile Phone 7.5 includes the Mobile Office feature that contains a mobile version of Microsoft Word, Microsoft PowerPoint, Microsoft OneNote, and Microsoft Excel. These mobile apps work very well to render a SharePoint Online document, allowing you to view and edit documents on your phone.

> **More Info** You can find a Microsoft-produced video about connecting a Windows Mobile 7.5 phone to Office 365 at *http://www.youtube.com/watch?v=7-cLV3DbD4E.*

If you have an older Windows phone, you're still in great shape. You can set up your phone as if it were connecting to an Exchange server. When connected, you have all the same benefits of Office 365, including calendar, contacts, alerts, and other features. However, keep in mind that the ease of use of a 7.5 phone is significantly advanced compared to Windows 6.*x* phones. With a 7.5 phone, you have threaded conversations, social networking, mobile office, Lync Mobile, and thousands of apps that you can easily download. For years, my Windows 6 Motorola Saga was a reliable partner that saved the day many times because it was connected to my Exchange Online account at Microsoft. Now that I use a Windows Phone 7.5, there is no going back.

Exchange ActiveSync Devices

The majority of modern mobile devices work well with Office 365 and Exchange Online. If the phone you have or are considering has Exchange ActiveSync support, chances are it will work fine. Exchange ActiveSync is the software provided by the phone's manufacturer for connecting to and synchronizing with an Exchange server, such as those used by Office 365.

Although Exchange ActiveSync was created by Microsoft, it is licensed to phone manufacturers who then create their own versions. As a result, the specific details of exactly how to connect to Office 365 can vary, as do the specific features. To bring some standardization to the feature set, Microsoft created the Exchange ActiveSync Logo Program (*http://technet.microsoft.com/en-us/exchange/gg187968.aspx*). The devices listed on the Logo Program page are certified to comply with the features needed to ensure a good experience with Office 365. As of this writing, Nokia, Apple, and Microsoft phones are listed.

In addition, Microsoft provides the following online resources to assist with setting up mobile devices:

- At *http://help.outlook.com/en-us/140/cc511380.aspx*, you'll find a video of setting up a Windows Mobile 6.5 device that uses ActiveSync.

- At *http://help.outlook.com/en-us/140/cc825479.aspx*, the Mobile Phone Setup Wizard walks you through the setup process for Droid, Android Tablet, iPad, iPhone, iPod Touch, Nokia, and Microsoft phones. This wizard is covered in more detail later in the chapter.

- At *http://www.microsoft.com/download/en/details.aspx?id=13602*, the 365 Mobility Solutions Service Description is the official document stating what is and is not possible and what is supported for mobile devices with Office 365. The nature of cloud services is such that features and capabilities change faster than software you normally purchase. Check this document regularly for updates.

BlackBerry

Office 365 supports BlackBerry operating systems 4.2, 4.3, 4.5, and 5.0, and Microsoft plans to support future releases. As of this writing, BlackBerry Enterprise Services (BES) services offered by RIM are not available in Plan P1. BlackBerry users can use BlackBerry Internet Service (BIS) to connect to Office 365. The difference between BES and BIS is that with BIS you are essentially accessing Outlook Web App (OWA) in your mobile browser. That's quite a bit different from having a mailbox client on your phone. The BES experience is preferred but, as mentioned, is available only in the Office 365 E plans. You can find more information about BlackBerry Cloud Services at *http://docs.blackberry.com/en/admin/subcategories/?userType=2&category=BlackBerry+Business+Cloud+Services*.

The Mobile Phone Setup Wizard

Microsoft publishes a wizard that provides instructions for a variety of phones. You can find the wizard at *http://help.outlook.com/en-us/140/dd936215.aspx*. Start the wizard, select your phone (see Figure 9-2), and then follow the subsequent instructions to set up your phone for Office 365.

FIGURE 9-2 The Mobile Phone Setup Wizard.

For some phones, such as a Windows Phone 7+, your email setup should require you to enter only user name and password. However, not all phones can take advantage of the behind-the-scenes auto-discover capabilities that make this possible. As a result, your phone's setup process might prompt you to enter server information about your Office 365 mail service. If your phone is listed in the Mobile Phone Setup Wizard, you might be guided through the following process. Also, if your device does not support Exchange ActiveSync, you can try connecting to the service by using other methods, such as POP, IMAP, or SMTP. POP is generally used for receiving mail and SMTP is used for sending mail, while IMAP can do both. Your phone might support these protocols to allow you to connect to a wide variety of services.

You can find connection details about your mailbox by logging on to OWA, clicking Options, and then clicking Show All Options. On the My Account page, click Settings for POP, IMAP, and SMTP access, as shown in Figure 9-3.

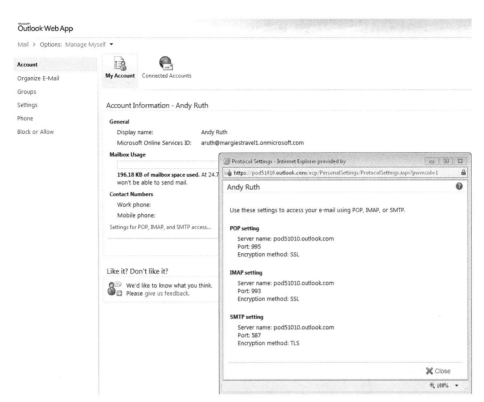

FIGURE 9-3 The settings for Pop, IMAP, and SMTP shown in OWA.

Note that the server name (in this example, pod51010.outlook.com) is shown in all the settings. Use this server name when asked by your phone setup wizard for the URL or server name for the mail server. Additional settings are shown for the other protocols you might use.

Important Microsoft recently introduced a new "universal" server name for mobile access. Rather than configuring your service with the server name shown in OWA, Microsoft recommends using *m.outlook.com*. The universal name was introduced because the server listed in OWA can change due to routine maintenance or because of a fail-over event at the data center. If your phone is configured to use *m.outlook.com*, when your phone connects to Office 365, the connection will be routed to the right server.

At the time of this writing, Microsoft documentation was not yet updated with this information. Android (and possibly other) phone users have reported problems using the *m.outlook.com* address. Both Microsoft and Google are working on updates. In this case, use the address found in OWA. If you are interested, you can read a technical article on this at *http://blogs.technet.com/b/exchange/archive/2012/02/07/cross-site-redirection-exchange-activesync-clients-in-office-365.aspx*.

Use SharePoint Online with a Mobile Device

SharePoint Online can interact with mobile devices in a variety of ways. The most commonly used activity is to access an Office document stored in a SharePoint document library. Some phones have apps either built in or downloadable, with which you can open and work with Office documents. The specifics of these capabilities depend on the combination of phone and application you use to access the documents.

Windows 7.5 or 6.5 Phone

Using SharePoint Workspace Mobile 2010, you can interact with and synchronize content from SharePoint Online; it is available on Windows 7.5 and Windows 6.5 phones. You can open and edit documents in Word Mobile 2010, Excel Mobile 2010, or PowerPoint Mobile 2010.

Windows Phone 7.5 interacts with SharePoint Online from the Office Hub (see Figure 9-4), where you can sync with the SharePoint Online site or download documents for offline work. You can then save the documents back to SharePoint Online to allow others to access your work.

FIGURE 9-4 Windows Phone 7 Office Hub.

Syncing to documents from SharePoint Online with a Windows Phone 7.5 device is easy:

1. Open the Office Hub on the phone.

2. Locate the SharePoint section, as shown in Figure 9-2.

3. Tap Open URL.

4. Type the URL of your team site, and then press the forward arrow. If you don't know the URL of the site, log on to *https://portal.microsoftonline.com* with your credentials, and then click Team Site.

Important Your phone will automatically enter "https://" and place the cursor so that you can start typing after https:// to complete the entry for the URL to your team site. As of this writing, SharePoint Online does not support https://. So to successfully connect, you must change https:// to http://, and then type the remainder of your URL.

5. Enter your Office 365 credentials, and then tap Sign In. You might be asked to log on a few times during the process.

6. Browse to the document library (such as Shared Documents) that contains the file that you want to take offline.

7. Press and hold the file name until a menu opens.

8. Select one of the two options presented. Download Now downloads the file to the phone for you to work on. When you save the file, it is automatically updated on SharePoint Online. Always Keep Offline saves the document to your phone. You can then edit the document and manually upload to SharePoint Online later.

Using the Office Hub that comes on the Windows Phone 7+, you can access and edit documents on SharePoint Online as well as take notes with OneNote Mobile and sync those notes back to SharePoint.

More Info You can find out more about the Office Mobile Workspace on Windows Phone 7.5 at *http://www.microsoft.com/windowsphone/en-us/apps/office.aspx*.

Special URL for Mobile Display of SharePoint Online Sites

Modern phones make it easy to navigate webpages simply by flicking the display up, down, right, and left, as well as magnify it by using gestures. However, older devices might not support this kind of browser. SharePoint Online has a special mode just for mobile devices that are HTML 4.0–compliant (and most are): just append **/?Mobile=1** to the URL to instruct SharePoint to deliver a page specially rendered for mobile viewing. For example, if your URL is *http://sharepoint.com/sites/contoso*, the mobile viewing URL would be *http://sharepoint.com/sites/contoso/?Mobile=1*. More up-to-date devices might not require this URL because with the built-in browser technology, you can effectively navigate larger, more complex webpages.

Other Phones and Mobile Devices

Most phones and mobile devices, such as an iPhone or iPad, can access SharePoint Online by using apps or the built-in browser. Because SharePoint Online is a web-based application, you can browse to the site and interact with the applications and content presented. You'll be able to open and work with Office documents, depending on the capabilities of your phone and apps.

Microsoft Lync 2010 Mobile

Microsoft offers Lync 2010 Mobile clients for several mobile devices, including:

- Android: *https://play.google.com/store/apps/details?id=com.microsoft.office.lync*

- iPad: *http://itunes.apple.com/us/app/microsoft-lync-2010-for-ipad/id484222449?mt=8*

- iPhone: *http://itunes.apple.com/us/app/microsoft-lync-2010-for-iphone/id484293461?mt=8*

- Microsoft Phones: *http://www.windowsphone.com/en-US/apps/9ce93e51-5b35-e011-854c-00237de2db9e*

- Nokia (Symbian) smartphones *http://office.microsoft.com/en-us/mobile/*

Using Lync Mobile, you can instant message others in your organization or other users of Lync Online who are accessible through Lync 2010. The ability to instant message users outside of your organization is covered in Chapter 12, "Working with Lync Online."

If you manage your own DNS services, depending on when you configured your services, you might need to update DNS for the mobile client to work. If Microsoft hosts your DNS services, the required settings for Lync 2010 Mobile are added for you. For details, see *http://community.office365.com/en-us/w/lync/1040.aspx*.

Mobile Device Administration

As the services administrator, you can log on to the administration portal and administer the services from your phone. In addition, you have several tools at your disposal to control how users of your service access Office 365 from a mobile device. You can control who can access their mail by using ActiveSync, and you can configure policies that apply to all users, such as requiring your mobile users to employ the use of a PIN on their device to unlock it. Office 365 has a rich set of capabilities in this area, extending beyond what most small businesses require. In general, you will want to learn how to turn off access for specific users and optionally set a simple policy. You can log on to the services as an administrator through OWA by clicking See All Options for the Options setting, hovering over Manage Myself, and then clicking My Organization. Alternately, you can log on via the Office 365 administration portal at *https://portal.onmicrosoftonline.com*; under Outlook, click General Settings.

Prevent ActiveSync Users from Accessing Email

Some organizations have individuals who need an email account but should not be synchronizing their Inbox with a mobile device. By default, the ability to synchronize is enabled for all users. To prevent this synchronization, you can disable ActiveSync for any user in your organization. The user can still browse to OWA and log on to view and send mail, but will not be able to create an Inbox on her phone by using ActiveSync.

From the Users & Groups page, select the user whom you want to configure, and then click Details. Scroll to the bottom of the settings window, and expand Phone & Voice Features, as shown in Figure 9-5.

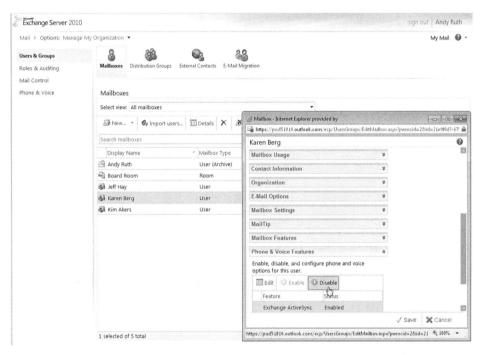

FIGURE 9-5 Disabling ActiveSync for a user.

Select Disable, and then click Save. Confirm the action, and then click OK.

The next time the user logs on with her phone, ActiveSync will be disabled.

Phone and Voice Administration

You can further control mobile settings by clicking on Phone & Voice in the left menu of the Manage My Organization page, as shown in Figure 9-6. Even though the options include the word "Voice" in the title, no voice features related to your phone are available in the Office 365 Plan P1. The Phone & Voice page presents you with two main choices for phones: ActiveSync Access and ActiveSync Device Policy.

ActiveSync Access

On the ActiveSync Access page, you can control the kinds of devices that can access your services (see Figure 9-6). By default, Office 365 allows any device that can authenticate to connect to the service, but you can set up Office 365 so that only specific kinds of devices are accepted. This is useful when company-provided phones are allowed to connect to the services but personal phones are prohibited. You can create rules in the Device Access Rules section to specify that only particular models of phones are allowed.

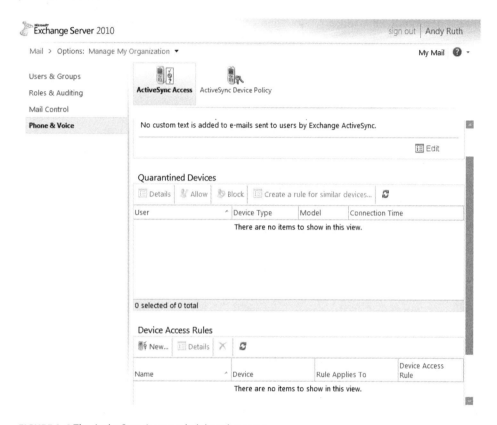

FIGURE 9-6 The ActiveSync Access administration page.

If you do set up such restrictions, devices that do not match your criteria are either quarantined or simply disallowed. You can specify a message be sent to you when a device is quarantined. You can then either authorize these devices or prohibit their access. In addition, you can customize a message to be sent to users when their device is quarantined.

Because most small businesses have only a few users, these settings are not likely to be needed. In most small business scenarios, you can simply allow or deny access on the per-user basis, as discussed earlier in this chapter. If you do need to control what kinds of devices have access, see *http://help.outlook. com/en-US/140/ms.exch.ecp.newdeviceaccessrule.aspx* for more details.

ActiveSync Device Policy

When a user connects to your Office 365 services by using ActiveSync, Office 365 enforces a "default policy" on the phone so that it behaves in compliance with settings that you specify. Using the settings on the ActiveSync Device Policy page, you can set up usage and access policies to fit the needs of your business. For example, you might want to protect business mail and other content by requiring a password to unlock phones that use your Office 365 service. In this way, if a phone is lost or stolen, the phone prompts for a password before allowing access.

If you don't have an unlimited email plan with your business phone service, you also might want to constrain the amount of mail that can be synced when a user first connects. Some people maintain large mailboxes, and downloading several gigabytes of data to your mobile device could be expensive. Likewise, if employees travel out of your home area frequently, consider enabling the Require Manual Synchronization When Roaming policy. In particular, be careful to manage your email downloads to your phone when traveling internationally.

 More Info You can find the complete list of device policies at *http://help.outlook.com/en-US/140/ms.exch.ecp.EditActiveSyncMailboxPolicy.aspx*.

The following sections detail the three settings categories you're most likely to need: General, Device Security, and Sync Settings.

General The settings in the General category are very straightforward, specifying which devices to grant permissions to and how frequently to refresh (update) policies for those devices:

- **Allow Devices That Don't Fully Support These Policies To Synchronize** Select this check box to allow users to synchronize devices that don't support policy enforcement or don't support some of the settings you've specified in this policy. If you don't select this check box, these devices will receive a 403 Access Denied error message when they try to synchronize with Microsoft Exchange.

- **Refresh This Policy On Mobile Devices** If you want policies to be regularly refreshed on devices, select this check box and enter how often you want ActiveSync to refresh policies on devices. Policies aren't refreshed unless this check box is selected. If you don't specify the time interval, policies will be refreshed every 24 hours.

Device security The following settings control security features for the mobile devices synchronizing with user mailboxes:

- **Require Encryption On Device** Select this check box to require devices to use encryption.

- **Require Encryption On Storage Cards** Select this check box to require devices to encrypt removable storage cards to protect the data on the cards.

- **Require A Password When Mobile Devices Are Not In Use**   Select this check box to require that devices be locked with a password. The other password options aren't available unless you select this check box.

- **Allow Simple Passwords**   Select this check box to allow devices to use simple password sequences, such as 1234 or 1111. Enabling this option makes it easier for users to remember their passwords but decreases device security by allowing passwords that are easy to guess.

- **Require An Alphanumeric Password**   Select this check box to require device passwords to contain both numbers and letters. The default is numbers only.

- **Passwords Must Include This Many Character Sets**   To enhance the security of device passwords, you can require passwords to contain characters from multiple character sets. Select a number from 1 to 4. The sets are lowercase letters, uppercase letters, numbers, and symbols. For example, if you select three, passwords must contain characters from three of these sets.

- **Minimum Password Length**   Select this check box, and enter the minimum number of characters that mobile device passwords must use.

- **Number Of Sign-In Failures Before Device Is Wiped**   Select this check box to wipe the memory of a mobile device if a user tries to sign in and fails for the specified number of times. This option isn't enforced unless this check box is selected and you have entered a number from 1 to 6.

- **Require Sign-In After The Device Has Been Inactive**   Select this check box to lock devices after they are idle for the number of minutes you specify, requiring users to sign in again. This option isn't enforced unless this check box is selected. You can specify the number of minutes from 1 to 60.

- **Enable Password Recovery**   Select this check box to specify whether users can recover their device passwords from the server. If you select this check box, the user can go to Manage Myself | Phones | Mobile Phones, and then select Show Recovery Password. If you clear this check box, the Show Recovery Password option isn't available.

- **Enforce Password Lifetime**   Select this check box and enter the number of days a password is valid before users are required to change their device passwords.

- **Password Recycle Count**   Enter how many different passwords users must use on their devices before repeating a password. You can enter a number from 0 to 50. Enter 0 to allow users to repeat passwords immediately.

Sync settings The following settings control what users can synchronize to their devices and whether they can synchronize when roaming:

- **Include Past Calendar Items** Select how far back in time past calendar items are synchronized. To help control data costs, specify a shorter interval.

- **Include Past Email Items** Select how far back in time past email messages are synchronized. To help control data costs, specify a shorter interval.

- **Limit Email Size** Enter a limit for the size of email messages, in kilobytes (KB). Emails that are larger than the size you specify are delivered, but they're truncated to the maximum size.

- **Require Manual Synchronization When Roaming** Select this check box to require users to manually start synchronization from their mobile devices while they are roaming. Clear this check box to allow mobile devices to synchronize on a schedule or to use Direct Push when they are roaming and data rates are traditionally higher.

- **Allow HTML-Formatted Email** Select this check box to allow HTML-formatted email messages to be downloaded to devices. If you clear this box, messages are converted to plain text before synchronizing to the device.

- **Allow Attachments To Be Downloaded To Device** Select this check box to allow attachments to be downloaded to devices. If you clear this box, messages show the attachment name but users can't download the attachment to their device.

- **Maximum Attachment Size** If you want to allow attachments but want to limit the size that can be downloaded, select this check box and enter the maximum attachment size, in kilobytes.

Apply Different Policies to Different Users

Most small businesses require only a single policy, but you do have the option of creating new policies and applying them to users, if necessary. For example, if you provide phones and email accounts for temporary workers, you might want to enforce a different set of policies for these workers than for your full time employees.

To create a new policy, go to the Manage My Organization page, click Phone & Voice, click the ActiveSync Device Policy icon, and then click New (see Figure 9-7). Give the policy a name, configure the desired settings, and then click Save. You will see the new policy listed with your default policy.

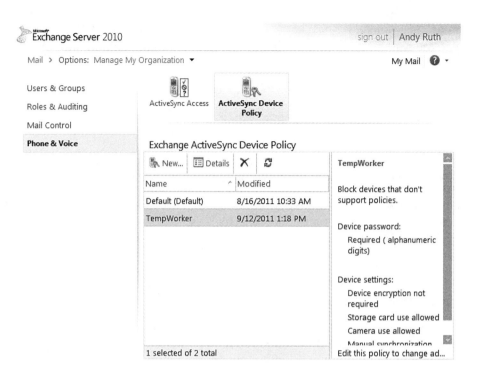

FIGURE 9-7 A new policy shown with the Default policy.

Next, you need to apply the new policy to the worker. To apply the policy, In the menu on the left, click Users & Groups, as shown in Figure 9-5. Then, double-click the desired user. Scroll down and expand Phone & Voice Features, also shown in Figure 9-5. However, instead of clicking Disable, click Edit (or double-click Exchange ActiveSync). This opens an entirely new menu from which you can specify what policy is assigned to control ActiveSync. Click Browse, and you can then select a new policy to apply. In Figure 9-8, you can see the series of windows that are opened.

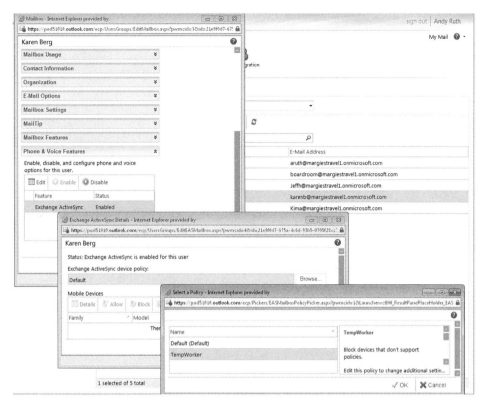

FIGURE 9-8 Applying a new ActiveSync policy to a user.

You can now apply the TempWorker policy by clicking OK.

Connection Is Key

Small businesses are big users of mobile technology. The ability to have your mobile devices connected to email, contacts, calendar, and online documents is one of the key drivers of adoption for cloud services such as Office 365. The small business plan for Office 365 allows all your users to connect to their mail and online services, including using Lync 2010 mobile as part of the base subscription. Of course, you will also want to use Outlook with Office 365, which is the subject of our next chapter.

CHAPTER 10

Improving Your Business Image and Productivity with Outlook

During my tenure at Microsoft, I had an up-close look at how large companies and their customers use technology to improve productivity. For example, in a bigger company, simply finding the person responsible for a specific program, feature, or product can be challenge. Microsoft uses SharePoint and internal search capabilities; thus, quickly locating teams, individuals, and content is easy.

You can see the online status of anyone in the company, worldwide, and start an instant message session with them. Need to schedule a meeting with a team? Just add them to a meeting request, and locate a conference room in their building by using the Global Address List. Seeing when key people are available and sending them all a meeting request is a fast and easy process. The conference room will automatically accept the meeting request and show it as booked.

These kinds of services are also available to you as the owner of an Office 365 Plan P1 subscription, meaning that you can reap the same benefits from improvements in productivity. Microsoft Office 365 not only can increase efficiencies but can also significantly enhance your image as a professional organization that takes its business—and its customers—seriously.

This chapter assumes that you know the basics of sending and receiving email and that you've already been using Microsoft Outlook. Rather than going into details about how to create folders, use tasks, and perform other useful tasks in Outlook, the chapter focuses on how to improve your professional image by using Office 365 and Outlook and provides some productivity-enhancing tips.

Improve Your Image

To project a professional image, you want your email to look professional. Using Outlook and Office 365, your email can have the look and feel of organizations many times your size.

Use a Custom Domain

Think of the impact of someone handing you a business card with an email address from a free service like Google Mail: It says "Too small to have my own domain." Even a one-person company should have a custom domain to set it apart from those that just don't bother. This is perhaps one of the most significant steps that you can take to improve your image, and with Office 365, there's no reason why you shouldn't do it. Details on how to add a custom domain are covered in Chapter 6, "Working with Custom Domains."

Create a Signature

When you add a signature to your mail, you brand every message with your company name, email, contact information, and any other information you want to include. My signature includes my email address, a link to my company website, and states that I'm an Office 365 MVP. Every time an email goes out, it's a potential contact or referral.

You can get creative with your signature as well. Try adding an electronic business card, hyperlinks, or custom graphics. If you add graphics, don't overdo the design, and be certain that your image does not add significantly to the size of your email. A basic text message is quite small, but even a modest graphic can triple the size of an email message. If you have more than one line of business, create a signature for each of your brands. Just insert the relevant one from the Signature icon when you're crafting an email.

Note Signatures in OWA are different from signatures in Outlook. If you use OWA and Outlook, consider creating similar signatures in both.

More Info Microsoft has a good online training session about creating signatures at *http://office.microsoft.com/en-us/outlook-help/create-great-looking-signatures-for-your-e-mail-RZ010186191.aspx?CTT=1.*

Reply to External Contacts with a Meeting Request

When you're talking to customers, vendors, or others outside of your organization, you can quickly show that you're serious about being efficient when you send them a meeting request that contains the date, time, contact information, agenda, and other details. Most businesses use Outlook as an email client, so they can accept the meeting or propose a new time very easily without having to handcraft an acceptance or proposal.

You can reply to an email with a meeting request simply by clicking the Meeting icon (shown in Figure 10-1) on the Message tab in an open message. This adds all the recipients to the meeting request and includes the email content in the body of the meeting request.

FIGURE 10-1 Reply with a meeting request.

Of course, in Outlook 2010, you can also create a meeting request manually by clicking Home, New Items, and then Meeting.

Frequently, in business communication, you will be on the phone with a potential customer or businesses associate and agree to meet at a future date. You can immediately send a meeting request containing your contact information and any other relevant information. Most businesses use Outlook, so your associate can accept, reschedule, or reject the request easily. This is an efficient way to ensure that you synchronize with one another, because the event will appear on both of your calendars.

The set of capabilities related to scheduling in Outlook, OWA, and Office 365 is enough for a full chapter or perhaps even a book. But for most businesses, the ability to create a meeting request by using shared free/busy schedules is one of the key values in Office 365.

Note Frequently, business communications cross time zone boundaries, so when setting a time, be clear about what time zone you are discussing. When sending a meeting request, always use your time zone for the agreed time. Outlook automatically adjusts the request for those in different time zones.

Online Meetings with Microsoft Lync Online

Another very effective way to improve both your business image and productivity is to hold online meetings. Using the Office 365 Lync Online service, you can easily send invitations for—and host—online meetings with people outside your company. Instead of emailing a document back and forth while talking about it on the phone, you can use Lync Online so that all meeting participants can view the same document simultaneously. You can even use Lync Online for voice and video, with external users, and for performing live demonstrations of websites, software, or anything you can access on your computer.

When your system is set up for Office 365, you will see Lync meeting options in Outlook. You can create an online meeting request or convert a normal meeting request to an online request, as shown in Figure 10-2.

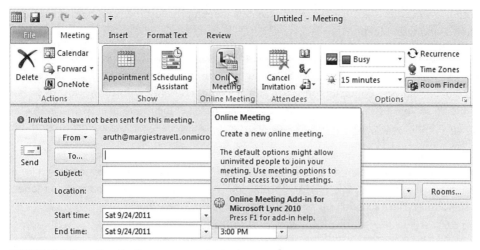

FIGURE 10-2 An online Meeting request in Outlook.

The online meeting request contains a URL, as shown in Figure 10-3, that when clicked connects the user to your online meeting.

When the user clicks the URL, his specific experience depends on his system setup. This also determines whether he can participate in two-way voice and video and other options. The minimum experience uses a browser-based interface through which the user can view a shared document, a product demonstration, a problem, or other activity on your computer. Exact details about how to manage the user experience for Lync Online meetings for people who are not in your organization are discussed in Chapter 12, "Working with Lync Online."

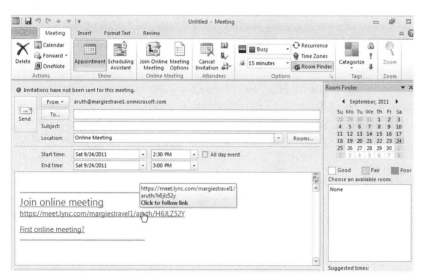

FIGURE 10-3 A Lync Online meeting request.

Publish Your Calendar

You can make your calendar visible to others by using the Publish Online option in Outlook. You can find this option in Outlook 2010 by clicking Calendar | Home | Publish Online on the ribbon, and then clicking Publish This Calendar. This option takes you to calendar publishing options in OWA, where you can enable calendar publishing as described in Chapter 9, "Working with Mobile Devices."

Improve Your Productivity

One of the benefits of Office 365 is that all the resources in your organization are available in a single directory called the Global Address List (GAL). This is particularly useful for businesses that have multiple locations or multiple business identities. Although normally associated with Outlook, the GAL also shows up in OWA as well as in Lync Online.

Use the GAL

Many small businesses have never had the benefit of a GAL. In fact, for a small business, the term "global" might seem a bit over-scoped. Even so, the GAL is actually very useful in small and large businesses alike.

Using the GAL, you can email anyone or anything in the list, which can contain users, resources (such as conference rooms), distribution lists, and contacts. External contacts that you add in OWA become available to everyone in the company. In this way, your GAL puts a directory of important customers, vendors, and other business associates at your fingertips.

When you click the To button in an email you are writing, Outlook 2010 shows you the GAL. In the example shown in Figure 10-4, the GAL includes two email groups (All Margies Travel Employees and Project Delta), individual users, a resource (Board Room), and an external contact (David Pelton), with their titles, phone numbers, and locations visible at a glance.

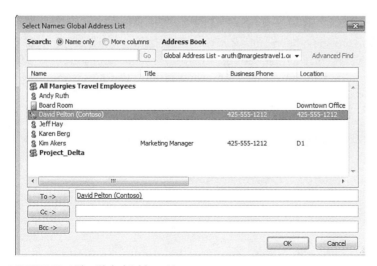

FIGURE 10-4 The Global Address List.

Right-click any name, and then in the context menu that opens, select Properties to bring up the additional details, such as those shown in Figure 10-5. In terms of productivity, it's a big help when anyone in your company can simply right-click to retrieve a cell phone number or mailing address, especially when you're on the road or it's after hours and you need to contact someone right way. Keep this in mind when creating your GAL. Your GAL will be much more useful if fully populated with addresses, extension numbers, phone numbers, and notes. When populating user accounts, resist the urge to only fill out a few fields with a minimum of user information.

FIGURE 10-5 The properties of a global contact in the GAL.

Share Your Calendar

By sharing your calendar, you provide other members of your organization with access to your schedule. By default, anyone in your organization can see your free/busy schedule, but you can choose to show more details on a person-by-person basis. You can even give rights to others to modify your calendar. In this way, an assistant can update your calendar without your involvement.

When you start Outlook 2010, you start out on the Home tab. At the lower left of the main window, click Calendar. Then, click the Share Calendar icon, as shown in Figure 10-6.

FIGURE 10-6 The Share Calendar option.

This displays a specialized form in which you can designate the recipients and the kind of detail to show when they view your calendar, as shown in Figure 10-7.

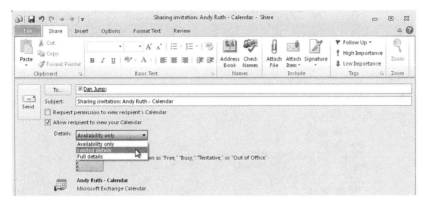

FIGURE 10-7 Calendar-sharing invitation.

Before you send the form, if you want to view the recipient's calendar, select the check box titled Request Permission To View Recipient's Calendar. When she receives your calendar-sharing message, she is prompted to allow you to view her calendar, as well.

The Details pull-down menu shown in Figure 10-7 gives you control over how much information is shown in your shared calendar. You can choose one of the following:

- **Availability Only**   Shows your time as Free, Busy, or "Out of Office." This is the default setting.

- **Limited Details**   Includes the availability and subject of calendar items.

- **Full Details**   Includes availability and full details of calendar items.

When you click Send, you are asked to confirm that you want to share your calendar. The recipient receives an email like the one shown in Figure 10-8.

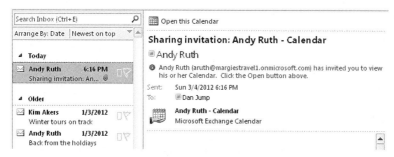

FIGURE 10-8 Receiving a sharing invitation.

When the receiver clicks Open This Calendar, at the top of the message, Outlook displays the receiver's calendar along with the shared calendar, side by side, as shown in Figure 10-9.

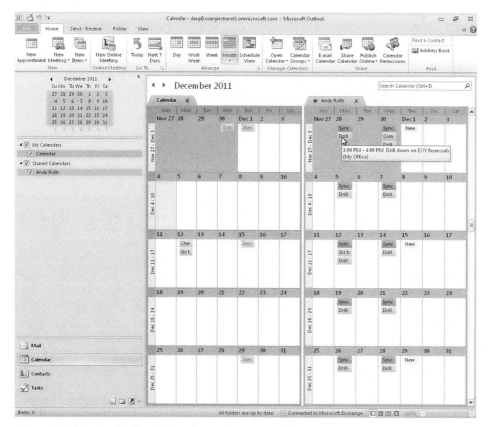

FIGURE 10-9 Viewing the shared calendar.

In this example, the calendar was shared with full details so that the receiver can see the meeting titles and details.

In the left column (see Figure 10-9), you can deselect the shared calendar by clearing the check box under Shared Calendar. The calendar remains available for you to view at any time by simply re-selecting the calendar.

A popular feature of Outlook is the ability to overlay one calendar on top of another. You can view both calendars in this way by clicking the arrow next to the name (in this case, Andy Ruth, shown in Figure 10-9). The resulting combined view is very useful because you can view multiple calendars as if they were one (Figure 10-10).

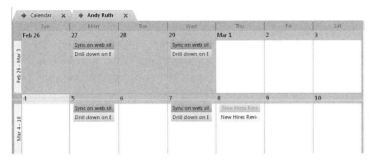

FIGURE 10-10 Calendars overlaid.

Finally, if you want to give someone permission to edit your calendar, click the Calendar Permissions button (the rightmost icon in Figure 10-6). This opens the permissions controls, as shown in Figure 10-11.

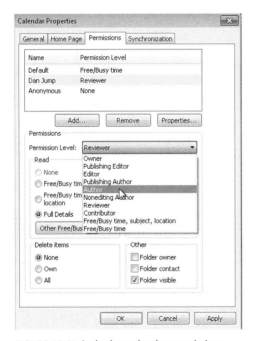

FIGURE 10-11 Assigning calendar permissions.

In the top box, you can choose to work with permissions that have already been assigned, add new people, or remove existing assignments. When you select the person to work with, their permissions are shown in the Permissions section.

While the Permissions Level list has many choices, the differences between these options are not obvious. However, when you make a selection, the permissions for Read, Write, Delete Items, and Other are set accordingly. For example, Figure 10-12 shows the Author permissions.

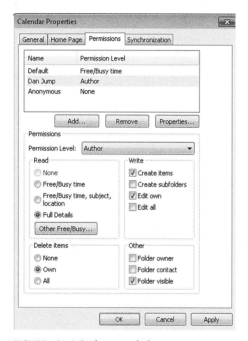

FIGURE 10-12 Author permissions.

Feel free to select a pre-defined set of permissions, such as Author, and adjust as you like. Notice that you can control whether people can add items to your calendar as well as whether they can edit or delete the items they add. In addition, you can allow them to edit or delete items you add to your own calendar. Using these permissions, you can create a permission set to fit most scenarios.

Designate a Delegate

Another benefit of using Office 365 with Outlook is the ability to delegate access to some or all of the content in Outlook to another person. Using the delegate features, you can have meeting requests sent to both you and the delegate. The delegate can accept or reschedule meetings on your behalf. You can also allow the delegate access, enabling him to reply to email you receive or to create tasks on your agenda. When a delegate replies to mail or a meeting request, the reply indicates that it was sent on your behalf. In this way, the receiver knows that you did not personally respond.

To assign a delegate in Outlook 2010, click the File tab, and then click Account Settings | Delegate Access, as shown in Figure 10-13.

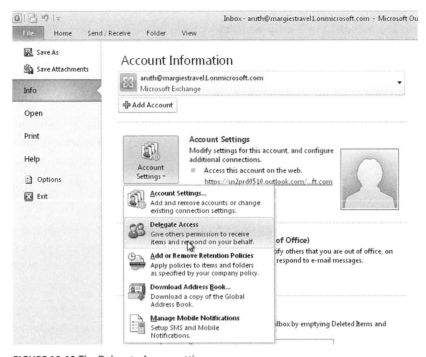

FIGURE 10-13 The Delegate Access setting.

You are then asked to select the person who is to receive delegate authority. Next, the Delegate Permissions form opens, as illustrated in Figure 10-14, in which you can refine the permissions.

FIGURE 10-14 The Delegate Permissions form.

When you click OK, you can specify how you want meeting requests managed. You can have meeting requests sent to your delegate and you receive a copy, sent to your delegate only and you do not receive a copy, or sent to both of you. You then click OK to complete the assignment.

The delegate can access content he is assigned by clicking File | Open | Other User's Folder, and then entering the name of the delegator. The delegate can then access the content in Outlook. For example, if the Inbox was delegated, the delegate would see their own inbox as well as the delegated Inbox.

Note that when you create meeting requests or appointments, you can choose to make them Private by clicking Categorize | Private. If the delegate is not allowed to see private content (which is controlled by the check box at the bottom of Figure 10-14), the calendar item is hidden from the delegate's view.

Use MailTips

Using MailTips, you can see information about a user, group, or contact in Outlook before you send a message. In Figure 10-15, you can see the MailTip assigned to David Pelton. It tells anyone in the company who sends him an email that he is an important business associate.

FIGURE 10-15 A MailTip shown before the mail is sent.

Only administrators can assign MailTips to external contacts. Both administrators and users can assign MailTips to public groups created in OWA.

Reply with a Meeting Request (Internal Recipients)

When inviting people within your organization to a meeting by using OWA or Outlook, you can easily see their free/busy schedule and arrange a time convenient to all. To create a meeting request and view the free/busy schedule, just click New Meeting in Outlook or OWA, select the time and date, and then click Scheduling Assistant. When you add people to the meeting, their availability is displayed, as shown in Figure 10-16. The ability to share calendars and book conference rooms without having to send separate emails to all parties asking when they are available obviously saves a great deal of time.

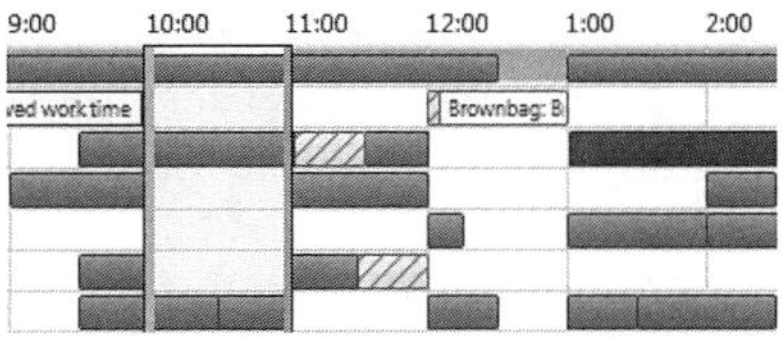

FIGURE 10-16 The Scheduling Assistant showing free/busy information of invited attendees.

Use Out-of-Office Messages

When you are going to be away, it's a good idea to get in the habit of setting up Outlook to send an out-of-office message while you are gone. You can improve productivity by including details about the duration of your absence, advising whether you are responding to email while out, and providing contacts for various projects or for situations that might arise. This also improves your professional image. If customers or business associates see an auto-reply when you're out of the office, particularly when it provides contacts for how they can take action to resolve their issue in your absence, it clearly saves time for those involved and tells your customers that you care about their business, even if you're traveling.

Here are some paraphrased messages I've seen:

"I'm on vacation till Oct 21st and will be back in the office on the 23rd. Contact Aruth@ margiestravel.com for issues related to cruise lines and Marge@margiestravel.com for all other questions. I will not have access to email, but will be checking voice messages occasionally.

"Traveling the first week of November, so contact will be spotty. Will return all messages as quickly as possible. Back in the Office Nov 15."

"Out of the office on parental leave, will not be available. Contact myboss@contoso.com for all issues."

To set up an out-of-office message in Outlook 2010, click File, Info, and then select Automatic Replies. This displays the form shown in Figure 10-17, in which you can create out-of-office messages for internal users and external users as well as designate the time frame when the messages should run. You can also configure an out-of-office message in OWA. Unlike signatures, if you configure an out-of-office message in Outlook, you do not also need to configure it in OWA.

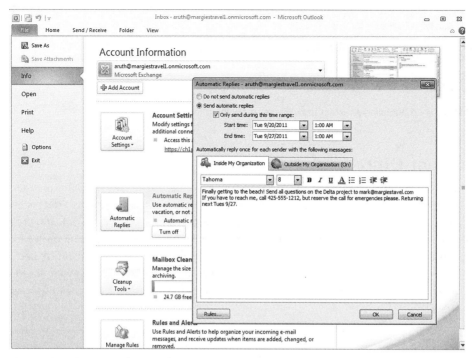

FIGURE 10-17 Setting up out-of-office replies.

Refine Your Junk Mail Filter

Office 365 uses a high-quality spam and virus filtering system based on Microsoft's Forefront server technology. You won't even notice that this is going on, except that certain mail will wind up in your Junk mailbox. In my experience, the filtering has been very good, but as with most junk mail filters, you will find mail in your junk mail that should not be there. Less frequently, you will find junk mail in your Inbox. In either of these situations, you can instruct Office 365 as to how to properly classify mail by right-clicking any message, or on the ribbon, on the Outlook 2010 Home tab, click the Junk icon, and then select one of the options shown in Figure 10-18.

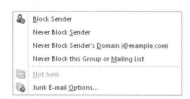

FIGURE 10-18 Junk options in Outlook 2010.

When you click Junk E-mail Options, Office 365 provides the additional options shown in Figure 10-19.

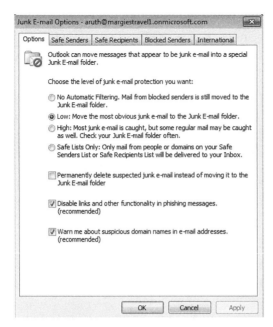

FIGURE 10-19 The Junk E-mail Options dialog box.

When you right-click an email and designate it as safe or junk, that information is recorded in the Safe Senders, Safe Recipients, or Blocked Senders list accordingly. You can manually add to these lists and view other options by selecting the appropriate tab. For example, in the Safe Senders list, you can designate domains or individuals that should not be treated as junk. As a best practice, if you receive email from a domain regularly, add that domain to your Safe Senders list. In addition, you can set up Office 365 to treat all your contacts as safe senders or automatically make safe anyone you email.

Use the Outlook Social Connector

Many savvy small businesses use social networking as a way to create connections, reach new markets, and stay in touch with business contacts. The Outlook Social Connector, installed as part of the Office 365 setup, shows you information from Facebook, LinkedIn, and a few other social networking sites, related to people you interact with using email (see Figure 10-20). The Connector is not actually an Office 365 feature, because it works without Office 365, but because it is installed with the Office 365 setup, many people will see it for the first time when they prepare for Office 365.

FIGURE 10-20 The Outlook Social Connector.

Figure 10-20 demonstrates that the Social Connector has very practical applications. Suppose that you are on the phone with a colleague who is not in your business and you're discussing a potential deal about which you have exchanged some email. Sure, you can click the Mail icon and see all mail associated with the person. But that's just mail, not a social connection.

Now imagine that, as you talk, the Social Connector is showing you the person's picture with the "In" logo on it, indicating the photo is from a LinkedIn profile. You click his name in the All Items list, see the colleague's LinkedIn profile, and discover that you both worked for the same company at some point in your careers. In addition, you can see that you know several people in common. You can bring this up during the conversation to help create a more personal connection with some-one who was previously just a business opportunity. Discovering these connections is fun, and the improved rapport can help close new business deals as well as improve your professional image with others.

> **Note** The Social Connector is minimized by default. In the reading pane, at the bottom, expand the Social Connector bar to see the rest of the content.

The Social Connector also has the following features:

- **Communication history** Your message history with the person is automatically shown. When someone you don't recognize contacts you, any messages you've exchanged with them in the past are easy to find.

- **Meetings** Meetings scheduled with the sender are shown.

- **Attachments** Remember sending an attachment to someone but you can't find the mes-sage? Let the Outlook Social Connector do the searching for you. All attachments are exchanged automatically.

- **Activity feeds** The activity feed from the network is displayed in Outlook.

Install a Social Connector Provider

By default, the Social Connector does not connect you to any networks. To add a network in Outlook 2010, click View, click People Pane, and then select Account Settings, as shown in Figure 10-21.

FIGURE 10-21 Selecting the People Pane account settings in Outlook 2010

The first time you select this, you see a welcome page with the message, You Can Now Connect Outlook To Your Online Social Networks. Click Next, and then click View Social Network Providers Available Online. This takes you to the URL on *office.microsoft.com*, where you can click the icon representing the provider that you want to install and add that to your setup.

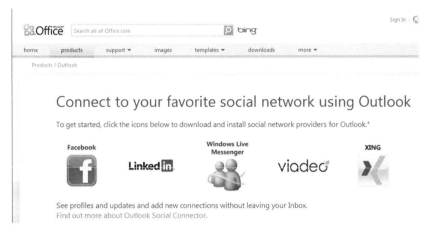

FIGURE 10-22 Social network connector providers.

After you install the Social Connector, you can configure it with your logon information and you'll receive information from any contacts involved with those networks right in Outlook.

For More Information

The Microsoft Office team has many online how-tos, tips, best practices, and other details related to using Outlook. Just look around *http://office.microsoft.com*, and you can find high-quality content directed at end users about how to best use Outlook as well as other Office products.

Here are a few that you might find useful:

- How to use email signatures in Outlook: *http://office.microsoft.com/en-us/outlook-help/use-e-mail-signatures-in-outlook-2010-RZ102000409.aspx*

- Get familiar with the Outlook Calendar: *http://office.microsoft.com/en-us/outlook-help/get-familiar-with-the-outlook-calendar-RZ101863385.aspx*

- Use electronic business cards: *http://office.microsoft.com/en-us/outlook-help/use-electronic-business-cards-in-outlook-2010-RZ102019638.aspx*

- Quickly create rules in Outlook 2010: *http://blogs.office.com/b/microsoft-outlook/archive/2010/07/21/quick-rule-creation-in-outlook-2010.aspx*

- Optimize Conversation view: *http://office.microsoft.com/en-us/outlook-help/view-email-messages-by-conversation-HA010362041.aspx#_Toc256606890*

CHAPTER 11

Working with SharePoint Online

Microsoft Office is the world's most popular software for creating business documents—for good reason. While the basics of Office are easy to learn, each Office product has tremendous depth. They allow for complex interactions with other Office products, personalization capabilities, multiple language support, and a dedicated programming language for developers to create new features and integrations with other systems.

Of course, like most well-established software products, Office has grown over the years, and with the advent of online services, with Office 365, you can now edit Office documents online as well as share them and collaborate with others.

Microsoft SharePoint Online is the Office 365 service by which you can work with your documents online in a totally new way. In this chapter, you'll learn how Office and SharePoint Online work together. For example, from within Office, you can open and edit documents that reside on SharePoint Online. You'll also learn how to set up version control when working with these Office documents, retain version history, check documents in and out, use Office Web Apps, and even publish a collection of documents to Outlook where they will be available to you offline. Need to ask a coworker about one of those documents? SharePoint Online lets you see who is online and then start an instant message (IM) session while you're within Microsoft Word or SharePoint. Finally, the chapter will explain some important security-related administrative tasks as well as how to add pages and invite external users to share your site.

SharePoint Online Structure and Terminology

To get the most out of this chapter and working with SharePoint Online, you need to understand a few key terms:

- **Site** The top level of a collection of associated pages. You can have multiple sites, each with one or more pages. Your subscription comes with a preconfigured *team site*. The team site has tasks and a document library added. You can customize this site to suit your requirements. Because the team site is the first site, it is always the "parent" of any new sites you create.

- **Page** A container for content in SharePoint Online. When you add a site, a page is created for you, and that page becomes the top level of the site. You can add additional pages as you choose.

- **Web Part** An application that you add to a page that provides a predefined capability. Using Web Parts, you can add ready-to-use functionality to your site, such as a document library, a calendar, task lists, contacts, a blog, or a wiki, without any coding.

- **Document library** A type of Web Part designed to work with Office documents, PDFs, and Zip files. You can use document libraries to check in and check out documents, keep document history, add customized workflows, attach notification of changes, add custom columns, and more.

- **Lists** A type of Web Part that can be customized to suit your needs. SharePoint Online's tasks and contacts are two examples of Web Parts that are based on lists.

To recap, your SharePoint Online site comes pre-configured with a team site. You can use the team site as-is or customize the site to your liking by adding pages or Web Parts. In addition, you can add additional sites to your system and customize the look, feel, function, and security of each.

Access SharePoint Online

With the Office 365 for professionals and small businesses subscription, you can find SharePoint Online by using the Team Site links from the Office 365 portal at *https://portal.microsoftonline.com*. The URL for your site will be unique and have the form *http://<company>.sharepoint.com*. The links and icons shown in Figure 11-1 take you to different capabilities provided by SharePoint Online.

Note You can access SharePoint Online from most any modern browser, but only the 32-bit versions of Internet Explorer 8 and Internet Explorer 9 can make full use of its features. If you use Firefox, Chrome, or Safari, specific features will not work or will be unavailable. For details about which features work with which versions of which browsers, see the article "Plan browser support (SharePoint Server 2010)" on TechNet at *http://technet.microsoft.com/en-us/library/cc263526.aspx*.

Team site

Collaborate on documents and share information and ideas using SharePoint Online.
Visit team site | Shared documents

Word   Excel   PowerPoint   OneNote

Website

View your public website.
http://margiestravel1.sharepoint.com/

FIGURE 11-1 Accessing SharePoint Online in the Office 365 Portal.

- **Visit Team Site**   The team site is a website created for you and designed for internal use. You can customize the site by adding content and features without any specialized or third-party software whatsoever. Technically, the team site is part of a *site collection*. Your Office 365 subscription allows you to have one site collection, which, as its name suggests, is a group of sites. The team site is one site in the collection. You can create additional sites in your site collection or just use the team site.

- **Shared Documents**   Clicking this link takes you to the part of your team site where you can store and share documents online. This is called a *document library*. You'll need to know this if you want to store documents in places other than the team site. We'll discuss using the Shared Documents feature in some detail, later in this chapter.

- **Office application icons**   Each of these starts Office Web Apps that are part of your Shared Documents features.

- **Website**   The Website section takes you to a link for the public website, which is also a feature of SharePoint Online.

But before investigating each of these links in depth, take some time to become familiar with the basic SharePoint navigation:

1. Click Visit Team Site. You will see the default team site, as shown in Figure 11-2.

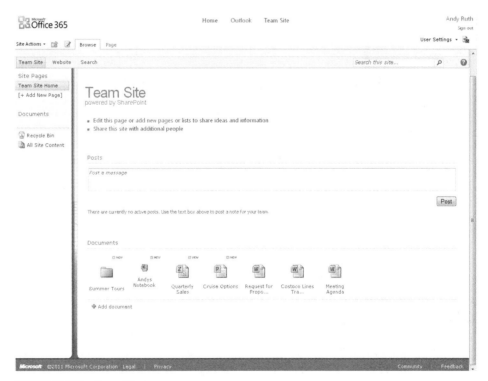

FIGURE 11-2 The Team Site page.

Notice that the URL now displayed in your browser is very different from the portal URL (*https://portal.microsoftonline.com/IWDeault.aspx* or similar). This is a key point: you are now working in SharePoint Online, which is completely distinct from the Office 365 portal. You don't need to go to the portal to access your team site. You can browse directly to your site by using its URL.

You can use the Posts section on the page to post messages that can be seen by anyone who views the site. You can use the Documents section to add documents to your site.

2. As you can see in Figure 11-2, one Documents link is in the main body of the page and one is in the left column. Click either to go to the same location, which is shown in Figure 11-3.

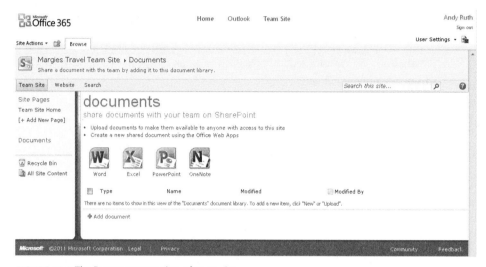

FIGURE 11-3 The Documents section of team site.

3. At the top of the page, click Home. This takes you back to the Office 365 portal. You've now gone full circle, from the Office 365 portal to SharePoint Online and back again.

4. Click Shared Documents. The link takes you directly to the same location as the team site's Documents link. The Shared Documents link in the Office 365 portal and the page it takes you to are actually both part of the team site and not a separate website or application. They are one and the same.

5. Click Home again to return to the Office 365 Portal.

Use Office Web Apps

On the Home page, you'll see icons for Microsoft Word, Microsoft Excel, Microsoft PowerPoint, and Microsoft OneNote. These are shortcuts to a SharePoint Online feature called Office Web Apps (OWA). OWA are online versions of Word, Excel, OneNote, and PowerPoint that work within a browser. You do not need Microsoft Office installed on your computer to create or print documents with OWA.

Because OWA is a browser-based application, you need to use one of the supported browsers listed in the Office Web App Service Description located at *http://www.microsoft.com/download/en/details.aspx?id=13602*.

The OWA Conundrum

The designers of OWA were faced with a daunting challenge. Office documents can be very complex, so building a way to create complex documents in a browser is not feasible due to the limitations of a browser-based environment. At the same time, the designers wanted to provide a browser-based ability to display Office documents with as much fidelity as possible. As a result, you can *view* documents by using OWA that you cannot *create* by using OWA. For example, Figure 11-4 shows a document using comments as presented in the Word Web App.

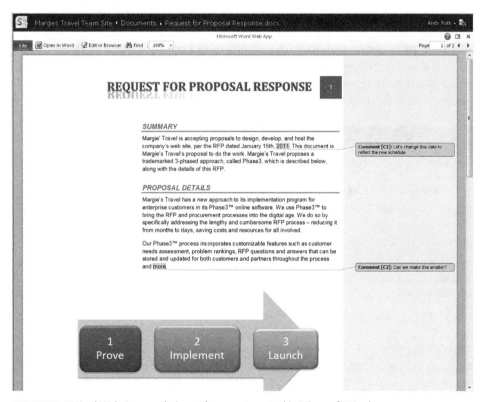

FIGURE 11-4 Word Web App rendering a document created in Microsoft Word.

As you can see, the document looks pretty good! Comments show as expected, and even the Smart Art is faithfully rendered. However, if you click Edit In Browser, you receive the message: "This document cannot be opened because it is set to track changes or contains tracked changes or comments. To edit this document, open it in Microsoft Word."

This highlights a key point. OWA has two distinct modes of operation, called *views*: Reading view and Edit view. Reading view can show Microsoft Office documents that are more complex than the

Edit view can actually create. So think of OWA as a way for you and others to easily view Microsoft Office documents on computers and portable devices when you don't have Microsoft Office available, and as a way to create simple, online documents.

Create Documents by Using OWA

Office 365 for professionals and small businesses makes it very easy to create basic online documents by using Office Web Apps. Simply log on to *https://portal.onmicrosoft.com*, and then click one of the Office document icons (refer to Figure 11-1). The Office icons are also available when you click Team Site.

After entering a file name, you are taken to the OWA you selected. You will then see the familiar ribbon at the top of the page from which you can begin to create your document (see Figure 11-5). You'll notice the ribbon has Home, Insert, and View options available, with which you can do common tasks like format the text, apply styles, insert images, and check spelling. This list will grow as you add features such as tables and images. When you want to use a feature that is not available, click Open In Word. Your SharePoint Online document will open for editing in Word, which means that you'll be editing your online document directly in Microsoft Office. This is one of the many ways that Office and SharePoint work together.

FIGURE 11-5 Creating a Word document in Word Web App.

When editing, you are, of course, in the Edit view. Except in the most basic documents, you will need to switch the view mode to the Reading view to see how your document will look when viewed by others or when opened in Office. To do this, click the View menu option, and then select Reading View.

Save Documents by Using OWA

Documents created by using OWA are saved online in your document library (called Shared Documents, by default). You cannot save Word Web App, PowerPoint Web App, or OneNote Web App documents to your desktop unless you open them with Microsoft Office.

The Excel Web App File menu is a bit different, as shown in Figure 11-6. If you click Where's The Save Button?, you see a message that your file is continually saved. You can click Download A Copy to copy the workbook to your computer. This allows you to store the file locally and edit it without being online. Keep in mind that you need to upload the local copy to SharePoint Online after making your changes.

FIGURE 11-6 The Excel Web App Save menu.

Print from Office Web Apps

Printing is a weak spot for Office Web Apps. The Word and PowerPoint Web Apps have a Print option that, as you will see, does not work as you might expect. The easiest way to print these documents is to first open them in Microsoft Office.

To print from the Word or PowerPoint Web App, you must first convert the document to a PDF file (Portable Document Format). To do this, select File, and then click Print. (If necessary, you will be prompted to download an add-on for your browser so that you can save the file as a PDF.) The next prompt you receive might seem counterintuitive: you are asked where you want to save the file, because the file must be saved as a PDF before it can be printed. After you save the file as a PDF, you are asked whether you want to open the file. If you select Yes and your computer can read PDF files, the document will open and you can then print it. If your computer cannot print PDF files, your browser will ask for permission to locate a program that reads PDF files. You can then elect to install the reader of your choice. Finally, you are ready to open and then print the file.

Note Because PDF files are so common, most people already have some kind of PDF reader installed on their computers. One of the most common is the free Adobe Reader available at *www.adobe.com*. However, if you need to download a reader, beware of other add-ons that might be automatically selected for you. Adobe, for example, will automatically install the Google toolbar as well, unless you opt out.

Microsoft is well aware that this is not an ideal end user experience and is likely to improve this feature in the future. However, there is a silver lining. Remember earlier when I mentioned how Word Web App doesn't allow you to save files to your PC without first opening the document in Office? As an alternative, you can save them as PDF files by selecting to print the document. This works well to email the document to someone, as long as the recipient doesn't need the file in the Office file format. This is actually a good solution for invoices, statements, finished papers, brochures, and other documents that are in their final form.

How to Disable OWA

The Library Settings menu (shown in Figure 11-14) includes an Advanced Settings page on which you'll find the Opening Documents In The Browser option. This option allows you to turn off OWA. If you want to always use Microsoft Office to view and edit documents, set this option to Open In The Client Application. In doing so, keep in mind that you commit to using Office to view the documents. If you find yourself at a computer without Office and need to view a document, you will be unable to do so.

Add Files to SharePoint Online

Adding documents to SharePoint Online is easy. Simply click the Add Document link as shown in Figure 11-7, browse to the file you want to upload, and you're done. You can also drag up to 50 documents at a time to SharePoint Online by using the Upload Multiple Files option.

 Note The Upload Multiple Files option does not appear when using the IE 64-bit version.

You can save many different kinds of files to SharePoint Online, including Zip and PDF files, but for the most part, SharePoint is optimized to work with Microsoft Office documents. There are some limitations, of course. The maximum file size is 250 MB for a single document. This limit has been increased steadily over time. It used to be 50 MB. In addition, you cannot generally upload executable files to SharePoint Onlne. The list of disallowed file extensions can be found in the appendix of the Microsoft "SharePoint Online Service Description for Enterprises" white paper, which is available for download from *http://www.microsoft.com/download/en/details.aspx?id=13602*. The enterprise service is the same one used in Plan P1, so many of the same limitations apply.

Create Folders for Shared Documents

Of course, when you have more than a few files, you will want to add folders to help keep them organized. This is easy to do when you find the right menu option. Figure 11-7 shows you the default shared documents page with a few documents posted. (Click the Documents link on the Team Site page to see this page.)

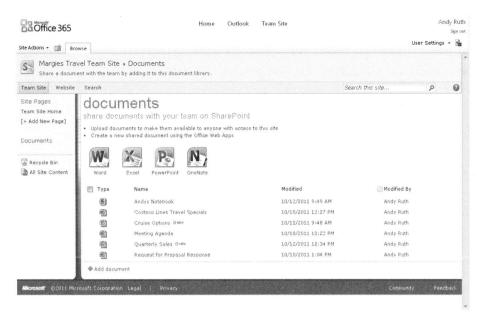

FIGURE 11-7 The default shared documents page with documents added.

You can see the Add Document link at the bottom and the icons for creating different kinds of Office documents, but how do you create a folder? It is not obvious, but the listing of files is a clickable area called a *document library*. Click in the white space beneath the column headers or to the right of any file name to view the Library Tools options available for managing a document library. If you're not sure, click just to the right of Add Document, where the mouse pointer is located in Figure 11-8.

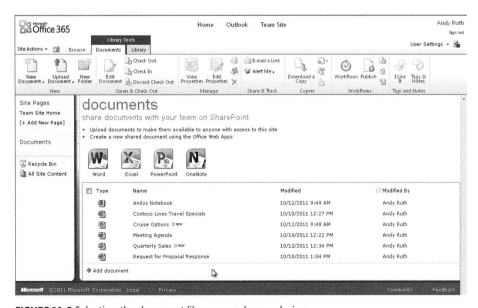

FIGURE 11-8 Selecting the document library reveals new choices.

Now, at the top of the page, you will see some entirely new choices, including New Folder. Use this option to create a new folder for your library. After you add the folder, when you select to upload files, the form you see for uploading will ask you what folder to place the files in. Also, note that you can select to create a new document or upload documents from this menu.

You can create nested folders to organize content just as you do on your computer; simply click a folder to add another inside it. In Figure 11-9, I've created a folder called Summer Tours and entered the folder. Now, how to get back to the parent folder, Documents?

At the top of the page is a breadcrumb trail that shows you exactly where you are and enables you to easily navigate upward.

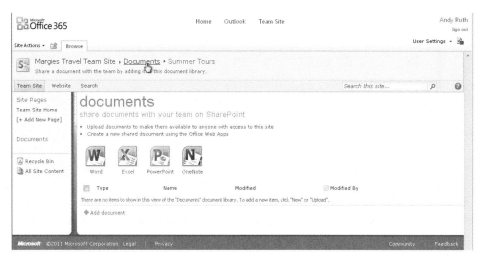

FIGURE 11-9 Navigating by using breadcrumbs.

Use the breadcrumb trail to take you back one or more levels in your directory structure. In addition, notice on the left a navigation menu with a link to Documents. This is your default document library. You can click that link whenever you want to return to your default library.

Open SharePoint Files by Using Windows Explorer

Rather than navigate your SharePoint Online documents and folders in your web browser, you can use Windows Explorer to manage your files and folders. In general, this is a much easier way to work with your files. To access this feature, you need to select the document library so that you are viewing the Library Tools options shown in Figure 11-8. Under Library Tools, click the Library tab to access the controls shown in Figure 11-10.

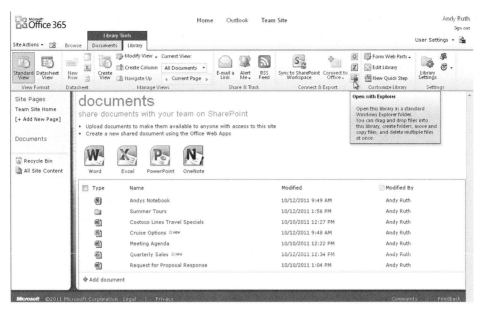

FIGURE 11-10 The Library Tools tab—the Library menu with Open With Explorer selected.

The Library menu contains some very useful features, such as Open With Explorer (shown selected in Figure 11-10). This feature is not named in the menu but is represented by a small icon with a folder and computer page, making it somewhat hard to discover.

When you click Open With Explorer, your document library opens in Windows Explorer, where you can manage your online documents as if they were in a local folder (see Figure 11-11).

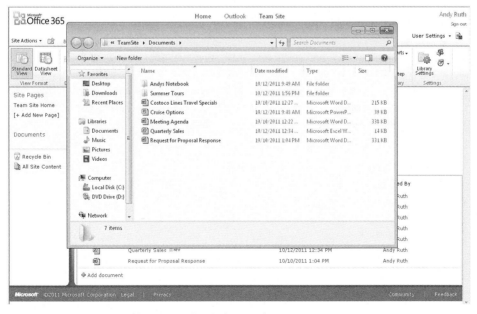

FIGURE 11-11 A document library open in Windows Explorer.

You can use this feature to rearrange your content. For example, remember how you added a new folder to the document library? That's great, but how do you get your documents that are already in the document library into the new folder? Explorer view is the easiest way. You can just drag the document into the folder as if it were a folder on your desktop.

In addition, when you want to add a folder that has existing content, you can drag the folder from your desktop to the opened Explorer window. The folder and its contents will be copied to SharePoint Online.

Placing Your Document Library on Your Desktop

This is one of my favorite SharePoint Online productivity tips: you don't need to open Share-Point Online in your browser to work with your online documents. You can add a shortcut folder to your desktop that will open the document library in SharePoint Online in Explorer whenever you click it. You can drag documents right into the folder *without opening your browser.*

First, open the document library in Explorer view, as shown in Figure 11-11. Next, *left-click and hold* on the folder icon in the address bar, as shown in Figure 11-12, and then drag the folder on to your desktop.

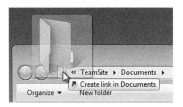

FIGURE 11-12 Dragging the folder icon.

Now you have a shortcut folder on your desktop that will open your document library in Explorer view! Note that if you delete this icon, your files and folders in SharePoint Online will not be deleted. Also, note that the Create Link In Documents tooltip appears in the figure only because it is a drag operation. The tooltip changes to Create Link In Desktop when the folder moves past the window boundary.

Troubleshoot Open With Windows Explorer

In some cases, when you click the Open With Explorer icon, you will receive the message Your Client Does Not Support Opening This List With Windows Explorer. The most common resolution is to add your SharePoint Online site to the list of Trusted Sites. Browse to your SharePoint Online site, and from Internet Explorer, choose Tools, and then click Internet Options. (If you don't see the Tools menu option, press the Alt key.) Click the Security tab and ensure that Trusted Sites is selected. Click the Sites button, and you should see your SharePoint Online site listed, placed there automatically. Before you close this form, be sure to clear the check box labeled Require Server Verification (Https) For All Sites In This Zone. Typically, you would not clear this check box for security reasons, but the Share-Point Online Plan P1 does not support https. Click Close. Clear the Enable Protected Mode check box, and then click OK. Close Internet Explorer and try again. This resolves the problem in many cases.

> Important Adding a non-https site to your trusted sites in Internet Explorer does create a security risk. If an attacker was able to successfully pose as your website and you connected to it, it could potentially inject harmful code that would run on your computer. Your browser would think it's connecting to a trusted site and provide elevated privileges. When your computer connects to a site by using an SSL connection (https://), the possibility of this is dramatically reduced because the traffic between you and the site is encrypted. As of this writing, Plan P1 does not support https connections, which makes it much easier for an attacker to implement this kind of attack. You have to assess for yourself if you consider the risk to be worth the convenience.

Create a New Document Library

The default document library works fine, but you might want to create different repositories to better manage your content, segregating it by team, project, security, or other grouping that makes sense for your business.

To create a new document library, browse to your team site, and then in the upper-left corner of the page, click Site Actions. From the menu, select New Document Library to reach the page shown in Figure 11-13.

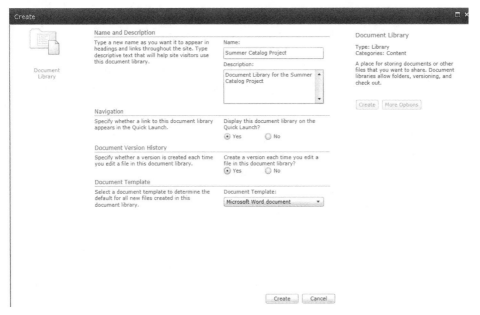

FIGURE 11-13 Creating a new document library.

Although the Name And Description settings are self-explanatory, the Navigation options are not so obvious. In Figure 11-13, notice the Document Library link listed on the left side of the page. The link is called a Quick Launch link. By default, when you create a new document library, SharePoint Online will add a Quick Launch link to this menu. This makes the document library easily discoverable by others using the system. However, if you do not want to "advertise" the document library, you can say No to the Navigation question. In this case, make a note of the URL when the library is created so that you can easily return to it later.

When enabled, Document Version History creates a new version of your file every time you save your edits rather than overwriting the existing file. When you open the file, you always open the latest version, but you have the option of reverting to any previous version. For more details about this feature, see the "Versioning Settings" section later in this chapter.

The Document Template setting determines what kind of file is created when you create a new file within SharePoint Online rather than uploading a file. In almost all cases, this remains set to the default.

When you've completed the form, click Create. You are now in the document library, where you can add documents or make further configuration settings. If you return to the Team Site page, you can now see the document library listed under Libraries on the left side of the page. This is the afore-mentioned Quick Launch link.

 Note After using SharePoint Online for a while, you might forget the link or name of a page or library that you created. You can find any content you created by clicking the All Site Content link on the left side of the Team Site page.

Add Alerts to the Document Library

Document libraries can be set to notify you when a document is added or changed. In some cases, this is exactly what you need to keep in touch with an active project that is time sensitive or material that is touch sensitive.

Setting alerts is easy to do. In the Library Tools group, select the Library tab (see Figure 11-10), and then click Alert Me (the ringing bell icon). Select Set Alert On The Library, and then complete the form that displays.

The alert options are self-explanatory. You can use them to specify when and where to send an alert via email or text message. For example, you can set up the alert to send an email when anyone changes any document, just your document, or when files are added, deleted, or modified. You can even elect to receive alerts one at a time, daily, weekly, or on a scheduled basis.

 Note You can have alerts sent to a distribution group if needed. This can be useful when a team is responsible for a set of documents, such as service requests. Any time a new one is added, several people will be notified.

Library Settings

The configuration settings for the document library are found on the Library Settings page. To access this page, on the ribbon, in the Library Tools group, select the Library tab, and then click Library Settings (see Figure 11-10). The page shown in Figure 11-14 opens.

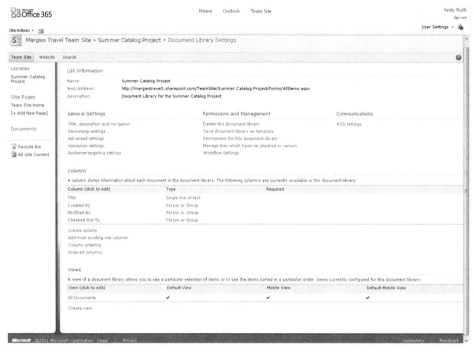

FIGURE 11-14 The Library Settings page in SharePoint Online.

This page provides many settings, but only a few that you will use regularly.

Title, Description, and Navigation

When you need to modify the title of the library, you can do so from the Title, Description, And Navigation page. In addition, you can add or remove a Quick Launch link for the library.

Versioning Settings

Click the Versioning settings link on the Library Settings page to refine the document history settings for your library, which you can see in Figure 11-15. SharePoint Online is designed to provide a framework for document version control and workflow. You can easily set up and control version history as well as require documents to be checked out when edited. The sections that follow take a closer look at key Versioning Settings page options.

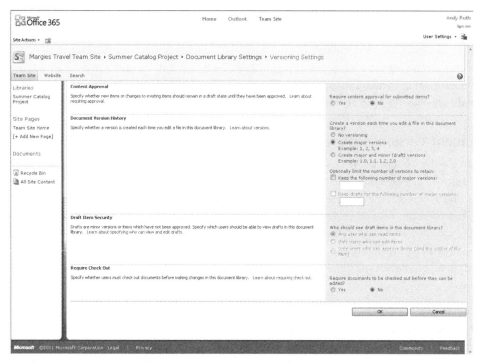

FIGURE 11-15 The document library Versioning Settings page.

Content Approval

Microsoft designed the Content Approval feature so that SharePoint sets the Approval Status of new documents added to the library to Pending and requires approval of the document before anyone other than the author or administrators can see it. For users of Plan P1, Content Approval should be disabled. With Content Approval turned on, Figure 11-16 shows the Pending status of a new document in the Approved Status column.

FIGURE 11-16 A new document showing Pending status after Content Approval enabled.

Because of the default permissions set for Plan P1, Content Approval *does not* work as you would expect from the description. In Plan P1, the default permissions allow all Office 365 users to contribute to the contents of your document library. As a result, when Content Approval is enabled, pending documents can be viewed and approved *by any user*. Even so, it can be useful to have all submissions automatically set to Pending status to note whether it has been reviewed. In the E plans, users do not automatically have rights to SharePoint Online, so this feature works as intended.

Document Version History

You can use the options in the Document Version History section to designate versions as major or minor versions as well as limit the number of versions saved. Major versions are whole numbers such as 1, 2, and 3, whereas minor versions are incremented in decimals, such as version 1.1, 1.2, 2.3, and so on. Everyone can view major versions, but only a select group of people can view minor versions, even though they are stored in the same document library as major versions. For larger organizations, this feature can be invaluable in preventing pre-release versions of important documents from being viewed. Small businesses will generally want to create a new version for both major and minor (draft) versions.

When you save a document to a document library that has versioning enabled, you are asked to specify the version number. If you don't, the version number is automatically incremented. Keep in mind that each version you keep consumes storage that counts against your SharePoint Online storage quota. It's a good idea to limit the number of versions kept for both major and minor versions; otherwise, the system will keep an unlimited number of versions, which could quickly consume your storage allotment.

Note The Draft Item Security setting works in coordination with the minor drafts feature as well as Content Approval, but most small businesses are not likely to need it. By default, in Plan P1, all users can read and approve a draft item. As a result, this setting has no effect unless you customize the security for the library.

Require Check Out

Turning on Require Check Out forces users to take ownership of the document they want to edit before they can open it, and it prevents others from editing the document at the same time. In addition, enabling this feature disables editing by using OWA.

Checking in and checking out documents is a major feature of SharePoint Online that you'll learn more about later in this chapter. In general, you will want to require check-out whenever your business involves collaborating on important documents and it's vital to avoid versioning issues, such as those that occur when two people are editing different versions of the same document.

Recommended Settings

For general use in a small business, I recommend the following settings based on the default configuration for Plan P1:

- Content Approval: No.

- Document Version History: Create major and minor (draft) versions; keep ten copies of both minor and major drafts.

- Draft Item Security: Disabled.

- Require Check Out: Depends on your use case. If the documents are actively being edited or reviewed by multiple people, requiring check-out can be useful. If the documents are finished, read-only, or templates, they do not require check-out.

Click OK to apply the versioning changes. The changes go into effect immediately.

Workflow Settings

The Library Settings page shown in Figure 11-14 includes a link to Workflow Settings, from which you can configure a three-stage *workflow,* or a set of predefined actions for a document. For example, you could create a workflow such as "When Kim adds a document with 'Budget' in the title, send an email to the Budget Committee group." However, the web-based interface for this feature is a bit awkward and quite limited.

Instead, I recommend using Microsoft SharePoint Designer 2010, which you can download from *http://www.microsoft.com/download/en/details.aspx?displaylang=en&id=16573*. With this free tool, you can create very useful workflows, without writing any code. To get started, go to *http://office.microsoft.com/ en-us/sharepoint-designer-help/introduction-to-designing-and-customizing-workflows-HA101859249. aspx*. You can attach these workflows to many items in SharePoint Online, such as lists, documents, contacts, and calendars.

Delete a Document Library or Document

You can delete a document library by clicking the Delete This Document Library option in the Library Settings. You will see a message confirming that you approve sending the item to the Recycle Bin. If you click OK, then the document library, the documents it contains, versions, and settings will be removed. To delete an individual document, select it in the document library, and then on the ribbon, click Delete or right-click the document, and then select Delete.

Recover from the Recycle Bin

Of course, not everything that is deleted should be deleted, and Microsoft has kindly added a two-stage safety net for deleted items. If you have deleted a document or library that you want to recover, the Recycle Bin holds a copy of the deleted items for 30 days. Selecting the Recycle Bin shows the items available to be recovered. This is called the End User Recycle Bin; it is available to all end users by default.

Figure 11-17 shows the Cruise World Overview PowerPoint file in the Recycle Bin. Kim can recover the file by clicking Restore Selection or she can delete the file from the Recycle Bin by clicking Delete Selection. If she deletes the selection, her Recycle Bin appears empty. If she does nothing, after 30 days, the file is permanently deleted.

FIGURE 11-17 Recovering a document from the team site Recycle Bin.

For purposes of example, Suppose that Kim deleted the file from the bin—even then, the file is still not lost. It is simply moved to stage 2. Kim can contact the service administrator (you, in this case), who has the ability to restore items that were deleted from the Recycle Bin by users.

As administrator, you go to the document library from which the item was deleted. At the top of the page are instructions on how you can access items deleted from the library by using the Site Collection Recycle Bin link. Click the link (also at the top of the page) to access the Site Collection Administration Recycle Bin page. Then, choose Deleted From End User Recycle Bin , as shown in Figure 11-18 (on the left). Now you can easily restore Kim's PowerPoint by selecting the file and clicking Restore Selection.

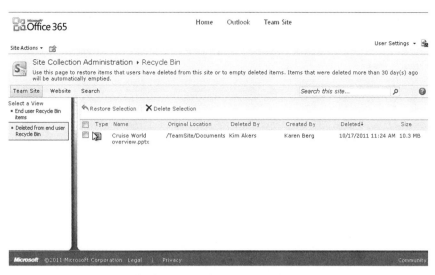

FIGURE 11-18 Recovering a file from the end-user Recycle Bin.

You can also restore any other item deleted from the Site Collection by using the option End User Recycle Bin Items, which shows you items that have not yet been deleted from the end-user recycle bins—those files are still in stage 1.

Note that when items are deleted, they must be recovered within 30 days or they will be permanently discarded.

Manage Permissions

As mentioned earlier, permissions in SharePoint Online for Plan P1 allow all your users to access your SharePoint Online site. In addition, they can write, delete, and create content on the site, but they are not full administrators.

Even if you have no need to create protected content for your users, you should have a basic understanding of how SharePoint Online security works. You will need this information when you start sharing content with users outside of your organization.

Using the Summer Catalog Project document library as an example, try setting up permissions so that only Kim and Karen can access the library. Of course, the service administrator can access any content, so the goal is not to block service administrators but to keep others from viewing the document library. When the document is ready, they will post the document to another location where people can view the document.

To access the permissions for the library, on the Document Library Settings page, in the Permissions And Management column, click Permissions For This Document Library link, as shown in Figure 11-14.

Clicking Permissions For This Document Library opens a page similar to Figure 11-19.

FIGURE 11-19 Document library default permissions.

The Name column lists all the groups, roles, and users who have permissions to the library. You can see that, by default, there are a number of assignments. The most important one is the strange-looking Tenant Users listing. This is the group that gives permissions to all your users. The Owners entry is also active, in that it contains an entry for the site administrator. Those two settings are the "active" entries in this list. You can verify this by clicking each entry; you will see that all the listings are empty except for those two groups.

At the top of the page is a very important note: This Library Inherits Permission From Its Parent. In other words, this document library does not have any *explicit* permissions assigned to it. The permissions you see flow down, or are inherited, from the overall team site to which it belongs.

As a result, to set up permissions that are different from the team site, you must first take a step called *breaking inheritance* by clicking the Stop Inheriting Permissions button.

> Important You can seriously impair the functionality of your SharePoint Online service by adjusting permissions. Specifically, be very careful when making adjustments to settings at the site collection level. There is only one site collection in your subscription, and due to inheritance, any adjustment will apply to everything in SharePoint Online. In the example, you are working in a test document library, so any changes you make to this library will apply only to items continued in the library. Be sure you have a good understanding of what you are applying and what it will affect before making permissions adjustments.

When you click Stop Inheriting Permissions, you will receive a warning that you are creating unique permissions for the document library and that the parent site permissions will no longer affect this site. That's exactly what you want, so click OK.

When you do this, you'll notice that the permissions do not change. That is because they are copied and applied from the team site. However, the document library now has its own unique permissions that can be adjusted individually. So even though they are at first exactly the same, you can now modify them.

You make these modifications by using the new menu items that appear after you break inheritance, as shown in Figure 11-20.

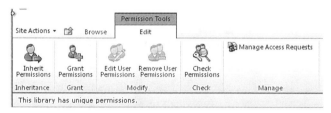

FIGURE 11-20 The Permission Tools ribbon.

- **Inherit Permissions**   Removes customized permissions and reverts to inheriting permissions from the team site.

- **Grant Permissions**   Used for adding new users, groups, or roles to the list.

- **Edit User Permissions and Remove User Permissions**   Use this to edit or remove permissions applied to a user, group, or role.

- **Check Permissions**   Gives you the effective permissions for a user, group, or role. This can be useful for situations in which users are members of more than one group or role.

- **Manage Access Requests**   Sets the options available when users receive an Access Denied message. In some cases, you might want to allow people to request access. In other cases, you might want no options at all.

 Important Before proceeding, ensure that you are logged on as the service administrator. Otherwise, you will remove your own access by taking the following actions.

For the example, you want to allow only Kim and Karen access to the collection, so you need to remove the Tenant Users from the list. Select the check box next to Tenant Users, select Remove Users Permissions, and then click OK when prompted that you are about to remove all permissions for the group. The group will disappear.

Next, click the Owners group. In the upper left, click New, as shown in Figure 11-21.

FIGURE 11-21 Adding new owners to the document library.

The Grant Permissions form opens, as shown in Figure 11-22. This form is easy to use but takes a bit of getting used to.

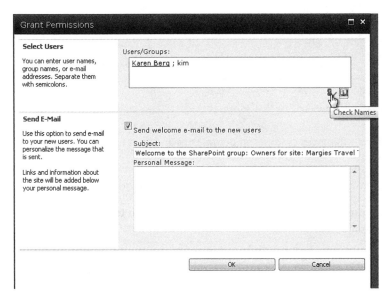

FIGURE 11-22 The Grant Permissions form with Check Names icon shown.

In the Select Users section, type the first part of the name you want to add, and then click the Check Names icon as shown in Figure 11-22. This will auto-complete the name for you, if it exists in your user directory. You can also click the address book icon next to the check names icon to locate and select multiple names. When you click OK, only Karen, Kim, and the site administrator have access to the site. Everyone else gets an access denied message.

 Note You can optionally send an email message to people who are granted access to a site. This is useful when adding people to a site, and they need to know that it is now available to them.

You can control who can do what with the page. In some cases, you will want people to view and download documents but not change them. Add those users to the Viewers group. Keep in mind, however, that rules are additive. If you are a member of the Contributors role and the Viewers role, you will have all the permissions granted to both.

Permissions in SharePoint

The "Manage Permissions" section covers how to change the permission for your SharePoint document library, but the same knowledge applies to permissions in general. With SharePoint Online, you can control access to lists, calendars, wikis, blogs, custom pages, and even individual documents. Just select the item that you want to manage, and then locate the security page. You can often find the security option on the ribbon; it is represented by the icon with two heads and a key, as shown in Figure 11-23.

FIGURE 11-23 Document Permissions on the document properties ribbon.

You can learn more about permissions at *http://office.microsoft.com/en-us/sharepoint-online-small-business-help/roadmap-grant-permissions-for-a-site-HA101966936.aspx*.

Add a "Checked Out To" Column

Suppose that you go to your document library to work on a document that's due for a review but see that it is checked out, as shown in Figure 11-24. You need to make edits to the document. You know you can open the document, save it as a new version, and then edit it, but by doing so, you then run the risk of creating multiple versions of the same document. How do you know who has checked it out? One way to find out is to hover over the document icon, which will pop up the name of the person who checked out the document.

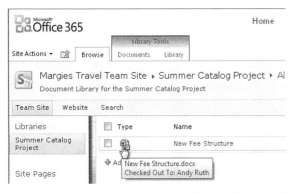

FIGURE 11-24 Hovering over the Checked Out To document icon.

This works well, but it would be easier if the library simply displayed a column that listed the people who have documents checked out.

The good news is that you can customize the view of your document library to suit your needs. The ability to modify and create new views in SharePoint Online is almost breathtaking in the number of options and capabilities you can control. You can add entirely new columns of information and designate their contents. For example, you could create a Status column and configure it to display one of a group of values, such as New, Edited, Approved, or Published. You can add columns that perform math based on the content of other columns. You can sort, subsort, query, and format contents in many ways. The online help available within SharePoint Online can get you started with any of these topics.

Adding a Checked Out To column is a simple matter because this is one of many predefined columns. First, on the ribbon, click Library Tools, and then select the Library tab, as shown in Figure 11-10. You'll see a section on the ribbon related to managing views. Click Modify View. Then, examine the Columns section, as shown in Figure 11-25.

FIGURE 11-25 Adding columns to a document library.

You can add any of the columns listed by simply selecting its corresponding Display check box. In addition, you can rearrange the columns by changing the Position From Left setting. This is a good example of how SharePoint Online gives you control over your sites and enables you to make changes without requiring any programming.

In this example, I've added the Checked Out To and Version columns. The document library now looks similar to Figure 11-26.

FIGURE 11-26 The document library showing Checked Out To and Version columns.

You can now see at a glance who has the document checked out and the latest version numbers.

Presence in SharePoint Online

You'll notice that something else appeared along with the Checked Out To name. The green box next to Karen and Andy's name is called a *Presence indicator*. It shows that both Karen and Andy are online and available. Presence is provided by the Microsoft Lync Online service in Office 365 and is shown in many places, including Microsoft Office, Outlook, Outlook Web App, and SharePoint Online. Andy can see that Karen is available. By hovering over her name, he can bring up the Lync contact card, as illustrated in Figure 11-27.

FIGURE 11-27 A Lync Contact card in SharePoint Online.

From this card, Andy can start an email, an instant message (IM) session, call Karen from Lync 2010, or look up her phone number and address in the address list. This is the kind of feature you would not normally find in a small business because the technology required to back it up is significant. Fortunately, with Office 365, it works automatically. In the right circumstances, this kind of capability can really save time because you can immediately connect with the right person.

Publish a Document Library to Outlook

Sometimes you might need a document when you don't have access to SharePoint Online. At other times, you want the same document available to everyone all the time. With SharePoint Online, you can connect a document library to Outlook, such that offline copies of the documents are available to you anytime. You can open the documents from within Outlook and make modifications that will be uploaded to the document library—presuming you have permissions—when you next connect. To connect Outlook to a document library, open the document library in your browser. On the ribbon, click the Library Tools group, and then select the Library tab, as shown in Figure 11-28.

 Note If you're using the default team site and having trouble finding the right menu, click the spot shown in Figure 11-8.

FIGURE 11-28 Enabling the Connect To Outlook option.

Click the Outlook icon as shown. You will then be presented with a series of approvals to confirm. When Outlook opens, a new folder will appear in the list of folders representing your document library. You can open and edit documents directly from Outlook, as shown in Figure 11-29.

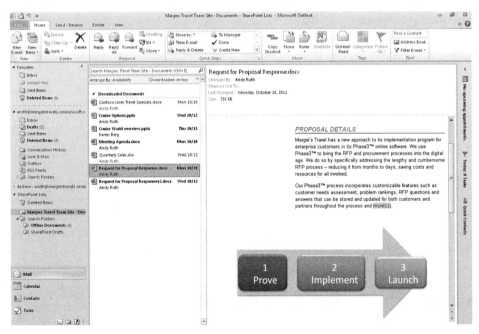

FIGURE 11-29 A document library connected to Outlook.

When you open a document, you will see the message shown in Figure 11-30, stating that you are editing an offline document and that you should save it to your computer for uploading later.

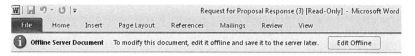

FIGURE 11-30 Offline server document.

When you click the Edit Offline button, you're presented with another message, informing you that your documents will be stored on your computer in SharePoint Drafts. That's useful but not fully informative. What if you want to store your drafts on a specific drive or location? You can customize the location by clicking Offline Editing Options in the Edit Offline prompt, as shown in Figure 11-31.

FIGURE 11-31 The Edit Offline dialog box showing offline editing options.

When you click OK, you can edit the document. When you close the document, if you are online, you will see the message shown in Figure 11-32, asking whether you want to upload the edited document.

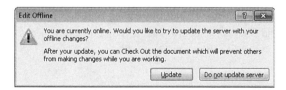

FIGURE 11-32 The prompt when closing a document edited offline, when you're online.

If you don't update the server, your copy stays local. You can upload it at any time by going to your SharePoint Drafts folder and opening the document. You will see the prompt shown in 11-32 when you do. If you do update the server, you replace the online copy with your version. If version history is turned on, the previous version is placed in the history.

Because you are editing an offline version of the file, using this method, if someone changes the file on SharePoint Online and you then copied your version to the library, you could potentially over-write the updated version with your version. SharePoint Online will catch this situation and prompt you with the message, Server Copy Of This Document Has Been Updated. Your Changes Conflict With The Changes Made To The Server Copy. Save This File To Another Location. In this case, you need to resolve the version issue by saving the file locally as a new file name and then upload it to SharePoint Online, or alternatively, delete the SharePoint Online file and then upload the document.

Work with SharePoint Online Documents in Microsoft Office

With Microsoft Office 2007 and 2010, you can manage your SharePoint Online documents directly within SharePoint. In particular, Office 2010 makes it very easy to interact with SharePoint Online documents. In this section, you'll learn how to open, save, check out, manage versions, revert to previous versions, and otherwise work with your online document from within Microsoft Office. I'll focus on using Word because it is most commonly used, and the features shown also apply to Excel, PowerPoint, and OneNote. Microsoft Access also interacts with SharePoint Online.

Open a Document in Microsoft Word

If you need a document that you've not opened previously, just browse to the document library and double-click the document. If it opens in Word Web App, click Edit In Microsoft Word. You can also hover over the line listing for the document, click the down arrow, and then select Edit In Microsoft Word (see Figure 11-33).

FIGURE 11-33 Select the menu options for a document.

After you have worked with the document, you can open it without having to return to SharePoint Online. Simply start Word, click the File tab, and then click Recent. The Recent Documents list contains the documents you've accessed in SharePoint Online, as shown in Figure 11-34.

FIGURE 11-34 Recent documents will open from SharePoint Online.

Editing Online and Coauthoring

When you open a document hosted on SharePoint Online, the document might or might not be checked out to you, depending on the settings for the document and document library. If the document is not checked out, other people can open and edit the document. This is a feature called coauthoring and can be very useful when you need to simultaneously edit a single document. If this occurs, you will be notified, as shown in Figure 11-35.

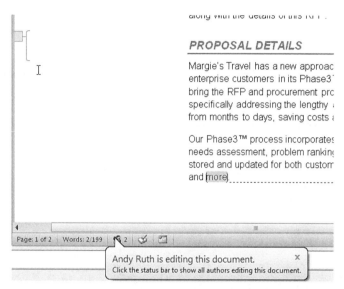

FIGURE 11-35 A notification that others are editing a document on which you're working.

You can click the group icon to see who is editing the document, as shown in Figure 11-36.

FIGURE 11-36 The authors editing this document.

Now that you know who is editing your document, you can contact them by clicking their tag and initiating an IM session, phone call, or email. You can also see the editors and contact them by using the File tab in Microsoft Word, as shown in Figure 11-37.

FIGURE 11-37 The People Currently Editing list.

In addition, you can see what content is being edited by other authors. When someone saves a version, you will be notified and your view refreshed. If a conflict occurs, Word has a special conflict view. In Figure 11-38, you can see that both Andy and Karen have saved the same heading. You can elect to keep your changes or reject your changes. This is a useful feature for handling conflicts that can arise from online editing.

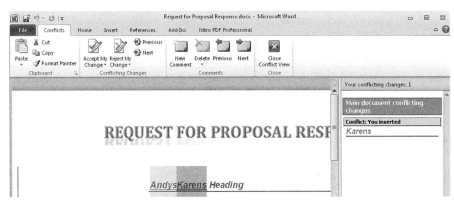

FIGURE 11-38 Conflict view in Word.

Note Coauthoring is an Office 2010 feature and not available in all Office products. For example, Excel does not support coauthoring. In addition, the experience is different if one user has Office 2007 and the other has Office 2010. You can read more about coauthoring at *http://technet.microsoft.com/en-us/library/ff718249.aspx*.

Check Out a Document

You can avoid the headaches of having more than one author on a document by checking out the document when you edit a file. In SharePoint Online, simply select a document, and then click Check Out to mark the document as belonging to you (see Figure 11-33). Note that checking out a document does not automatically open it. When you check out the document, you are asked whether you want to use your local drafts folder. If you do not select to use your local drafts folder, you will be editing the document directly on SharePoint Online. There's nothing wrong with this, but in general, you will want to save a copy locally for editing because it is faster and allows you to work on the document when you are not connected to your SharePoint site.

After you have opened a document with Microsoft Office, you do not need to return to SharePoint Online to reopen it and check it out. Just open the document from your Recent Documents list, and it will open from SharePoint Online. You can then check out the document without leaving Microsoft Office. Click the File tab to display what Microsoft calls the "Backstage view." (I just call it the File tab, because that's what you click to see the page, similar to Figure 11-39.)

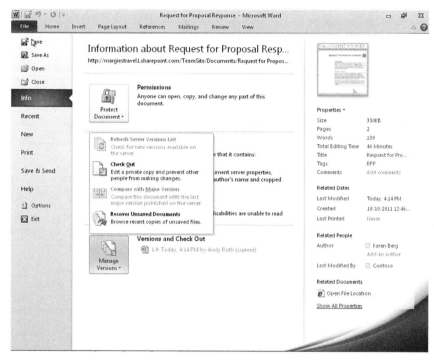

FIGURE 11-39 Checking out a document while in Microsoft Word.

When a document is checked out, anyone attempting to open the document sees the message shown in Figure 11-40.

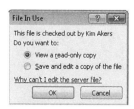

FIGURE 11-40 The File In Use message.

Users can select to view the file or make a copy of the file and edit the new copy. They cannot upload and overwrite the existing document in SharePoint Online without first changing the name of the document.

The Downside to Checking Out Documents

Checking out documents is a great feature and works well to prevent versioning issues. The downside is that if someone checks out a document and forgets to check it back in, he then blocks progress by other team members. In Plan P1, the default permissions are such that a user can discard any other user's checkout by accessing the menu shown in Figure 11-39. If you have modified permissions so that this not possible, the service administrator can discard the checkout.

Check In a Document (Offline Editing)

When you're ready to check in the document, you do not need to go to SharePoint Online. Just open the document from your Recent Documents list, click File, and then click Check In, as shown in Figure 11-41.

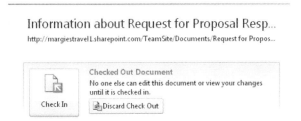

FIGURE 11-41 Checking in a document within Microsoft Word 2010.

You will be asked to add comments related to the checked-in version. These comments can be viewed by others when reviewing the version history.

After checking in the document, the document will revert to Read Only, as shown in Figure 11-42.

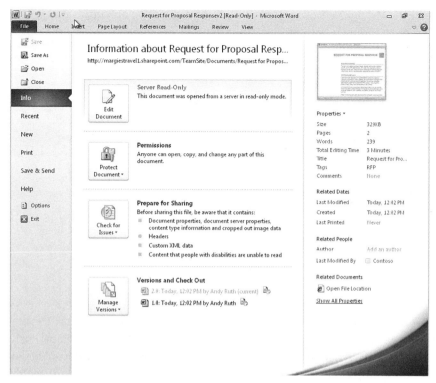

FIGURE 11-42 Selecting Server Read-Only mode.

You can click the Edit Document button to edit the document. The difference is that, because the document is now checked in, you are directly editing the online document instead of a local copy.

As you can see, you can easily switch between editing online and offline, checking in and checking out. Be sure to keep in mind the mode you're in, and make sure it's the mode that matches your intention.

Notice the Manage Versions button at the bottom of Figure 11-42. You can see that multiple versions of the document are on SharePoint Online and that you can manage them. One of the actions you can take is to hover over the icon to the right of an entry, as shown in Figure 11-43. This displays the Comments the author added when checking in the version.

FIGURE 11-43 Showing Comments in Word 2010.

When you click the Manage Versions button, you see some surprising options, as shown in Figure 11-44.

FIGURE 11-44 The Manage Versions menu in Word 2010.

From this menu, you can check out a document without going to SharePoint Online! This is a very nice feature that shows how well Office and SharePoint Online work together. This choice simply appears automatically, without having to install anything or turn on any special features. This and other features in Office simply "wake up" when Office works with documents stored in SharePoint Online.

In addition, you can open any previous version shown. This is useful when you want to review part of a previous edition that was not carried forward into the most recent edition. If you open a prior version, Word lets you know that you're not working on the latest version and offers to compare the two versions. Use this feature when someone has made changes to a document you are working on and you need to inspect every change. Also, the compare options give you a quick way to locate content in a prior version that you want to bring forward.

You should click Refresh Server Version List to ensure that your version history is current and has not been updated while you are looking at the document.

Again, the key point here is that all of this activity is happening directly in Microsoft Word without having to go to SharePoint online. Excel and PowerPoint both have the same kinds of capabilities built in.

Recover Unsaved Documents

SharePoint Online includes a feature to recover unsaved documents, which can be a real lifesaver. In fact, it saved this chapter. While directly editing the chapter on my own SharePoint Online site, I logged on to a different SharePoint Online site to conduct a test. When I opened a different Word document from that site, I inadvertently closed without saving the working draft of this chapter. I was sure I'd lost several hard-fought pages! Upon returning to my own SharePoint Online site and reopening the chapter, I was relieved to see a prompt asking whether I wanted to recover the unsaved version of my file. Answering yes restored the complete file to Word—a testament to the kind of resiliency built into the service.

SharePoint and OneNote

OneNote is an underappreciated Office application with which you can capture and organize unstructured information. I use it extensively to store technical details that I can then easily search for. I also use it for capturing important facts that I reference frequently. It integrates with Internet Explorer for easy capture of interesting webpages; simply click Send To OneNote in your browser to store the page in a OneNote *notebook*. At meetings or at any other time, you can toss untreated bits of information (Windows key+N) into the notebook and sort them out later. In addition, OneNote integrates with Windows 7 Phone and SharePoint Online.

You can create a OneNote notebook by using the OneNote Web App. Click the OneNote icon, and you will see the prompt shown in Figure 11-45.

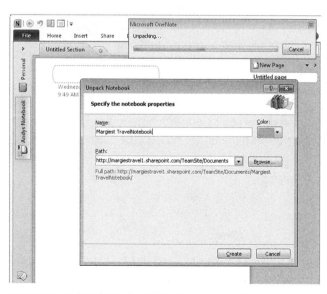

FIGURE 11-45 Creating a shared OneNote notebook.

Complete the form, and then click Create. You are now looking at a traditional OneNote notebook and can begin making entries. If you click the File tab, you'll see similar Word-like options tailored to OneNote, as shown in Figure 11-46. Anyone who has rights to the online notebook can access the notebook by using the URL shown in the Path field in Figure 11-45.

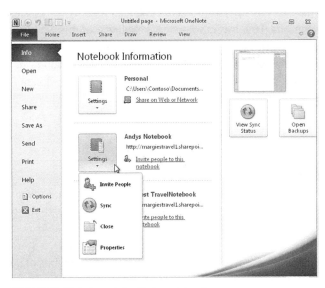

FIGURE 11-46 A shared OneNote notebook.

You can get creative about how to use OneNote for meeting items, outlines, capturing details for later review, and other ways your team might benefit from having a common, shared notebook. For example, you could create a notebook for a research project and have a tab for each person on the team. As they discover useful information, links, screen shots, or other suitable material, they simply post it to their sections. When you sync the notebook, everyone is updated.

Note As of this writing, a Hotfix is required for OneNote notebooks to properly synchronize. You can find details at *http://support.microsoft.com/kb/2522098*. Also, it is not recommended to enable minor versions in your Version settings for a shared copy of an OneNote notebook. To learn more about OneNote in general, see *http://office.microsoft.com/en-us/onenote/*.

Edit the Team Site Page

Although the default template for your SharePoint Online site works fine for basic document sharing, you can easily customize the look of the page to suit your preferences. To edit the page, at the top of the team site, click the Edit This Page link.

Note Any new pages you create will not have the Edit This Page link, so you will need to select Site Actions | Edit Page to enter the Edit mode for them.

When editing a page, the top menu bar changes. You will see the Editing Tools ribbon and its two tabs, as shown in Figure 11-47. Use the Format Text options to change fonts, format lists, insert paragraphs, and other standard formatting functions. You add or edit text simply by typing on the page.

Change the Title

When you are in Edit mode, you can change or add the title by typing on the page as if it were a Word document. You can add text anywhere you want, but some space is taken by the various parts already laid on the page. For example, you can add text above and below the Getting Started section (shown in Figure 11-47), but you cannot edit the Getting Started section itself.

FIGURE 11-47 Customizing the Team Site page title.

If you click the Insert tab, the ribbon changes, and you can insert pictures, tables, links, upload files; or insert features such as a shared calendar, announcements, contacts, or other Web Parts.

Note The Getting Started section is a predefined Web Part added automatically to the team site for Plan P1. You can remove, but not edit, this section. The links contained in Getting Started are quite useful while you are, appropriately enough, getting started. You can access any of the features from other menus, but the links are handy.

SharePoint Online Web Parts

To insert or remove Web Parts, on the ribbon, in the Editing Tools group, click the Insert tab (refer to Figure 11-47). You can now work with a variety of Web Parts, including a document library, calendar, announcements, contacts, and more. To see the full list, click the More Web Parts option, but don't expect to understand how to use all of the options you see there. The Content Editor Web Part is the one to add when you just want to type in some text and format it accordingly. Some of the options, such as the XML Viewer, require technical expertise to understand and use. In general, the tools you will use with SharePoint Online are documents and lists, so you don't need to spend much time learning how to implement the various other options unless you have a specific need.

> **Note** Remember, a Web Part is an application that you can add to your site that provides interactive capability. Using a Web Part, you can add functionality to your site without having to write any software. SharePoint Online comes with many pre-built Web Parts.

The Web Parts you can place on a page are configurable but not customizable. This means that you can't add or remove functionality from the predefined Web Parts by modifying the code, but you can change their size, color, content, and other settings. For example, suppose that you want to change the Posts Web Part on the team site to say Announcements instead of Posts. First, hover over the downward-facing triangle on the top right of the Web Part. The menu shown in Figure 11-48 will display, in which you can select Edit Web Part. Note that you can also delete the Web Part if you choose.

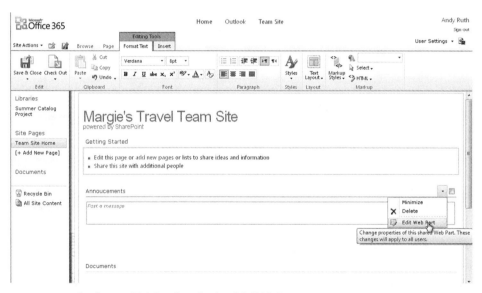

FIGURE 11-48 Configure a Web Part by selecting Edit Web Part

This opens a configuration-setting menu to the right of the Web Part with various sections that you can expand and configure. Expand the Appearance section to see the Title property. Enter **Announcements**, and then click OK. The title of the Posts section will be changed to Announcements.

If you are the adventurous type and like to explore what happens with various settings, be careful because it is possible to configure your Web Part so that it does not appear or function as expected. As a tip, notice in the upper-left portion of Figure 11-48 that you can check out the page. This functions similarly to checking out a document. If you check out a page and then discard it, your edits are not published.

Add an Image

You can add images to your page from your computer, a network location, or the Internet. Just place the cursor where you want the image to appear, click the Insert tab, and then click the Image button. You'll be prompted to browse to a file or provide a URL. The URL option makes it easy to populate a page with pictures from Facebook, Linked In, your public website, or other resource.

> **Note** If you use a URL for a publicly available image and you have added your SharePoint URL to Trusted Domains, every time the photo appears you will receive a warning message that the content from the page is coming from both trusted and untrusted sources. In this case, it's best to upload a picture to SharePoint Online rather than use a URL.

Back on the page, the ribbon will change once again to show Picture Tools options that appear only when an image is selected. You can resize the image dynamically by dragging the handles or by entering a specific size for the picture. In addition, you can specify whether you want a line drawn around the picture as well as how the image should be placed in relationship to the text. Figure 11-49 shows an image from the Microsoft Office clip art collection placed on the page by clicking Float | Left.

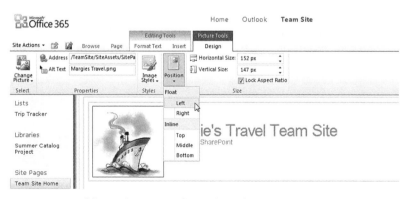

FIGURE 11-49 Adding an image to a SharePoint Online page.

Change the Page Layout

You might want to change the layout of your team site or other sites that you create. Using the layout options, you can apply different pre-existing templates to a page. You select from two-column or three-column, pages with headers, pages with footers, and other configurations. To change the layout, select Text Layout from the Format Text menu, as shown in Figure 11-50.

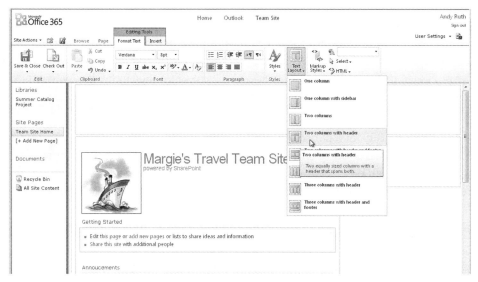

FIGURE 11-50 Changing the page layout.

The new layout provides an additional column for new content or Web Parts.

With just a few minutes of configuring, you can create a simple but pleasant page, as shown in Figure 11-51, complete with announcements, a calendar of events, and a document library—and no coding was required.

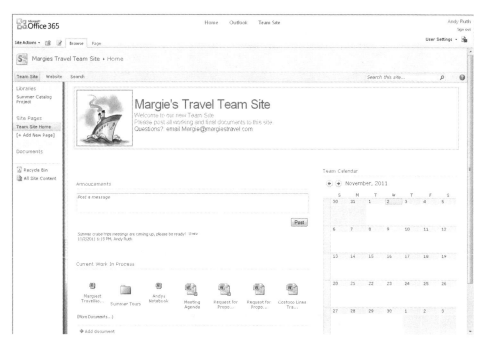

FIGURE 11-51 a customized team portal.

Calendars, Contacts, and Tasks

The calendar Web Part shown in Figure 11-51 is worth exploring a bit. Click the Team Calendar link to display the Calendar Tools options, as shown in Figure 11-52.

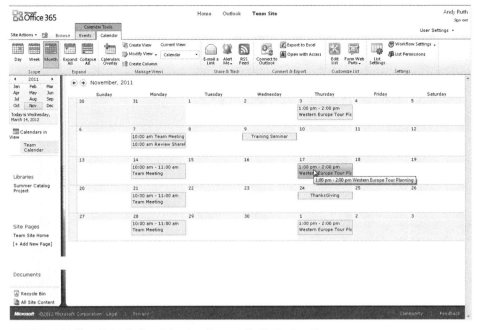

FIGURE 11-52 SharePoint Online Calendar–Connect To Outlook option.

You can add events to the calendar that viewers can see when they are on the SharePoint site, which is nice. But wouldn't it be great if you could open this in Outlook? You then could view the team calendar side by side with your personal calendar. Wouldn't it be even better if events you placed on the calendar in Outlook automatically appeared on the SharePoint Online team calendar? That's exactly the functionality built in to to SharePoint calendars. Click the Calendar Tool's Connect To Outlook option (see Figure 11-52); Outlook shows the SharePoint Calendar and your personal calendar, side by side, as in Figure 11-53.

This can be very useful for setting a team calendar that is shared with team members via Share-Point and is viewed in Outlook. As discussed in Chapter 10, "Improving Your Business Image and Productivity with Outlook," you can overlay one calendar atop the other by right-clicking either calendar and selecting Overlay. The resulting single calendar view allows you to easily spot conflicts.

To add an event to the calendar in Outlook, right-click a date and select whether to add a meeting or an appointment. You can also drag meetings from your Outlook calendar to the SharePoint calendar. It's best if you don't send meeting requests associated with the SharePoint Online calendar, because that is a function that involves email and tracking who and who hasn't accepted. Those are features provided in Exchange Online, not SharePoint Online. In other words, you can add events and key dates such as project milestones, holidays, recurring meetings, training events, and other activities, and they will automatically appear on the SharePoint Online calendar.

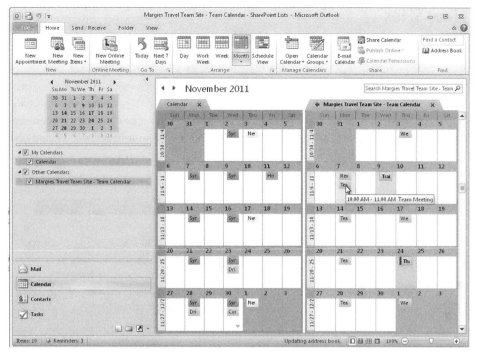

FIGURE 11-53 The SharePoint Online Calendar shown in Outlook, side by side with a personal calendar.

Similarly, you can add tasks and contacts to SharePoint Online and share them by using Outlook. Sharing contacts is a popular feature by which you can have a unified set of contacts available to all Office 365 users. Just add a Contacts Web Part to a page, and populate the list with information. Select the Contacts Web Part, and then in List Tools, click List | Connect To Outlook. The shared contact list will now be available in Outlook. You can drag existing contacts to the list, which then become available to other users of the SharePoint Contacts list.

Add Pages to Your Team Site

Suppose that you need to create a page on your team site for a special purpose, such as for a specific project or for new or temporary employees to use as they come onboard. Or perhaps you want to create a specific list integrated with Access on its own page in the team site. The default team site page provides two links for adding a page: in the left menu, under Site Page, you can click the + Add New Page or in the Getting Started section, you can click the Add New Page link (see Figure 11-47). Either way, you'll be prompted for a page name, and then you are presented with a blank page that you can configure as you like. Don't forget to set page permissions according to your requirements. You can then access the new page in the Quick Start links on the left side of the page under Site Pages.

Create New Sites

So far, you have been working within a single site team site. However, you can create other kinds of internal-use sites for different purposes. Each site can have its own look and feel, security, feature set, and content. To create a new site, click Site Actions, and then select New Site. You will see a preview of the site templates you can add. You can scroll through the pages and see whether there's one that suits your needs, keeping in mind that you can add or remove features and relocate content as you see fit. The predefined templates are just starting places and suggestions of ways you could build the simple Group Work Site, as shown in Figure 11-54, but you have many other ways to configure such a site, as well.

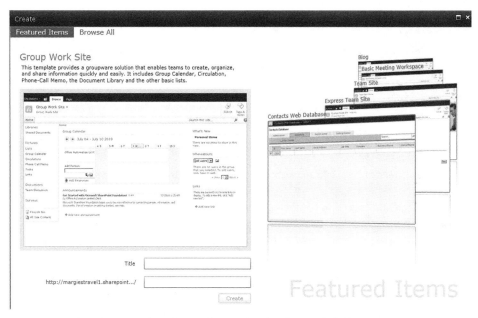

FIGURE 11-54 Creating a new site—Featured Items showing Group Work Site.

The Featured Items list does not show you all the choices. At the top of the window, click Browse All to view the remaining choices. Perhaps the most commonly used template is the Document Workspace. Figure 11-55 shows a sample of it.

In this example, the new site is called Italian Tours and can act as a shared workspace for a group creating a new tour offering. As you can see, the site is just a page with announcements, shared documents, tasks, users, and links Web Parts added. If you need more, check the document libraries and lists under Libraries and Lists, respectively, on the left. You can add, remove, or redesign the site to suit your requirements.

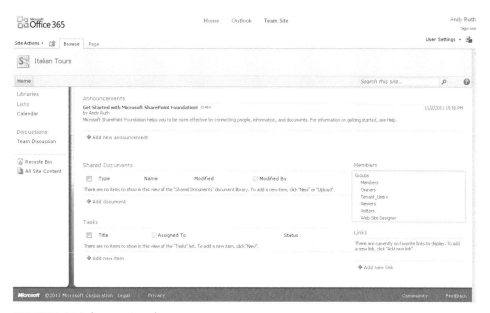

FIGURE 11-55 A document workspace.

When working with new sites, it's important to pay attention to navigation. How do you get to the new site? Where are the links for the site going to appear? To view the navigation tree that reveals the hierarchy of the content, in the upper-left portion of the page, click the Folder icon, as shown in Figure 11-56.

FIGURE 11-56 Navigating sites in SharePoint Online.

You can see that the the new site, Italian Tours, is actually under the team site. So you can navigate back to the team site by clicking Margies Travel Team Site. When you do, you'll see the familiar team site, but now there is a new menu option: Italian Tours, as shown in Figure 11-57.

FIGURE 11-57 Italian Tours is now a menu option on the Team Site page.

You can experiment further with the navigation elements by clicking Site Action | Site Settings and then exploring such options as Quick Launch, Top Link bar, Tree View, and Site Theme.

Roadmap to How SharePoint Sites Are Organized

If you're confused about where sites are in relationship to each other on SharePoint Online, you're not alone. Here's how it works: with SharePoint Online and Plan P1, you are provided with a single *site collection*. A site collection is just what the name says—a collection of sites.

To make it easy to use right out of the box, Microsoft creates a team site in that site collection. Otherwise, when you start to use SharePoint, you would see nothing there at all. So when you start out, you have one site in your site collection. In this case, the team site URL is http://margiestravel1.sharepointonline.com/*TeamSite*/SitePages/Home.aspx.

When you create a new site, you would expect it to be a peer of the existing site, so it might have a URL like http://margiestravel1.sharepointonline.com/*NewSite*/SitePages/Home.aspx. But that is not what happens. Instead, the new site is under the team site. In this example, you see that the URL for Italian Tours is http://margiestravel1.sharepointonline.com/*TeamSite/Italy*/default.aspx. This is because in SharePoint Online, the first site in the site collection is the parent of all other sites. So even though you are adding a new site, it would be more technically correct to call any new site a subsite. You can configure these subsites to have very different properties and capabilities from the parent site. In addition, you do not need the top site to have links to the subsites. As a result, these subsites can look and act more or less as independent sites but cannot have unique URLs.

Create Pages for New Sites

Adding pages to a new site, other than the team site, requires a slightly different process. On the new site page, click Site Action, and then select New Page. You'll then be prompted to enter a page name, and the page will be created using a default template. The specific appearance and layout of the new page depends on the kind of site that hosts the page. Experiment with different kinds of sites to see how pages are added to each and how they are laid out. When you find one you like, you can edit the page and populate it with Web Parts.

Using SharePoint Designer 2010

In addition to creating workflows, SharePoint Designer 2010 can help you build highly customized pages. Assuming you installed this free tool (using the link in the "Workflow Settings" section, earlier in this chapter), browse to the desired SharePoint Online page, click Site Action, and then select Edit In SharePoint Designer, as shown in Figure 11-58. The page will open in SharePoint Designer for editing. Using SharePoint Designer is an advanced topic not included in this book, but you can find many references and guides to SharePoint Designer by searching for "SharePoint Designer" at *http://office.microsoft.com*.

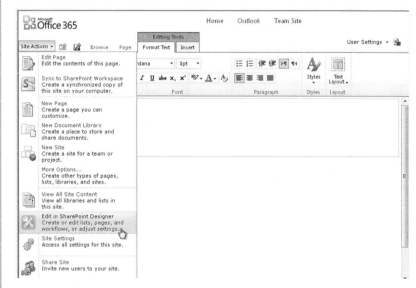

FIGURE 11-58 Edit in SharePoint Designer.

Work with Lists

For many businesses, just using SharePoint Online for document sharing and collaboration is well worth the cost of the entire Office 365 subscription. But SharePoint Online has many other capabilities, including the ability to work with predefined and customized lists—for example, inventory, sales leads, employee lists, phone numbers, email addresses, or business assets. You can add lists to SharePoint Online just as you can with document libraries. Lists can be highly customized to have columns that you choose, that can be sorted how you like, and can even interact with other lists. Features you've already learned, such as applying permissions and setting alerts, apply to lists as well as documents. You'll find that as you learn how to do something in one area of SharePoint Online, you can often apply that knowledge to another area.

Create a List from an Excel Spreadsheet

If you're like many businesses, you use Excel from time to time to keep lists of information, such as services, email addresses, inventory, attendees of an event, and reviews of your service. You can import these simple Excel lists into SharePoint, where others can see and interact with the content. For example, Margie's Travel has several group travel offerings. The company uses a spreadsheet to track how many travelers are signed up for each, which agent owns the event, notes, and whether the event is a go or no-go. Rather than track this information in a spreadsheet, management decided to convert the content to a SharePoint Online list. Agents can then review and update the list in real time as well as sign up for alerts to changes.

> Note To import an Excel spreadsheet, the SharePoint Online site must be listed in Trusted Sites. See the section "Troubleshoot Open With Windows Explorer," earlier in this chapter.

To create a list from a spreadsheet, in the upper-left corner, click Site Actions, and then select More Options. From the list of options, select Import Spreadsheet, as shown in Figure 11-59.

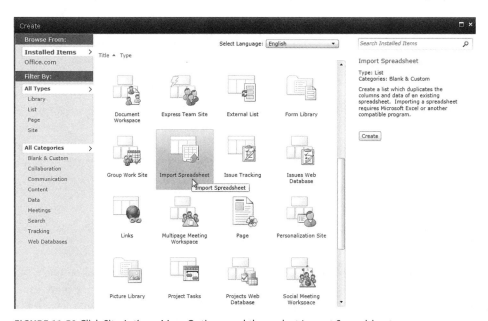

FIGURE 11-59 Click Site Actions, More Options, and then select Import Spreadsheet.

Click Create. A dialog box opens, in which you must provide a name for the list and description. Next, browse to the file containing the list, and then click Import. Excel opens and asks what part of the spreadsheet you want to import. You can designate one of three types: Table Range, Range Of Cells, or Named Range. Table Range is selected by default. For the example, you want to designate a range of cells to import, so click Range Type, and then select Table Range, as shown in Figure 11-60.

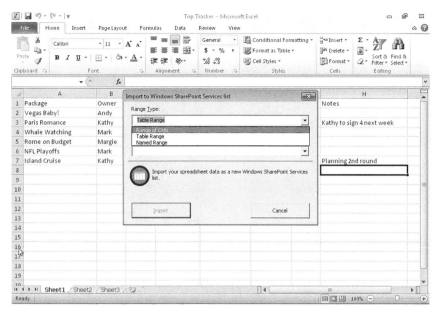

FIGURE 11-60 Selecting Range Of Cells in preparation for import.

After selecting Table Range, there is an important next step: you must click the Select Range text box before you do anything else! By placing the cursor in the Select Range box, as shown in Figure 11-61, you can click the spreadsheet underneath and select the range to import.

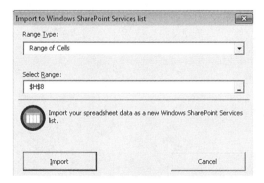

FIGURE 11-61 Put the cursor in the Select Range box.

When you've selected the correct range, click Import. Your list will import and will be hosted on SharePoint Online, as shown in Figure 11-62.

FIGURE 11-62 A list imported from Excel.

You can manage any individual item by clicking the down-arrow that appears when you hover over a line, as shown in Figure 11-63.

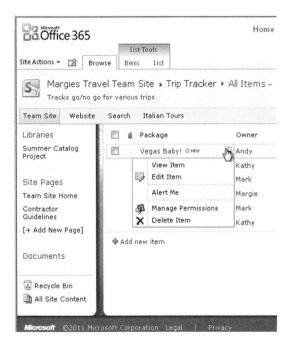

FIGURE 11-63 List item options.

At the top of the window, you can see the List tab, as illustrated in Figure 11-63 . When selected, many new options appear that allow you to work with and customize the list.

Add a Quick Launch Link

Now that you have your list in SharePoint Online, how do you find it again? You could make a note of the URL, but it's best to create a Quick Launch link for the list. The Quick Launch link will appear on the left of the page when you are on the site that hosts the list.

To access this option, first select the list so that the List Tools tabs are shown. Next, select List (see Figure 11-65), and then click List Settings. Under General Settings, select Title, Description, And Navigation. In the Navigation section, select Yes for the option Display This List In The Quick Launch Bar, and then click OK. Now, when you go to the team site, you can click your list from the Quick Launch bar. You can see the Trip Tracker list in the Quick Launch bar in Figure 11-64.

FIGURE 11-64 Adding a list to the Quick Launch bar.

DataSheet View

One of the most useful features for working with lists is the Datasheet view. When selected, you can work with a list in columns and rows, as shown in Figure 11-65. It's like an Excel spreadsheet except that it's hosted on SharePoint Online. Using this view, you can easily filter, add, edit, or delete entries.

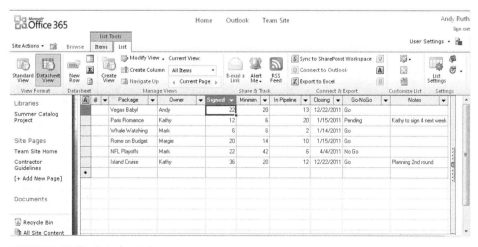

FIGURE 11-65 The Datasheet view.

Edit Existing Columns

One of the most powerful features of lists in SharePoint Online is the ability to create your own custom columns. You can add one of many predefined columns; create your own column; change the sequence; sort, add, and calculate columns; link two lists together by a shared value; add validations for content in any list; and more.

As a basic exercise, try changing the Go-NoGo column in the example so that it appears as set of predefined choices: Go, NoGo, or Pending. To do this, in the upper-right portion of the page, click the List Settings icon, as shown in Figure 11-65. In the center of the page, the existing columns are listed as shown in Figure 11-66. Note that in the Type column, Go-NoGo is described as a Single Line Of Text.

Columns

A column stores information about each item in the list. The following columns are currently available in this list:

Column (click to edit)	Type	Required
Package	Single line of text	
Owner	Single line of text	
Signed	Number	
Minimim	Number	
In Pipeline	Number	
Closing	Date and Time	
Go-NoGo	Single line of text	
Notes	Single line of text	
Created By	Person or Group	
Modified By	Person or Group	

Create column
Add from existing site columns
Column ordering
Indexed columns

FIGURE 11-66 A List of existing columns.

By clicking the Go-NoGo column, you can reconfigure the column type and other details, as shown in Figure 11-67.

FIGURE 11-67 The Go-NoGo column as single line of text.

To change this to a set of predefined choices, change the setting from Single Line Of Text to Choice (Menu To Choose From). After you make the change, your options change to those shown in Figure 11-68.

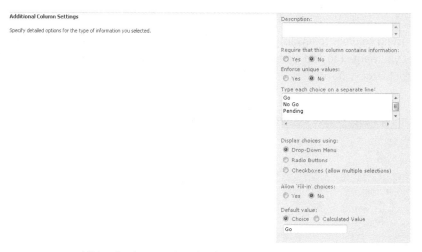

FIGURE 11-68 Additional column options for the Choice (Menu To Select From) setting.

You now have some nice options with which you can control how the column behaves. For example, you can require that an entry be made for new lines and designate the default value. Note that SharePoint Online kindly reads your existing values and suggests those as the options for you.

After setting the values you want, at the bottom of the page, click OK, and then return to the list. When you select to edit an item in the list or use Datasheet view, you will now be presented with a drop-down list from which you can choose one of the designated options, as shown in Figure 11-69.

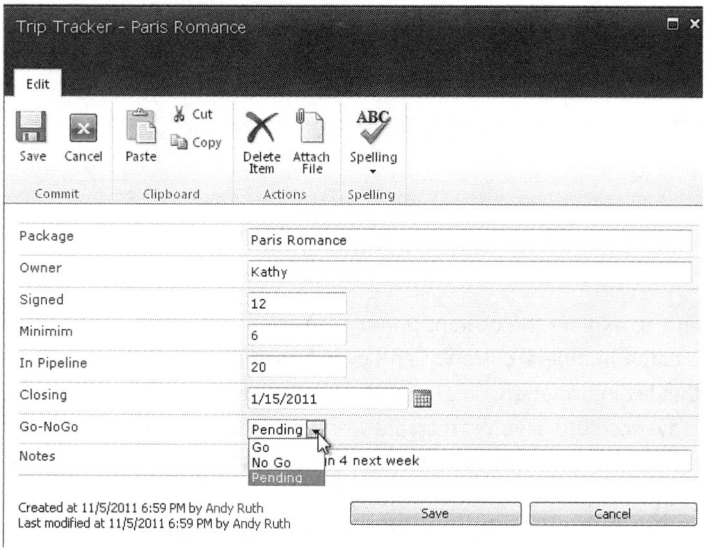

FIGURE 11-69 The Go-NoGo drop-down list.

Add New Columns

Often, the easiest way to create a list is to start with Excel and import the list, as described earlier. But sometimes you will want to build a list from scratch or add new columns after your list is already started.

You can add existing columns to any list from a set of predefined columns, or you can create your own. Suppose that you wanted to add a new column to our trip tracker list to indicate whether the trip is a new one for Margie's Travel.

To do this, in the upper-right part of the page, select the List Settings option, as shown in Figure 11-65. Under Columns, select Create Column. The form shown in Figure 11-70 opens.

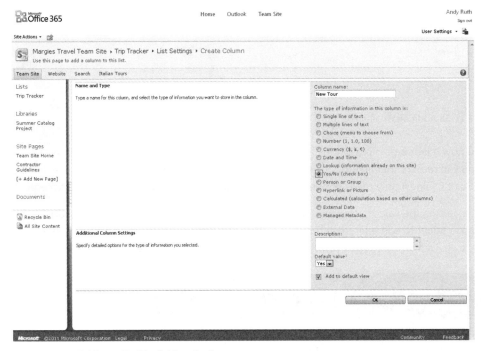

FIGURE 11-70 Adding a Yes/No field to the list.

After entering **New Tour** for the column name and selecting Yes/No, when you click OK, the new column is added.

It's worth taking a bit of time to explore the options under each column type. You can add columns for information such as dates, numbers, currency, and even hyperlinks. In addition, you can add calculated fields based on other list information. This lets you generate dynamically calculated values that can be quite useful. For advanced users, you can create workflows that trigger when these calculated events hit specified values. In this way, you can automate processes that alert you to important events, such as an inventory item dropping below a threshold, or be notified when a sales region hits or exceeds its projections. In addition, you can mark columns as required or optional.

Add Columns to Document Libraries

Here is a yet another way that Microsoft Office works with SharePoint Online—and it's one that you almost never hear about. You can add columns to document libraries just as you can to a list. This means that you can add information about a document to the document library, such as "last review" or "project owner." When you do this, the custom fields actually display in Microsoft Office when you open the document. You can use this to update the fields when you edit the document, as shown in Figure 11-71.

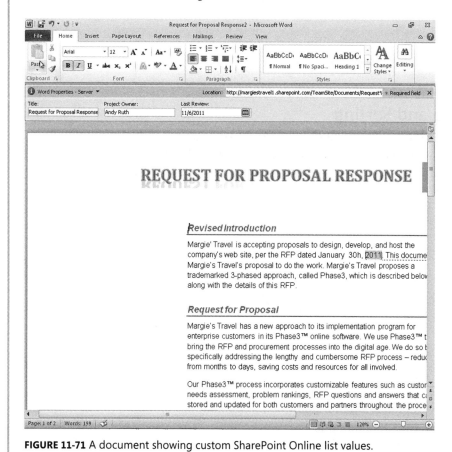

FIGURE 11-71 A document showing custom SharePoint Online list values.

Reorder Columns

To change the column order, from the List Settings page, select Column Ordering. You can then indicate which sequence you prefer by selecting Position From Top, as shown in Figure 11-72.

FIGURE 11-72 Changing column order.

Filtering and Sorting

Lists (and other libraries) can be sorted and filtered. First, select the column title you want to work with. To order the entire list, click A On Top or Z On Top, as shown in Figure 11-73. To filter the view, select the entry you want to view and the list will be instantly filtered to show only those that match the selected entry.

FIGURE 11-73 Sorting and filtering columns.

Invite External Users to Share Documents

Small businesses often hire contractors and other business associates to work on content. Typically, a person needs an Office 365 logon and password to access your SharePoint Online site, but Plan P1 includes the capability of inviting up to 50 outside users to a SharePoint Online site. These users do *not* need to be assigned an Office 365 license.

Microsoft promotes this feature as *external sharing*, and it's an excellent value for the service. But you need to know about a couple of issues before you start inviting people to a document library.

Limited to Live ID Authentication

For people to authenticate to your SharePoint Online site, they must use a Windows Live ID (*https://login.live.com*). This is a free service by which you can create a new email address or validate an existing email address by using the Live ID mechanism. In other words, a contractor or business associate could go to *https://login.live.com* and enable her email address for use with a Live ID and then use it to log on to your SharePoint Online document site.

Send an Invitation

Inviting someone to your site is simple. From the team site, click Share This Site or select Site Actions | Share Site. You can then enter the email address (or addresses) you want to invite in either the Visitors or Members column. If you select Visitors, as shown in Figure 11-74, the user cannot edit or publish documents. This is a good choice when you need people to view frequently updated documents that are too large for email. Select Members when you want to allow the user to edit and post documents as well as interact with lists. Use the Message field to type a personal welcome to the site, which will be included in the standard email invitation sent to the specified user. Click Share to send the invitation.

FIGURE 11-74 Inviting an external user as a visitor to your site.

Although you can customize the standard invitation with a personal message, you cannot change the design of the email, which is shown in Figure 11-75. When the user accepts, she is authenticated and taken directly to your site.

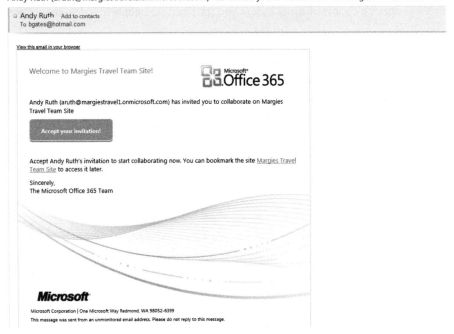

Andy Ruth (aruth@margiestravel1.onmicrosoft.com) has invited you to collaborate on Margies Travel Team Site

FIGURE 11-75 An invitation to collaborate sent to the user.

Restrict External Users to Specific Content

Although sharing the site is a great feature and is easy to do, you must keep one important consideration in mind: if you share the team site with an external user, he will by default have permissions to view all your content. When you invite the user to join the site as a Visitor or Member, he is placed into a predefined security group by that name. By default, both these groups have permissions to view all the content on SharePoint Online. (See "Manage Permissions," earlier in this chapter and Figure 11-19.)

Even though this is the scenario that Microsoft has enabled by placing a Share This Site With Additional People link on the Team Site home page, it is likely that you will want to limit external users to only a specific document library. Here's how to do it:

1. Create a new site to contain the content that you share with outside users. From the Team Site home page, click Site Actions, and then click Create New Site. Select the type of site that you want to create. The Document Workspace is a good basic template for a document-sharing site.

2. Within the new site, click Site Actions, and then select Site Settings. Under Users And Permissions, click Site Permissions.

3. Click Stop Inheriting Permissions, and then click OK.

4. Click Create Group. Provide a suitable name for the group, such as External Users.

5. Set the permissions level of the group to a suitable level, such as Contribute. Leave other settings the same, unless you have specific reasons for changing them and understand their purpose.

6. Click Create to open a page on which you can add and edit settings for the group.

7. Under Settings, click Make Default Group, as shown in Figure 11-76. You can now send invitations to external users to join the External Users group rather than the Members group.

FIGURE 11-76 Selecting Make Default Group.

8. At the prompt Do You Want To Make The Current Group The Default Members Group, click OK—that's exactly what you want.

Now when you click Site Actions | Share Site, the form looks a bit different, as Figure 11-77 illustrates. Instead of listing Members as the second option, your new security group appears (shown in the figure as External Users).

FIGURE 11-77 The updated form shows custom security group.

When you enter a user's Hotmail address in the External Users field, she will be added to the External Users security group and limited to the content in the new site. Clicking any links to other content results in an access denied message. Using this method, you can create multiple sites and security groups, keeping each isolated from the others.

Mobile Devices

Most mobile devices have browsers that permit users to log on to SharePoint Online. As of this writing, the following mobile devices are supported:

- Windows Phone 7+

- Windows Mobile 6.1+ (Internet Explorer mobile and Office Mobile 2010 for 6.5.x devices)

- Nokia S60 3.0 or later E series and N series devices

- Apple iPhone 3.0 or later

- Blackberry 4.2 or later

- Android 1.5 or later

As a result, you can interact with lists, calendars, tasks, and other content through the mobile browser. In some cases, it might be best to view the content through a specialized page by appending **?Mobile=1** to the URL. For example, if your URL is *http://margiestravel1.sharepoint.com*, the mobile URL would be *http://margiestravel1.sharepoint.con?Mobile=1*.

If you have a phone running Windows Phone 7, you can access your SharePoint Online site by using the Office Hub. The Office Hub lists the content from SharePoint Online sites and allows you to access the content from your phone. You can find instructions for connecting the Office Hub to SharePoint Online at *http://office.microsoft.com/en-gb/sharepoint-online-small-business-help/use-a-mobile-device-to-work-with-sharepoint-online-sites-HA102109237.aspx*. Alternatively, search for *Use a mobile device to work with SharePoint Online* sites.

Other mobile devices, including iPhones and iPads, have applications available specifically for working with SharePoint sites and Office documents. Search your device's application store for apps to connect your device to SharePoint Online.

More Info For a deeper discussion of mobile devices and Office 365, see Chapter 9, "Working with Mobile Devices." In addition, the most accurate and up-to-date information about which devices are officially supported for use with SharePoint Online is always available in the SharePoint Online Service Description. Finally, Microsoft publishes an Office 365 Mobility Services Description. Both of these documents can be found at *http://www.microsoft.com/download/en/details.aspx?id=13602*.

Publish a Public Website

SharePoint Online comes with a public website that can be accessed anonymously on the Web. The site is built using a feature called the Site Designer that configures the pages for you. Site Designer is well-suited for a business that only needs a low-traffic, public website with basic information about the business, such as contact information, a description of your business, location, hours, bios, or other details. You can add downloadable content as well as other useful functionality.

Use a Custom URL

The default website, shown in Figure 11-78, is created for you when you subscribe to Office 365 and can be accessed from the URL located in the Home portal, listed under Website. In our example of Margie's Travel, the website URL is http://margiestravel1.sharepoint.com/Pages/default.aspx.

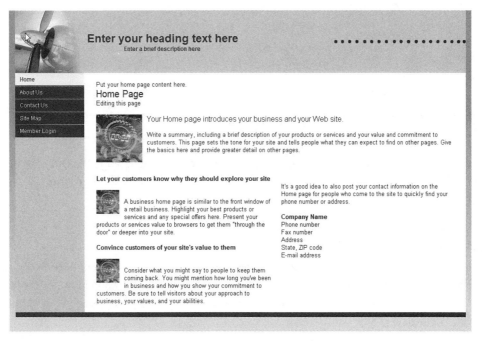

FIGURE 11-78 The default public website.

You can change the URL to a custom URL such as http://margiestravel.com by validating the custom domain in the Admin portal and delegating DNS services to Microsoft. When the custom domain is validated and delegated, you can open *https://portal.microsoftonline.com* and select Domains from the left side of the page. There you will find a link line that states, Your SharePoint Website Address Is Http://<*Yourcompany*>.Sharepoint.Com (Change Address), as shown in Figure 11-79. When you click the Change Address link, you will have the option of assigning your custom domain name to the site.

 More Info For details about adding custom URLs to Office 365, see Chapter 6, "Working with Custom Domains."

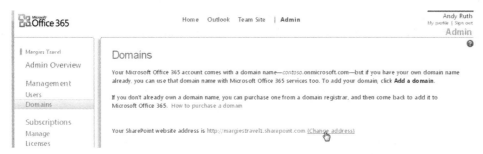

FIGURE 11-79 Changing the website address.

 Note Be sure you have finished creating your website before you change the URL, because the website will be available to the general public as soon as you make this change.

Customize the Website

You can change the content and appearance of your site. To begin, browse to your website and click Member Login. Alternatively, you can log on to SharePoint Online with your administrator credentials, click Website (in the top menu bar), and then click Home. The home page will open in the website designer, as shown in Figure 11-80.

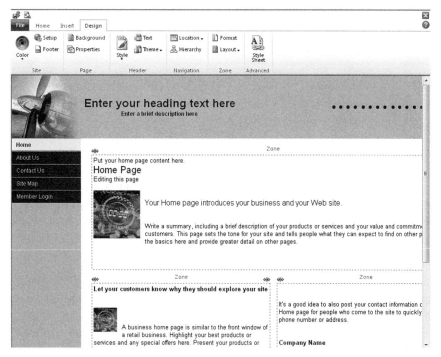

FIGURE 11-80 The Public Website Wizard.

You can quickly customize the look of the page by using the Color, Setup, Footer, Text, Theme, Style, and Format options. In addition, you can add pages and arrange the hierarchy of pages.

The boxes in the body of the page are *zones*. You can resize each zone independently by clicking the handle at the upper-left corner of each. Right-click in a zone to open a properties menu in which you can configure the background and other settings, as shown in Figure 11-81.

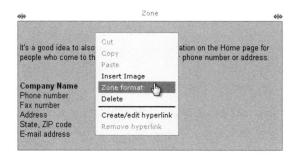

FIGURE 11-81 The Zone Format menu.

If you click the Insert tab at the top of the page, new options become available, as shown in Figure 11-82. Using this ribbon, you can insert images, tables, links, and gadgets, with which you can embed slideshows, maps, videos, a "contact us form" so that users can email you, and other elements.

FIGURE 11-82 The Insert ribbon for the webpage designer.

As you can see, Microsoft has made it simple for anyone to configure a nice-looking website with the basic information needed for many small businesses. In addition to adding basic text, the dynamic, predefined gadgets help provide a polished look-and-feel as well as useful functionality.

More Info It is beyond the scope of this book to cover all the design capabilities provided by the public website feature in SharePoint Online. You can find a good description of each of the options at *http://office.microsoft.com/en-us/sharepoint-online-small-business-help/CL102040066.aspx*, or search for "design a public-facing website." Also, you can watch a good introduction video at *http://office.microsoft.com/en-us/sharepoint-online-small-business-help/video-design-your-business-website-VA102586182.aspx*, or search for "Video: Design your business website."

Limitations of the Public Site

Before you make a choice about the SharePoint Online public site, you should be aware of some limitations:

- The public-facing website is not intended for high-traffic scenarios.

- There can be only one public website.

- You cannot use SharePoint Designer to manage the site.

- You cannot transfer a site from Windows Live Small Business to the public site.

- You cannot connect to a database-driven application or pre-built applications such as Word-Press or other open-source web applications.

A business that needs dynamic content, such as an online shopping cart, user forums, blogs, or a registration system, should not consider using the SharePoint Online public website because it does not currently support this kind of functionality.

Advanced Topics and Resources

SharePoint online has many features that we have not discussed. Some of these might interest you but would require entire books to explain. This chapter has focused on features and capabilities that you can implement without custom code or specialized technical skills, such as designing a database. However, you can write custom applications for SharePoint Online by using *sandboxed solutions*. This gives you tremendous flexibility to provide specific features—such as custom workflows, integrated mobile applications, forms processing, and other line-of-business integrations—that go beyond what you can create using pre-built Web Parts. These applications are referred to as sandboxed because they have some limitations enforced by the host environment. In other words, Microsoft limits the scope of custom SharePoint Online applications so that they do not risk the performance and availability of the service.

In addition, Plan P1 includes Access Web Services, with which you can integrate Access databases with SharePoint Online. Consider the possibilities of having an Access database available online that all of your users can view, add to, and edit. This can normally be achieved only by using a shared in-house database. For example, just as you can create a list from Excel, you can publish a basic database to SharePoint Online. In this way, the database itself is on SharePoint Online, but you can use Access as a front end. Access has some templates provided that can be published to SharePoint Online, and SharePoint Online has several templates in the Web Database category (as shown in Figure 11-83) that can be opened by using Access or run as an online database.

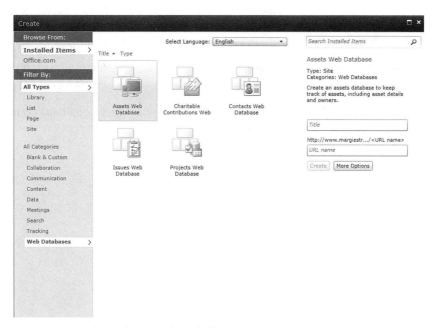

FIGURE 11-83 Web Database templates built into SharePoint Online that can interact with Access.

Having your data on a centralized, Internet-available repository can provide creative ways to solve business problems. For example, when gathering data from personnel in the field, you can aggregate information for everyone to see and use, or you can create specialized lists and workflows, based on incoming data.

For More Information

As you've seen, there is a lot to learn about SharePoint Online but not enough space in this book to describe it all. To delve deeper into many of the topics we've discussed, consult these links:

- Get-Started-with-SharePoint videos created by the SharePoint End-User Content team at Microsoft: *http://www.youtube.com/user/GetStartedSharePoint?feature=watch*

- SharePoint Online for professionals and small businesses Help and How-to: *http://office.microsoft. com/en-us/sharepoint-online-small-business-help*

- SharePoint Online planning guide for Office 365 for professionals and small businesses: *http:// office.microsoft.com/en-us/sharepoint-online-small-business-help/sharepoint-online-planning- guide-for-office-365-for-professionals-and-small-businesses-HA101988914.aspx*

- SharePoint Online Developer Resource Center: *http://msdn.microsoft.com/en-us/sharepoint/ gg153540*

- About the workflows included with SharePoint: *http://office.microsoft.com/en-us/sharepoint- online-enterprise-help/about-the-workflows-included-with-sharepoint-HA102420739.aspx*

- Build and Publish an Access database to SharePoint: *http://office.microsoft.com/en-us/sharepoint- online-enterprise-help/build-and-publish-an-access-database-to-sharepoint-HA102435342.aspx*

- The Access Show: Access 2010 demo of Access Services and web databases: *http://channel9.msdn. com/shows/Access/Microsoft-Access-2010-Demo/*

CHAPTER 12

Working with Lync Online

Some technologies, such as cell phones and the Internet, we just take for granted. How did businesses ever get along without out them? Microsoft Lync Online is like that, revolutionizing business communications so subtly that we don't really notice it until we discover that we don't want to manage without it.

Crafting an email and waiting for a response takes time, which is a commodity you might not have when you're facing a deadline. Instead, with Lync Online, you can check to see whether the person you need to contact is online and instant message her. If she isn't online, you can right-click her name and set a "flag" to be notified if her status changes. The second she logs in, you'll be notified.

If you want to make a voice call to someone, with Lync Online it's one click away, no matter where in the world he is or whether you remember his phone number. While you're on the phone, you want to send the URL you're discussing to your colleague—just paste it into Lync 2010. There's no need to hassle with email; a record of the URL instantly appears in your Conversation History folder in Microsoft Outlook. Need to pull others into the conversation? Even arranging an online meeting with a shared workspace is just a click of a button in Outlook.

With today's distributed workforce, the ability to stay connected with Lync Online adds a lot of value. Throw in its many other features, such as hosting online meetings for people outside of your organization and the ability to remotely control another person's desktop, and you'll wonder how you ever managed without it. In this chapter, you'll learn how to use the Lync 2010 client to make the best of your Lync Online services. In addition, the chapter reviews how Lync Online interacts with other services and describes some administrative settings for Lync Online that you should know how to use.

Get to Know the Lync 2010 Client

First, some basic terminology: Lync Online is the online service hosted by Microsoft. The Lync 2010 client is a specialized application that is installed on your computer, which communicates with Lync Online. After Microsoft Office 365 is set up on your computer, the Lync 2010 client appears each time the computer is started. It automatically logs on to Office 365 and makes your presence known to other Office 365 users.

At first, the Lync 2010 client looks rather plain. As shown in Figure 12-1, it contains no picture of you or anyone else, no contact information, and no groups. But it takes only a few minutes to have your client fully customized and connected.

FIGURE 12-1 The Lync 2010 client.

Lync at Work

A company like Microsoft relies heavily on the services provided by Lync, but does a small business need the same features as an enterprise? Although a large, international company like Microsoft makes daily use of almost all the features of Lync 2010, smaller businesses will primarily use those key features of Lync Online that will be most helpful to their productivity.

The degree to which you use any particular Lync Online feature depends on the type of business you have. Is your work force geographically separated? If so, Lync can help you keep in touch with presence, voice, and online meetings. Without Lync, you simply don't know what's going on with your staff. With Lync Online, you can see at glance who is online, who is available, and any current status information that they want to share ("Cell phone dead, call hotel!"). Scenarios like these and many others are well served by Lync Online.

Also keep in mind what Lync Online will not do. You cannot use Lync Online to dial phone numbers. You can call other Lync Online users regardless of their location, as long as they are on the Internet, but you can't punch in a phone number and dial it. For that kind of service, consider Skype.

You should also be aware of limitations when using Lync Online in specific countries. For example, Lync Online uses Voice over IP (VoIP) for voice conference calls, but that capability is restricted in some countries. You can find the current list of countries that have such restrictions at *http://www.microsoft.com/en-us/office365/licensing-restrictions.aspx*.

Sign In to Lync Online

Normally, Lync 2010 will open and sign in to Office 365 automatically when you start your computer. If Lync 2010 doesn't start for some reason, you can start it manually from your Start menu. Click Start | All Programs | Microsoft Lync, and then select Lync 2010.

The first time you open Lync 2010, you will be asked to provide your logon credentials, as shown in Figure 12-2.

FIGURE 12-2 Signing in for the first time.

It's important to use your Office 365 email address for both Sign-In Address and User Name so that Lync 2010 can connect to Lync Online. After the first time you start Lync 2010, you do not have to enter the credentials again until your password changes. By default, password changes are required every 90 days.

Open the Options Menu

The Lync 2010 client doesn't take up much space, but it has a surprising number of options. If you aren't familiar with the user interface, it can take a bit of time to find key features. For example, where are the configuration menus? To open the Options menu, in the upper-right side of the Lync client, click the Cog icon, as shown in Figure 12-3. Take a moment to find it now, because you'll be using the Options menu throughout this chapter.

FIGURE 12-3 The Lync 2010 Options menu.

Configure Audio and Video

Lync Online can use a USB headset (or one that uses plugs) and a video camera for online communications. Often, laptops have built in microphones that work with Lync Online, but if you plan to regularly use Lync Online for voice calls, it's preferable for call quality, as well as privacy, to have a headset with a microphone. Webcams also often have microphones. As a result, it's pretty common for a single system to have more than one microphone available for use. For this reason, you should click Options | Audio Device, and then ensure that the specific microphone and speakers you plan to use regularly are selected, as shown in Figure 12-4.

When you plug a headset into your computer, set Lync 2010 to use the device and then remove the headset. Lync 2010 will automatically change its settings to use an available device. Later, when you plug the headset back in, Lync 2010 will automatically use the headset.

Even so, if you try to make call and can't hear or be heard, check this setting, because periodically, your system can lose its configuration.

After selecting the device you want, you can adjust the levels for the microphone and audio by using the sliders under each device.

Of special interest is the Secondary Ringer setting. This should be set to your computer speakers so that you can hear incoming calls without using your headset.

If you select Custom Device, you can select different devices for different purposes. For example, you could use the built-in microphone from your computer or webcam, but use a headphone for audio.

Setting video is similar. Simply click Video Device, and then select the webcam to use. You will see a video feed from the selected device, and you can tune the picture by using the Webcam settings options.

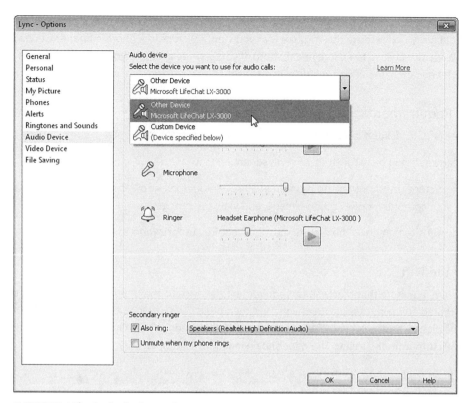

FIGURE 12-4 The Audio Device settings page.

Personalize Lync 2010

One of the first actions I recommend is to take a few moments to personalize Lync 2010. There are a number of possible options, including adding a photo that will display for you and anyone else who adds you as a contact.

Add Your Picture

As explained in Chapter 4, "The Dual Purpose Office 365 Portal," the best way to add a picture is in the Office 365 portal. When you add a photo to the Office 365 portal, the picture is automatically displayed in Lync 2010. By placing a picture in the portal, Microsoft can use it in other services. If you added a picture to the portal, you can skip this section because your picture will already be shown.

Any picture you add is visible to you and other users and makes the service more user-friendly. In larger organizations, having photos in Lync is quite important because people can associate a face with a name. In smaller organizations, having pictures in Lync 2010 can help with temporary workers and other new hires. But in my experience, the real value is how adding pictures makes Lync 2010 more attractive and communication more interesting.

Alternatively, you can link to a picture from a public website. In my testing, sites such as Flickr and SkyDrive did not work because they require that you view a picture in a photo album or webpage and do not provide direct links to an individual photo. If you provide a URL to your photo that does not require authentication, the image will display.

Picture Requirements

The picture and its location need to meet three general requirements:

- The size should be a 1-inch to 1.5-inch square.

- The picture size should be no more than 30 KB. If you don't know the size of a picture, save it to your computer, right-click the image, and view the properties.

- The website that hosts the picture must not require authorization to access it.

Specify the URL

After you have a picture that meets these requirements, browse to the Internet location where the photo is located and copy the URL (highlight and then press Ctrl+C). Open the My Pictures form by clicking the picture profile in Lync 2010, or open the Options menu shown in Figure 12-4, and then select My Picture from the menu. The page shown in Figure 12-5 opens.

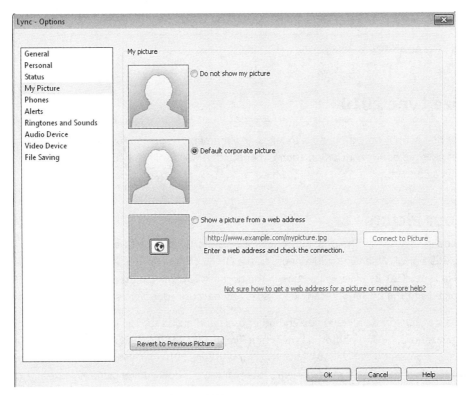

FIGURE 12-5 The My Picture page in Lync 2010.

Select Show A Picture From A Web Address, and paste (Ctrl+V) or type in the URL. Click Connect To Picture to load the picture into Lync 2010, as demonstrated in Figure 12-6.

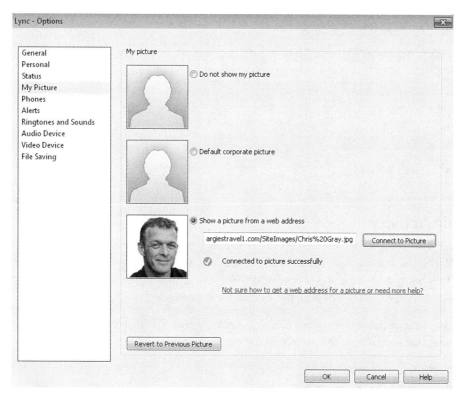

FIGURE 12-6 A picture added to Lync 2010 from website.

Click Close; the photo appears at the top of Lync 2010, as shown in Figure 12-7.

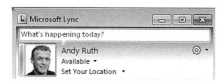

FIGURE 12-7 Lync 2010 configured with a photo.

Set Your Location

In Figure 12-7, notice the small downward-facing triangle next to the Set Your Location setting. This little jewel can be very helpful in communicating your current location to others. For example, it could be useful for coworkers to know when you're in the office, working from home, at a convention, hotel, or other site. From my experience, it has been very helpful to see that someone whom you're trying to reach is actually "in the building" or "on vacation."

To set a location, just click Set Your Location and start typing. You can disable showing others your location, if you choose, or clear custom locations by clicking the down-arrow, as shown in Figure 12-8.

FIGURE 12-8 The location menu.

Set Your Activity

At the top of the Lync 2010 client is a text balloon that asks, "What's happening today?" You can enter anything in this box, and it will appear to others in your contact card in their Lync 2010 client. This is a great way to broadcast what's going in your world, from personal ("Go Seahawks") to business ("Traveling, expect delayed response") or both ("At doctor, back tomorrow").

It's not well known, but you can add a URL in the activity area. This makes it easier to communicate online content that's interesting or informative to your colleagues.

FIGURE 12-9 Activity with URL.

Add Your Phone Numbers

The Options menu also has a section for you to add your phone numbers. This can be quite important when people need to reach you and can easily access your mobile phone or home phone number. When added, your numbers are available using the Lync Contact card (covered later in this chapter), which appears in a number of places.

Set Ringtones and Sounds

You can further personalize the Lync 2010 client by setting the ringtone you want to sound when someone calls you by using Lync. Open the Options menu, and select Ringtones And Sounds. Then test the different sounds to find one that you like. If you cannot hear the ringtones, check the Audio Device settings.

Add Contacts

When installed, Lync 2010 has no contacts listed. You can easily add contacts from within your company or other Office 365 organizations. In addition, Microsoft intends to allow MSN Messenger and Windows Live Messenger users to interact with your organization, but as of this writing, this feature has been temporarily disabled from Plan P1. E plan users do have this capability.

From Your Organization

Adding people from your organization is a simple process of typing their names (or some portion of their names) in Lync 2010. You will see the list of available contacts as you type. Click the plus sign (as shown in Figure 12-10), and select Pin To Frequent Contacts to add the selected person to the list of your frequent contacts, or choose All Contacts to add her to the All Contacts list.

FIGURE 12-10 Adding a contact.

When someone adds you as a contact, you receive a notification, as shown in Figure 12-11, and you have the option to add the person to your own contact list.

FIGURE 12-11 The notification that you've been added as a contact.

When you've added more contacts than you can easily manage in a single list, you can create a group and assign a contact to that group. This helps when you have teams of people with whom you work on specific tasks.

To create a group, just right-click Frequent Contacts or All Contacts, and then select Create New Group. You can then right-click any contact and select to move the contact to the group.

With most small businesses, you won't have enough contacts for people in your organization to make it difficult to manage, but with Lync Online, you can add people outside of your company, as well.

Add Contacts From Outside Your Company

Lync Online has the ability to communicate with Office 365 users at other companies through a feature called *instant messaging federation*. To add a user who is not part of your organization but is an Office 365 Lync Online user, simply type his email address into the Lync 2010 client. You can now interact with the user, provided his Lync Online system is configured to permit communications outside his company. By default, this capability is enabled in Plan P1. Using this feature, you can instant message, transfer files, use voice and video, and share applications and video with Office 365 users, worldwide. In addition, you can instant message with users of Windows Live Messenger, but you cannot engage in voice communications or advanced features of Lync 2010. You'll learn how to configure these capabilities in the "Lync Online Administration" section later in this chapter.

Note As of this writing, the ability to communicate with other instant messaging service providers, such as Yahoo, Google Talk, ICQ, and Skype, is not available. Microsoft is working on expanding the list of services with which Lync Online can interact.

Use the Contact Card

After you've added a contact, you can use the person's contact card in Lync 2010 and other applications to start an instant message (IM) session, email the user, start a call, share your desktop, or look up information such as a phone number.

Hovering over the name of the contact (and you need to point to the name, not just the picture) or clicking on the entry in Lync 2010 opens a contact card fly-out panel (see Figure 12-12). Each of the icons on the card initiates the actions you would expect. Email, instant messaging, and voice calls are all indicated by the envelope chat bubble and handset, respectively. The last icon is for the Additional Choices menu.

FIGURE 12-12 Hovering over a contact's name shows the person's contact card.

You can click the down-facing triangles shown in Figure 12-12 to reveal more options. When you click the phone icon, Lync initiates a call. If you click the down-facing triangle next to the phone, you'll see the contact's phone numbers and a little-known feature: you can present the conversation subject to the contact when the call is made (see Figure 12-13). This can help the person receiving the call to distinguish between an urgent business matter and a casual call.

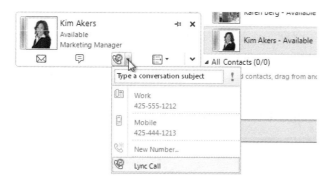

FIGURE 12-13 The phone menu from the contact card.

This menu also shows you the contact's phone numbers. Sometimes the ability to quickly locate a person's mobile phone number is exactly what you need.

> **Note** Figure 12-13 shows phone numbers, but you cannot call those numbers directly by using Lync Online. There is even a New Number option that is dimmed (unavailable). Why is there a New Number menu option when you can't dial out? The Lync 2010 client you use for Lync Online is the same one used for an on-premises server system called Lync 2010 Server. When Lync 2010 is used with the on-premises server, it is possible to dial out using Lync 2010. In this way, Microsoft has only one client to maintain, which reduces its costs and helps keep the service price low. The downside is that features can appear in Lync 2010 and other applications that are not actually available when used with Office 365.

Also, the Additional Choices menu (shown in Figure 12-14) has useful options for quickly starting a video call (which is the same as a voice call, but a video session is initiated, as well), sharing your desktop, adding the user to your contacts, or tagging the user for status change alerts.

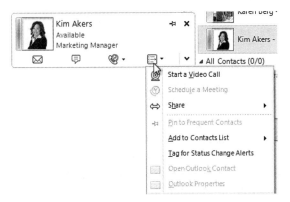

FIGURE 12-14 The Additional Choices menu.

When you need to reach someone the moment they become available, tag them, using the Tag For Status Change Alerts setting. When she logs on, using OWA or Lync 2010, or when the person's status changes in any other way (for example, from busy to available), you will be notified. This is a great way to be flagged when someone you must speak with right away becomes available.

The larger down-facing arrow on the contact card expands the card to phone numbers, organizational information, email address, and other details.

The contact card appears in Microsoft Office applications, including Outlook 2010. Because the contact card is so accessible, you can easily initiate a call or IM session without leaving Outlook.

Presence and Lync Online

Connecting with someone is just a click away with Lync 2010, but before you start a call or IM session, be mindful of the person's online status. Although it's great to be connected to others when you need them, it can be less than thrilling to have an instant message appear when your laptop is projected in a meeting, conference, or otherwise shared with coworkers. Also, before sending personal or sensitive messages, keep in mind that other people might be in the room with your contact.

The ability of Lync Online to broadcast your online status and availability is called *presence*. Your presence can be any of several status conditions, ranging from Available to Offline.

Status Indicators

The different status indicators that you can manually set are shown in Figure 12-15.

FIGURE 12-15 Status indicators and messages.

A variety of colors and accompanying status messages can be shown. You can set your status manually or allow the system to manage your status for you. Lync Online displays Busy automatically when you're scheduled to be in a meeting and will also display the message, In A Meeting. Similarly, if you're available and then receive or make a Lync Online call, your status changes to Busy and shows the message, In A Call. I've found the automatic management to be quite accurate and useful.

The Do Not Disturb status is of particular importance. When your status is Do Not Disturb, you cannot be contacted via Lync 2010. Lync 2010 will never automatically place you in Do Not Disturb mode. Use this setting or sign out of Lync Online when you do not want any interruptions.

Manually Set Status

The automatic management of your status works quite well, but sometimes you will want to make adjustments. If a meeting on your calendar is canceled but still listed on your calendar, your status will change to busy when the meeting was scheduled to start. You can manually set your status by using the Available pull-down menu, as shown previously. Note that you can also use this menu to sign out of Lync 2010; in fact, this is the easiest way to do so.

Another way to change your status is to hover over the Lync 2010 icon in the taskbar at the bottom of your screen, as shown in Figure 12-16.

FIGURE 12-16 Hover to quickly change status.

Presence in Other Programs

One of the great aspects about Lync Online is that you can also see the status of your colleagues in Outlook Web Access and Microsoft Office applications. Figure 12-17 shows presence in an Outlook Web App email.

FIGURE 12-17 Presence in Outlook Web App.

The Special Case of Outlook Web App

Outlook Web App (OWA) is unique because presence and instant messaging are built in. In other words, you can change your presence, see other's presence, and instant message others in your organization directly in OWA, even if you do not have Lync 2010 installed on the system that you are using.

This means that if you are traveling and have access to a trusted system, you can instant message others from your browser. Also, when you log on to OWA, your presence is changed to show that you are online.

You can add an IM contact to OWA, just as you can in Lync 2010. Click Add Contact, and select the person to add, just as you would select someone to email. They are added to the list, as shown in Figure 12-18.

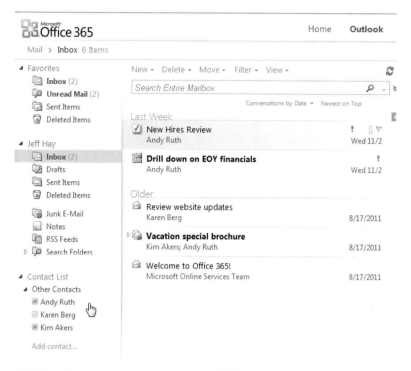

FIGURE 12-18 Instant messaging contacts in OWA.

To start an IM session, just double-click the contact name.

Figure 12-19 shows where to change your status in Outlook Web App. Simply click your name in the upper-right side, and then set your status. It will automatically be updated in everyone's Lync 2010 application and other presence-aware applications.

FIGURE 12-19 Updating status in OWA.

If you have the Lync 2010 client installed, Outlook 2007 and Outlook 2010 also provide presence. This is one of those features you might not think much of at first but which can be a real time saver. For example, suppose you are crafting an email and it starts to get a bit longer than you thought. You can see from the presence on the To line that the person to whom you are writing is "green" (online and available). Instead of sending an email, you can just call him by using Lync Online to make a quick voice call. He's available to clarify the issue you were writing about, and you are back to work without writing a detailed email and waiting for response. (And when was the last time you had a complete response to a detailed email?)

Without the presence indicator, you would not have known he was online and available. Plus, it's only a click away to be "dialing," which helps make it easy to choose to call when you can. You're better informed, faster, and you didn't have to do much to make it all happen, courtesy of Office 365.

Microsoft Office

Presence is also available in Microsoft Office applications. Shown in Figure 12-20 is the Authors section, as it appears when you click the Home tab in Microsoft Word.

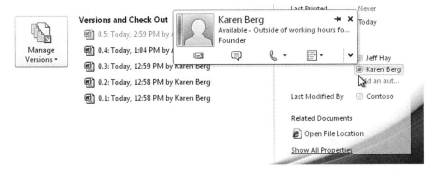

FIGURE 12-20 Presence in Microsoft Word.

In practice, I have found the presence indicators in Microsoft Office applications other than Outlook to be useful but not highly reliable. However, you can hover over the user's name, as shown in Figure 12-20, which opens the contact card fly-out. The contact card presence represents the same status as Lync 2010, so it tends to be more accurate.

As of this writing, in Office 365 for professionals and small businesses, SharePoint Online does not show presence by default because Secure Sockets Layer (SSL) is required for presence to be determined. If you add the SharePoint Online URL (discussed in Chapter 11, "Working with SharePoint Online") to Trusted Sites in your browser, presence will be shown.

Caution For security reasons, adding the SharePoint Online URL to Trusted Sites is not recommended by Microsoft. Microsoft has stated it is looking at providing SSL at for Plan P1 in a future release. See the online help for Office 365 for Small Business and Professionals (*http://office.microsoft.com/en-us/sharepoint-online-small-business-help/step-1-plan-sites-and-manage-users-HA102029292.aspx*) for details.

Microsoft Lync Mobile 2010

As discussed in Chapter 9, "Working with Mobile Devices," Microsoft has Lync Mobile 2010 clients for iPhones, iPads, Microsoft Phones, Nokia, and Android. If your phone is not listed, check the apps store for your device, because the list of supported devices is subject to change. Presence and instant messaging are provided in Lync Mobile 2010. Go to *http://lync.microsoft.com/en-us/what-is-lync/Pages/what-is-lync.aspx*, and then click the Mobile Apps tab.

IM

IM in Lync 2010 is very much like it is in other IM applications; you just start the conversation, and if the other person is available, she will respond (hopefully).

Start and Accept an IM Session

Start an IM session by double-clicking the person's entry in Lync 2010 and typing your message. At the receiving end, the user receives a prompt that is accompanied by an audio alert. The message appears along with a couple of options, as shown in Figure 12-21.

FIGURE 12-21 Karen initiates an instant message.

In this example, Andy can click the green bubble to open the chat window (which opens automatically if he takes no action). Andy can also click Redirect, which presents the options Respond With Lync Call or Set To Do Not Disturb, as shown in Figure 12-22.

FIGURE 12-22 Redirect options.

Andy can also just ignore the request, of course.

When the chat window is open, Karen and Andy are conversing, as you would expect in a typical IM application.

Note that you can change fonts, font color, and display emoticons by using the A and happy-face icons. Also, don't forget that you can send complex URLs in instant messaging, as shown in Figure 12-23.

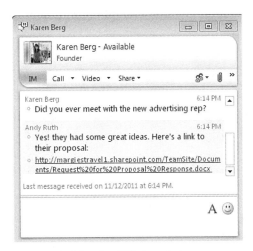

FIGURE 12-23 Sending URLs in a chat.

Add Others to Your Chat

You can easily add other people to your chat session. You can click the group icon adjacent to the paper clip shown in Figure 12-23, but that's the hard way. All you need to do is drag the person's entry into the chat window, and she will automatically be added.

When you add more than one person, the chat window changes to a group chat, as shown in Figure 12-24.

FIGURE 12-24 A group conversation.

In this case, Karen just added Kim to the conversation. Both Kim and Andy received an invitation to the group conversation.

Conversation History

Some IM conversations hold important details about costs, contacts, phone numbers, email addresses, URLs, and other specific information that might be needed after the conversation is over. One of the disadvantages of a traditional IM session is that it is like a phone call. After the call is over, information in the call is no longer available, unless you took good notes. Lync Online solves this problem by keeping a transcript of all IM sessions. After a session has been idle for a while or is closed, a transcript of it is placed in the Conversation History folder of Outlook, as shown in Figure 12-25.

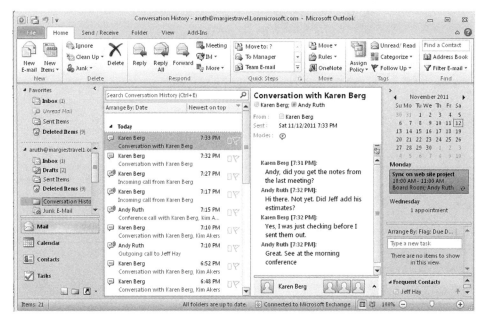

FIGURE 12-25 Conversation history is kept in Outlook.

The same content is also available in OWA.

Note that you can elect to disable this feature in the Lync 2010 Options menu, under the Personal settings.

File Transfer

When you are discussing specific content and one of you would benefit from having the file under discussion, you can transfer the file by using the paper clip icon located in the upper-right corner of the page, as shown in Figure 12-24. Just click the paper clip, and browse to the file. When the file is sent, the receiver will be prompted, as shown in Figure 12-26.

When received, the location of the file displays, along with the suggestion that you scan the file with an antivirus program. In other words, Lync Online does not inspect transferred files for viruses. Even so, certain kinds of files cannot be transferred. You can find a list of blocked file extensions in the Office 365 Security and Service Continuity Service Description at *http://www.microsoft.com/download/en/details.aspx?id=13602*.

Microsoft does not specify a maximum size for a transferable file, and a recent query to a technical source at Microsoft indicated there is no set limit.

To customize the location of the file drop for transferred files, click Options | File Saving, and then click the Browse button adjacent to the File Transfer path.

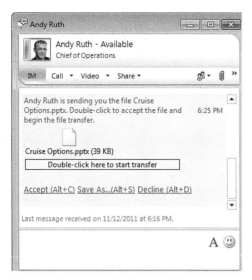

FIGURE 12-26 Receiving a file during an IM session.

Voice Calls

One of the most popular features of Lync Online is the ability to make VoIP phone calls to others by using Lync Online. You can place calls to Lync Online users inside and outside of your organization.

Lync Online works with a wide variety of hardware. Almost any headset that is suitable for VoIP or gaming will work. Even so, Microsoft publishes a list of approved devices at *http://technet.microsoft.com/en-us/lync/gg278164.aspx*. If you refer to this list, remember that it is for Lync 2010 Server, which supports phone systems as well as the kinds of calls possible with Plan P1. Focus on the USB headsets rather than the phones.

After you set up your audio and microphone as covered under "Configure Audio and Video," you are ready to make and receive calls.

Start and Accept a Lync Online Call

Calling is simple. Just click the phone icon on the contact card or entry in Lync 2010. The receiving party is notified via a ringtone and a prompt, as shown is Figure 12-27.

FIGURE 12-27 An incoming call.

When connected, Lync 2010 shows you the ongoing call status and provides choices you can use during the call, as shown in Figure 12-28. Also, note that the status of the participants is automatically changed to busy and shows In A Call.

FIGURE 12-28 Options available during a Lync 2010 call.

You can click the appropriate icons on the bottom (from left to right) to do the following:

■ Mute or unmute your microphone.

■ Adjust the speaker volume.

■ Present a dialing pad for issuing touch-tone sounds.

■ Display the duration of the call.

■ Monitor the network quality.

■ Place the call on hold.

Also, you'll see that using the top menu items, you can instant message during a call, start video, or share an application or your desktop with others.

Add Others to Your Call

Adding people to your call works the same way as adding people to an IM session. Just drag the user to the call. If the user is not listed, you can add him by clicking the people icon next to the paper clip, as shown in Figure 12-29.

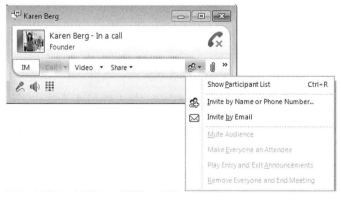

FIGURE 12-29 Inviting participants who are not in the contact list to a call.

As mentioned earlier, this capability is not avaible in all countries.

Share

One of the most powerful features of Lync 2010 and Lync Online is the ability to share content with others. In short, Lync Online can act like a virtual digital projector so that all participants in the meeting can view the same content. You can even give control of the shared content to others.

Share an Application

When you click the Share menu option (shown in Figure 12-30), you can select to share your desktop, a specific program, or other options. You'll see how to do this in the section "Real-Time Annotation and Demonstrations," later in this chapter.

FIGURE 12-30 The Share menu.

In the example, Karen asks Andy to share a document. Andy can, of course, direct her to a SharePoint Online link, transfer the file by using Lync 2010, or email her an attachment. Andy knows that simply sharing the same document creates a better shared experience and ensures that no confusion arises about which section of a document you are referencing.

In my experience with conducting online meetings, for which everyone has their own copy of a document, people tend to look through the document at different paces and explore whatever areas interest them. The group focus on the topic under discussion is frequently lost, and it is necessary to continuously call out page numbers and headings to keep the group together. Also, the document is difficult to navigate unless it is well-structured with clear landmarks. All of this is avoided by simply sharing the same document at the same time.

To share the Word document, Andy opens the document in Word, and then clicks Share | Program. A window similar to the one shown in Figure 12-31 appears. After selecting the Word document, he clicks Share.

FIGURE 12-31 Selecting the program to share.

The Presenter's View of a Shared Application

Immediately after he clicks Share, Andy's desktop changes, now looking similar to Figure 12-32.

The shared application is clearly designated by the Now Sharing frame around it. Any activity that happens in other applications is not visible to others. For example, in Figure 12-32, the section of the Lync 2010 chat window that overlaps the shared windows is not shown as part of the shared application.

At the top of the screen is a status bar that indicates you are currently sharing content. From this bar, you can also give control to other attendees or stop sharing the application.

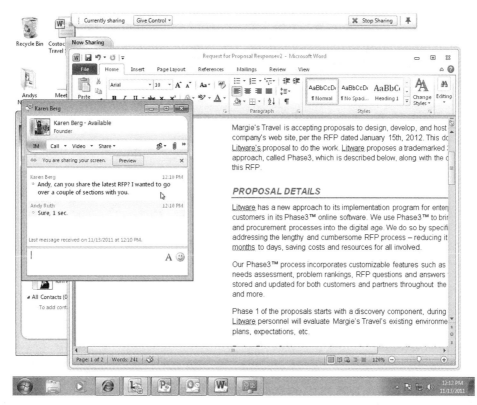

FIGURE 12-32 The presenter's view of a shared application.

The Participant's View of a Shared Application

When Andy clicks Share, Karen receives a prompt to accept the sharing request, as shown in Figure 12-33.

FIGURE 12-33 The Accept Sharing Request prompt.

Karen's screen now changes to show the shared application (called the *stage*) and the IM session, as shown in Figure 12-34.

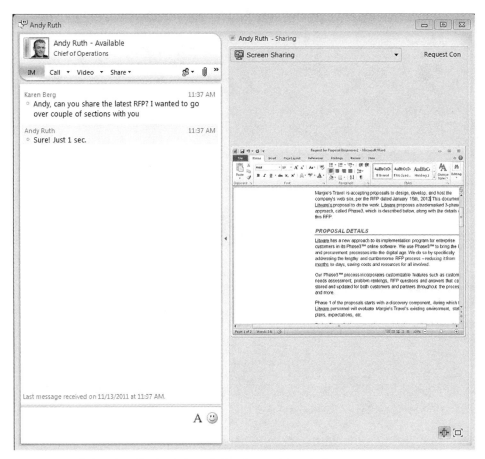

FIGURE 12-34 A shared application in Lync Online: the participant's view.

The shared document seems small compared to the rest of the window. This size might be fine for a slide or graphic image, but not for a document, Karen can click the icons on the bottom right to improve her viewing experience. Using these controls, she can switch to actual size and full screen views.

Request and Grant Control

If Karen wants to "drive," she can click the Request Control button in the upper-right corner of the page. Figure 12-35 shows the same screen as Figure 12-34, with the document in Actual Size mode, as Karen clicks Request Control.

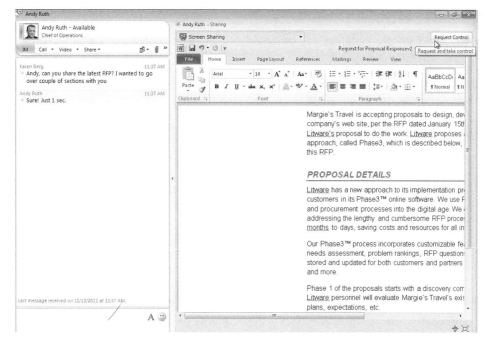

FIGURE 12-35 Requesting control.

On the presenter side, at the top of the screen, Andy is alerted that Karen has asked for control, as shown in Figure 12-36.

FIGURE 12-36 You can accept or decline a request for control.

Andy could also elect to offer control to Karen on his own. Referring to Figure 12-32, Presenter View, you can see the Give Control button. Using this option, Karen would receive an invitation to take control and, if she accepts, can manage the shared document remotely.

Designated Driver

Keep in mind that all participants with control have control at the same time. It is important to be clear about who's responsible for controlling the view. It can be quite confusing when two or more people are managing the shared source at the same time. In practice, you should agree on who is driving. You can hand off control by asking for or passing this role. "Karen, you drive," or "Let me drive for this part," are often heard in situations like this.

Share a Desktop

Just as you can share an application, you can share your entire desktop. Alternatively, someone you are chatting with can share their desktop.

Sharing a desktop has some extremely useful applications:

- **Demonstrations**   There's nothing like a demo to drive a point home. Sharing your desktop is the best way to demonstrate multistep processes that involve multiple applications.

- **PowerPoint Presentations**   Of course, you can just share PowerPoint, but during a presentation you might be asked about a resource or topic that is outside of the deck. If you have shared your desktop instead of just the application, you can simply minimize PowerPoint, browse to the requested information, and then return to PowerPoint. If you have shared only PowerPoint, you need to share any other application you use during the meeting, as well.

- **Troubleshooting**   This works in two directions. If you are troubleshooting someone else's technical issues, there is no substitute for having the user let you see what's going on. He can give you control, as well, so you can check settings and attempt fixes without having to explain each step, click by click. In the right situations, this feature, in and of itself, pays for the subscription costs of Office 365. On the other hand, if someone is troubleshooting your desktop and you can offer to share it, you can dramatically decrease the time it takes to solve the problem.

Invite Others to Online Meetings

Meetings come in a lot of different shapes and sizes, including planned, unplanned, public, and private. The specifics on how to invite others to a meeting depend on when the meeting occurs and on whom you want to invite.

Meet Now

As you have seen, a meeting can start between two people and simply escalate as others are added to the call or IM session. When you know you want to create a meeting workspace for multiple parties right now, you can use the Meet Now option in Lync 2010.

First, you have to locate the Lync 2010 menu, which is not shown by default. In Figure 12-37, notice the cursor arrow located on the downward-facing triangle *next to but not on* the Options menu icon. Click that triangle to show the well-hidden Lync 2010 menu.

FIGURE 12-37 The Lync 2010 menu can be hard to find.

 Note Select the Show Menu Bar option to display the menu items at the top of Lync 2010. This setting is persistent. The menu will show the next time you launch Lync 2010.

When you choose Meet Now, you are prompted to provide information about how you want users to connect to the meeting for audio, as shown in Figure 12-38. You can have users dial a designated phone number (when using a conferencing service), use Lync audio, or just use IM.

FIGURE 12-38 Meeting Audio choice for an online meeting.

Lync Online can integrate with specific audio conference providers as provided in the Office 365 administration portal. This is discussed in the "Lync Online Administration" section at the end of this chapter.

As soon as you click OK or Cancel, you are placed into the Group Conversation page, as shown in Figure 12-39.

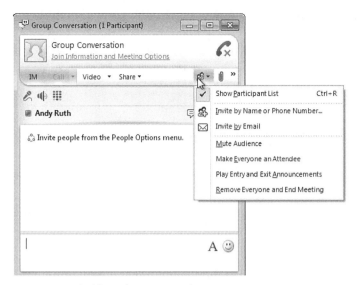

FIGURE 12-39 Inviting others to a meeting.

To invite others, you can drag users into the attendee list, click Invite By Name Or Phone Number, or click Invite By Email.

Also, notice the Join Information And Meeting Options link at the top of the client. Clicking that link reveals some very useful information, as shown in Figure 12-40.

FIGURE 12-40 The Meeting Link for your meeting.

The meeting link is the unique address for your meeting. Anyone with this link can click to join the meeting, but they might or might not be admitted, depending on how you have configured Meeting Options (Figure 12-41).

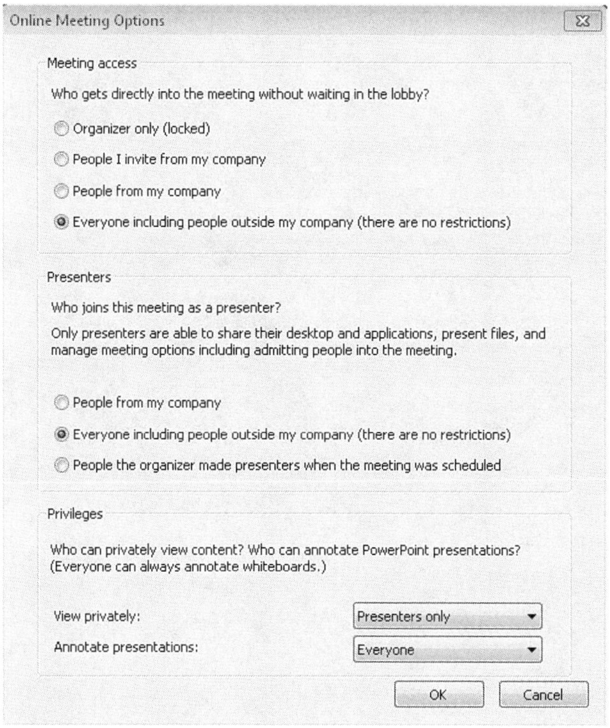

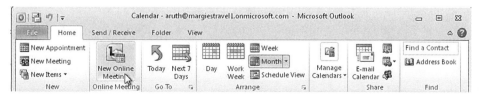

FIGURE 12-41 Online meeting options.

The default meeting options allow everyone with a link to join the meeting without first holding them in the "lobby" for approval. Also, everyone who joins is a presenter. These settings work fine for ad hoc meetings, created on demand, but if you were going to host a meeting for people outside of your company—such as a webinar—you would want to modify the settings to suit the occasion.

Schedule an Online Meeting with Outlook

When you install the Lync 2010 client and the Office 365 connector, Outlook is configured with a button that automatically inserts the meeting URL into a meeting request. Just click the Net Online Meeting button to open a new meeting request, which contains a link to the online meeting (see Figure 12-42).

FIGURE 12-42 New Online Meeting button in Outlook 2010.

Clicking the button opens a meeting invitation window, as shown in Figure 12-43.

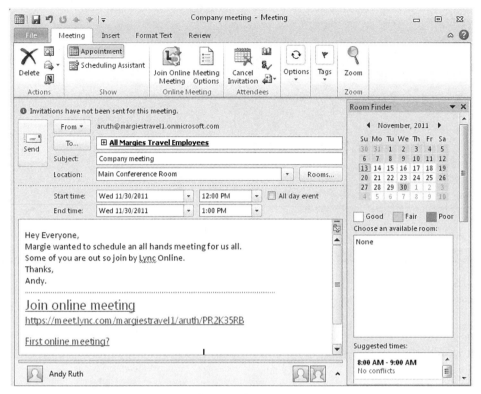

FIGURE 12-43 Online meeting request with Lync Online meeting information.

On the To line, invite anyone you want to participate in the meeting. You can add internal or external addresses. For example, if you want to invite a group outside your company for an online demonstration or training, you can use this method to send them a Lync Online Meeting request.

Those who accept the meeting request have all the information they need to join the meeting. This actually works very well in practice. As the meeting time arrives, Outlook notifies the attendees of the upcoming meeting. They click to open the meeting request and can then click Join Online Meeting in that request to connect to the meeting.

As the organizer, you can customize the settings of the meeting by using the Meeting Options button in Outlook shown in Figure 12-40, located next to the Lync Join Online Meeting icon shown in Figure 12-43. This opens an Online Meeting Options form (see Figure 12-44) that is similar to the Online Meeting Options menu in Lync 2010 shown in Figure 12-41.

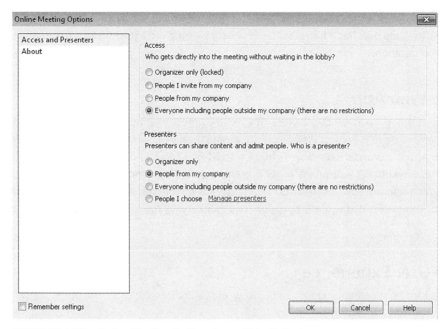

FIGURE 12-44 The Online Meeting Options from within Outlook.

You can use the options menu to determine who is directly admitted to the meeting without waiting in the lobby and who will be a presenter. A key difference in this menu relates to the Presenters section. People From My Company is the selected default option rather than Everyone.

Join Meetings

Lync Online meetings can be attended by those inside or outside your organization. So how do people join a meeting if they do not have Lync Online? Two choices are available.

The Lync 2010 Attendee Client

The Lync 2010 Attendee client can be installed in place of Lync 2010. It provides a great online experience for Lync Online meetings. This is by far the preferred way for users to connect to your meeting if they do not have Lync 2010, but it needs to be installed before they can join. By the way, do not confuse the Lync 2010 Attendee with the Lync 2010 Call Attendant, which is a completely different product for a different scenario (integration with the on-premises Lync 2010 Server).

If you are holding online meetings that include people outside of your organization, include a link to the Attendee client (*http://www.microsoft.com/download/en/details.aspx?id=15755*) in your meeting request, and advise them to install it if possible.

When the user clicks the meeting request link, the Attendee client will automatically open. Using the Attendee client, the user has a better visual experience with the stage and can participate in video and VoIP communications.

The Lync Web App

Many users do not want to install client-side software to connect to a meeting. If Lync 2010 or the Lync 2010 Attendee client is not installed, users are automatically connected to the Lync Web App. The Lync Web App is a browser-based application with which users can connect to Lync Online meetings. Microsoft Silverlight 4.0 is required. If not present, the user is prompted to install Silverlight 4.0. The Lync Web App provides a very good experience for meetings visually, but does not support voice or video. This means that *you must provide a way for users of the Lync Web App to hear the presentation.*

The End-User Experience

When a user clicks the meeting request, Lync 2010 or the Lync Attendee client will open, if installed. If not, the user sees the webpage shown in Figure 12-45.

FIGURE 12-45 Alternatives for joining a meeting.

Note that users can click the Supported Browser button if they are concerned about their browsers not working for the meeting. In this example, Silverlight is not installed, so the link for installing it is presented. Most users will access the meeting without installing the Lync Attendee, unless they are directed to do so. The Lync Attendee client link is provided under View Alternative For Joining The Meeting but is not expanded by default.

> **Note** Silverlight is a technology created by Microsoft and is similar to Adobe Flash. Many sites, including Netflix, make use of Silverlight to provide a rich graphic experience over the web. Silverlight installs quickly, directly in the browser, and does not require a reboot.

In short, when the user clicks the meeting request, he will automatically connect using the best method available: Lync 2010, the Lync 2010 Attendee, or the web browser, in that order.

Meeting Setup and Preparation

You can use Lync Online to conduct an online meeting for up to 50 people. In your meeting invitations, be sure you have included audio dial-in instructions, if available, and links to the Lync 2010 Attendee client or supported browsers. Test the links you include to ensure that they work and are current.

If there are other presenters, conduct a trial meeting to ensure that voice and other issues are resolved. For example, shared content needs to be uploaded to the stage before the meeting, and make a plan for who will control the stage and in what order.

At any time, you can click the meeting URL to display the meeting stage. The stage is on the right, as shown in Figure 12-46. This area is visible to all users when application sharing is not in use.

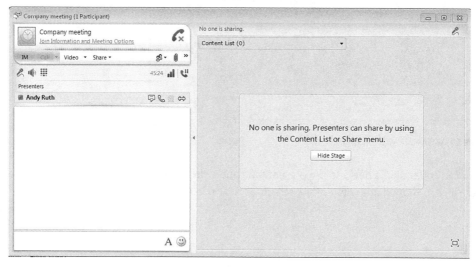

FIGURE 12-46 An empty Lync 2010 meeting stage.

Meeting Configuration

Take a moment to ensure that the Online Meeting Options (see Figure 12-40) are set up as you require. If everyone joins as a presenter, for example, that's likely to cause a problem during a large meeting. Also, be sure the setting for annotations is correct. Those who can annotate can write messages on the stage during the presentation (more on this topic in "Real-Time Annotation and Demonstrations," later in this chapter). Typically, this should be set to Presenters Only.

Upload a PowerPoint Deck

Frequently, PowerPoint decks are used as the core of a presentation. To add a deck, click the Share menu option, and then select PowerPoint Presentation. Browse to the deck, and then click Open. The deck will be opened and prepared for presentation. The first slide is displayed. You will want to manage the display of the slides during the presentation, using the thumbnails of each deck. To show the thumbnails, click the Show Thumbnails icon on the lower-right corner of the stage, as shown in Figure 12-47.

FIGURE 12-47 The Show Thumbnails icon.

You can add multiple decks to the presentation and switch between them by using the pull-down under You Are Sharing at the top of the screen, as shown in Figure 12-48.

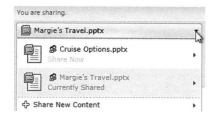

FIGURE 12-48 Switching decks.

Navigate the Deck

During the presentation, with thumbnail view enabled, you just click the slide that you want to show. As shown in Figure 12-49, you can easily go back and forth between slides during the presentation.

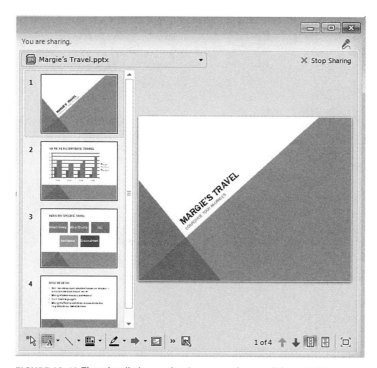

FIGURE 12-49 Thumbnail view makes it easy to change slides quickly.

Animated slides should render properly, but they have been known to act differently when displayed in the presentation. For slides that require click events, click the slide in the stage area when you are ready to start animations. It's a good idea to test animations before the presentation so that you know what to expect.

Polls

You can add simple polls to your Lync Online presentation. To do so, choose Share, and then click Poll. The Create A Poll form open, as shown in Figure 12-50. The poll is added to the content that you can share.

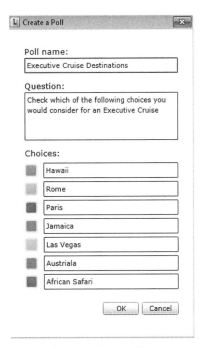

FIGURE 12-50 Creating a poll.

When you are ready to take the poll, just select it from the You Are Sharing pull-down (Figure 12-47). Use the choices at the bottom of the stage to open, close, show results, hide results, edit, clear, and save the poll, as shown from left to right in Figure 12-51.

FIGURE 12-51 Managing the poll during the meeting.

Manage the Meeting

When the time comes for your meeting, people will start to join.

Admit People from the Lobby

If you are using the meeting lobby, you need to approve users before they can be admitted, as shown in Figure 12-52. With multiple people in the lobby, you can select Admit All.

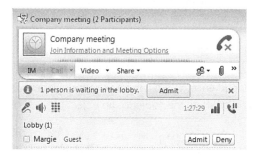

FIGURE 12-52 Admitting people from the lobby.

Be mindful of people showing up late to the meeting, because they must be admitted while you are presenting.

Mute Audio

Be alert to audio issues, such as broadcasting chatter to everyone in the group, or having an open mike in the audience, which is heard by all. Some very embarrassing and annoying situations can occur when personal or inappropriate commentary is sent to the entire meeting without the person knowing that there is an open microphone.

When using the Lync Online Voice feature, you can mute the entire audience by using the Mute Audience feature, as shown in Figure 12-53.

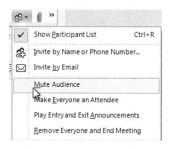

FIGURE 12-53 The Mute Audience option.

Keep in mind that if you are using a conference call service that is completely independent of Lync Online, clicking Mute Audience has no effect on the audio.

Also, notice the other options on the menu that can be very handy during a meeting. Make Everyone An Attendee is the solution if everyone attending the meeting is a presenter and you didn't intend for that to be the case. If this occurs, first select Make Everyone An Attendee. Next, in the participant list, select the individuals who should be presenters. (Right-click the entry for each, and then select Make Presenter.)

You can also select individuals in the participant list and mute their microphones. Conversely, if everyone but the presenter is muted and you want to grant someone the opportunity to speak, you can unmute her while she asks a question or makes a point.

Use Video

During the meeting, you can transmit video to your audience. Video can be very useful when you want to provide personal presence or when you want to show the audience an object not well represented by a picture.

With more than one presenter, Lync Online automatically switches to the speaker. Not only is this a lot of fun, but it provides interactive and interesting content during a presentation.

To start broadcasting, just click the Video button in Lync 2010.

Real-Time Annotation and Demonstrations

During the meeting, you can use the tools located at the bottom of the stage to interact with the stage without modifying the original content. You've probably seen something similar to this on sports broadcasts where the announcers draw lines on a frozen frame to call out a certain player or action. You can do the same with your presentations by using the annotation tools. You can add comments, circle key points, underline, and otherwise interact with the audience as you talk.

A common use of this feature is to place a note on the opening slide if the starting time is delayed. A slide that says "The meeting will begin at 10:05," easily informs all participants.

Annotation Tools

Each of the tools shown in Figure 12-54 has a unique function.

FIGURE 12-54 Annotation tools for use during the presentation.

The most commonly used is the laser point tool (selected in Figure 12-54). When selected, clicking the slide causes a point to appear momentarily on the shared screen at the location where you clicked. You can drag the point around (click and hold down the mouse button) as if you were using an actual laser pointer.

You can use the text box tool (second from left) to type on the shared screen.

The blue arrow is the stamp tool that stamps an arrow where you click. Click the down-facing triangle next to the stamp tool (or any other tool with that option) to reveal other choices.

In the meeting options, note that you can limit the use of these tools to presenters only or allow everyone to annotate.

The White Board

Another useful real-time annotation feature is the whiteboard. You insert a whiteboard just like a poll. Choose Share | White Board to display a white space on the stage and enable the annotation tools for everyone in the meeting. The whiteboard is a great brainstorming tool for small group use. You can save the whiteboard by using the save icon (shown in Figure 12-54) for later reference.

Present Demos

Many presentations are accompanied by demonstrations. You can easily switch to showing a live demonstration during a presentation by using application sharing, as previously discussed. Just select the Share menu option, and then share your desktop or the program you want to show. The stage switches from the slide show to the demonstration. During the demonstration, keep in mind that you do not want to constantly change your screen because it can take a moment or two for the displayed version of your demo to reach all attendees. For example, if you open a Word document and are constantly moving up and down in the document as you speak, there might not be enough time for the display to catch up with rapid updates.

Develop the habit of showing a screen and letting it settle for few seconds before moving on. This helps to ensure that everyone's display is fully in sync with your presentation.

When your demo is finished, close the application or click Stop Sharing at the top of the screen (see Figure 12-32). If you want to return to the slide show during the presentation without closing your demo, just switch to the Lync meeting window, and then under You Are Sharing, select the content to share from the stage drop-down menu, as shown in Figure 12-55.

FIGURE 12-55 Switching the stage content.

Lync Online Administration

The Office 365 Admin portal contains a few settings that you can manage related to Lync Online. In general, the default settings work well for most small businesses. You can modify the features of Lync Online service-wide and on a per-user basis, as well as manage additional capabilities such as adding a teleconferencing provider to your service. First, log on to the portal, using your administrator credentials. Click the Admin menu at the top of the page, and then under Lync Online, click General Settings. You will see the Overview page, as shown in Figure 12-56.

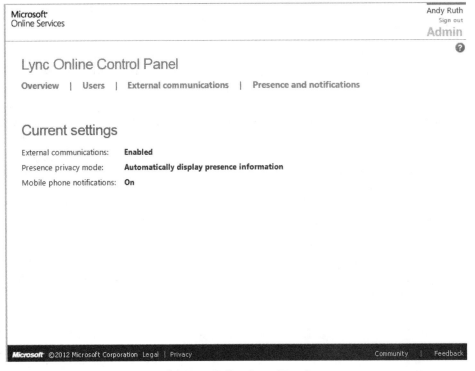

FIGURE 12-56 The Overview page of the Lync Online Control Panel.

The Lync Online Control Panel overview page shows the status of the settings available in Lync Online. Take a look at each of your options.

Users

When you click Users at the top of the page, you'll see a list of your users. Select one or more users from the list, and then click Edit User to show the Edit User Settings page, as shown in Figure 12-57.

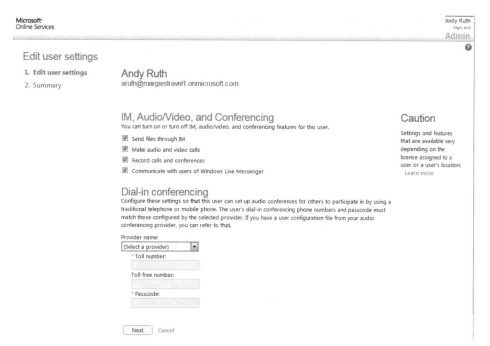

FIGURE 12-57 The Edit User Settings page.

Use the settings under IM, Audio/Video, and Conferencing to enable or disable each feature on a per-user basis. They are all enabled by default. Note that the ability to communicate with users of Windows Live Messenger is dependent on enabling the External Communications feature for the service, which is disabled by default. This is discussed in the next section, "Enable or Disable External Communications."

A significant feature that appears here is the ability to add dial-in conferencing service providers to Lync Online. You would use a dial-in conference provider to add traditional phone line conference call capabilities to your Lync Online meeting requests. This capability is not provided by Microsoft and comes with additional fees through service contracts with specific service providers. As of this writing, the companies providing this service are as follows:

- PGI: *http://www.pgi.com/us/en/conferencing/web-meetings/ms-lync-audio.php*

- British Telecom: *http://www.btconferencing.com/unified-communications/audio-for-microsoft-lync-online/*

- InterCall: *http://www.intercall.com/services/web-conferencing/lync-online.php*

When provisioned, conference call information is included in the Lync Online meeting request. This allows users of Lync Web App to participate in the audio portion of a meeting. You can find online help for configuring dial-in conferencing at *http://onlinehelp.microsoft.com/en-us/office365-smallbusinesses/gg591295.aspx*.

Enable or Disable External Communications

The External Communications page shown in Figure 12-58 determines whether your users can connect to those outside of your organization by using the Lync 2010 client.

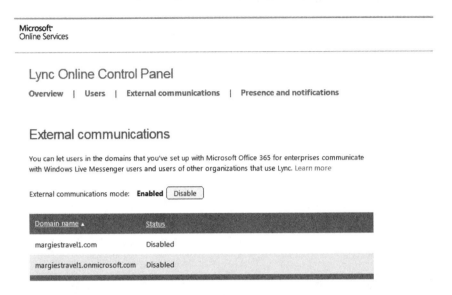

FIGURE 12-58 External communications settings in Lync Online.

When this feature is enabled (the default), you can communicate with users outside of your organization who use Lync Online or Lync Server 2010, presuming they allow connections from outside users, as well. In addition, you can instant message users of Windows Live Messenger.

You can use the Presence And Notifications page (Figure 12-59) to control presence privacy mode and mobile phone notifications. When you click the Edit button next to Presence Privacy Mode, you are presented with two options, as shown in Figure 12-60.

As you know, by default, Lync Online is set to allow you to communicate with other Lync Online users outside of your organization. Conversely, they can also contact you. The first step in this process is type your email address in the Lync 2010 client. Lync 2010 then shows your contact card to the other users so that they can see your status information before they initiate a conversation with you. Some people consider this to be too much information to expose to people whom you don't know or didn't authorize. If you enable Display Presence Information Only To User's Contacts, Lync 2010 shows presence only to users who are in your contact list.

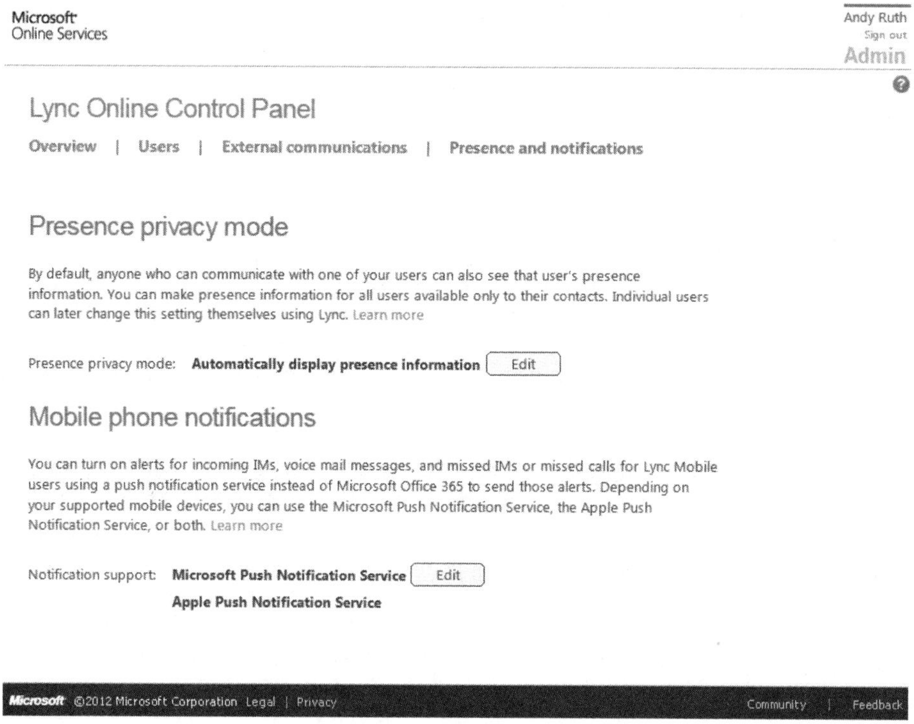
Microsoft Online Services
Andy Ruth
Sign out
Admin
Lync Online Control Panel
Overview | Users | External communications | Presence and notifications
Presence privacy mode
By default, anyone who can communicate with one of your users can also see that user's presence information. You can make presence information for all users available only to their contacts. Individual users can later change this setting themselves using Lync. Learn more
Presence privacy mode: Automatically display presence information Edit
Mobile phone notifications
You can turn on alerts for incoming IMs, voice mail messages, and missed IMs or missed calls for Lync Mobile users using a push notification service instead of Microsoft Office 365 to send those alerts. Depending on your supported mobile devices, you can use the Microsoft Push Notification Service, the Apple Push Notification Service, or both. Learn more
Notification support: Microsoft Push Notification Service Edit
Apple Push Notification Service
Microsoft ©2012 Microsoft Corporation Legal | Privacy
Community | Feedback

FIGURE 12-59 Presence and notifications.

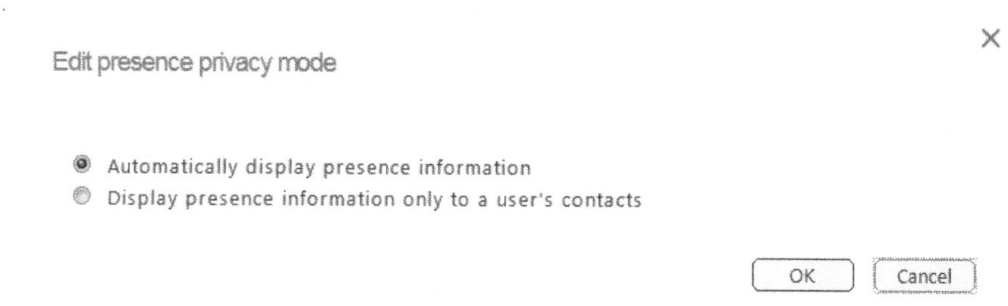
Edit presence privacy mode
Automatically display presence information
Display presence information only to a user's contacts
OK
Cancel

FIGURE 12-60 Presence privacy mode settings.

It is important to note that a user can override the Display Presence Only To A User's Contacts setting in Lync 2010. See *http://onlinehelp.microsoft.com/en-us/office365-smallbusinesses/hh831847.aspx* for more information.

The next setting on the Presence And Notifications page is Mobile Phone Notifications, which controls the behavior of Lync Online with Windows Phones or Apple devices. A "push" occurs when Lync Online initiates an update to your mobile device because of an event that occurs online. If the Lync 2010 Mobile client is not active and someone instant messages you, a push event might be required. By default, these settings are enabled.

For More Information

"Working with Lync Online" is a fitting final chapter. It's the service that most people think will have the least impact, but as you can tell, I'm a fan and believe it delivers quite a bit more value than people expect. This is based on my personal experience using Lync Online in my own business as well as those of businesses I work with.

Before ending, it should be restated that Office 365 is a continuously updated service. By far, the most valuable resource for information about Office 365 is *http://community.office365.com*. There, you can find blogs, wikis, forums, news, and other important details about the services. Often, information appears there before it is formalized into help files or white papers.

On the site, you'll find a wiki where Microsoft posts its most recent updates to the service at *http://community.office365.com/en-us/w/office_365_service_updates/default.aspx*. In addition, there is a forum focused on Plan P1 such as plan administration at *http://community.office365.com/en-us/f/146.aspx*.

Finally, Appendix A of this book provides a deployment checklist that you might find helpful.

Deployment Checklist

This checklist is representative of a general Microsoft Office 365 deployment process. The specific steps and stages required will vary depending on your requirements.

TABLE A-1 Typical Deployment Workflow

Task	Notes	Chapter
Select the right plan for your business	Understand the capabilities and limitations of Plan P1.	2
Sign up for trial or paid account	30-day free trial is available.	3
Set up admin account for password recovery	Automatically prompted for a cell phone number that receives text messages when you first access the site.	3
Create a second administrator account	Best practice in case first administrator account becomes accessible.	3
Survey desktops and mobile devices; identify upgrades required, if any	Office 2003 is not supported. Apple systems require different considerations. Check mobile devices for compatibility with Office 365. Acquire headsets and video for Lync Online if needed.	7, 9
Determine whether Office Professional Plus is a good value for your business	Review pricing and features plus needed upgrades.	2
Clean up current email, contacts, junk mail, deleted mail, and so on	Housekeeping in preparation for migration if required. Reduce mailbox size to reduce migration time.	7
Optional: Configure Connected Accounts in Office Web Apps (OWA)	Copies mail to Office 365 from existing service.	8
Document current DNS settings for custom domain	Need administrative access to your DNS management services.	6
Validate domain(s)*	Do not transfer DNS services to Office 365 yet.	6
Add needed setting to DNS Manager*	If necessary, add website and other settings.	6
Add users and assign to new domain	Instruct users to change initial password. Inform users that they can access OWA and Microsoft SharePoint Online with the onmicrosoft.com address.	5
Add additional identities if required for users	Users can receive mail for more than one domain.	8
Configure Microsoft Exchange Online	Add global contacts, public groups, mobile policy, and personal archive as required.	8
Configure Microsoft Lync Online	Allow or restrict settings for external communications, file transfer, and so on in Admin portal. Acquire conference bridge provider if needed.	12
Configure SharePoint Online security and features	SharePoint Online configuration can occur any time after users are created.	11
Export user mail, calendar, and other settings as needed in preparation for new Office 365 Inbox	Timing and activities depend on type of services currently in use and how you plan to migrate the data.	7

Task	Notes	Chapter
Transfer DNS to Microsoft*	This step starts mail flow to Microsoft. Alternatively, add Office 365 DNS settings to your existing DNS service, including the MX record.	6
Deploy Desktops	Be prepared for changes when new account is added to Outlook.	7
Import historical mail, calendars, and other information as needed to Office 365	Attach or import PSTs. Drag and drop messages to Office 365. If you used Connected Accounts, mail is already there.	7
Configure Lync 2010 Client	Add contacts, photo; set up audio and video hardware.	12
Configure mobile devices	Cannot occur before users are created and initial passwords are changed.	9

* If your account has the Domain Quickstart Wizard, the domain validation workflow will be different. See Chapter 6, "Working with Custom Domains," for details.

Index

M

About the Author

 BRETT HILL, Office 365 MVP, is a consultant, trainer, speaker, and author, living in Bellevue, Washington. Brett was an IIS MVP for three years before joining Microsoft as the IIS Technical Evangelist. He was one of the key authors for the IIS Resource Guide for Microsoft Press on IIS 7. He then transitioned to online services and was instrumental in creating technical training and content for Microsoft related to Business Productivity Online Suite (BPOS) and Office 365. Brett left Microsoft to start *Office365training.com*, which hosts online training and other content for end users of Office 365. Since then he was named Office 365 MVP by Microsoft for 2011 and 2012. You can find out more about Brett at LinkedIn *http://www.linkedin.com/profile/view?id=8088527* and at *Office365answers.com* or *Office365training.com*.

What do you think of this book?

We want to hear from you!
To participate in a brief online survey, please visit:

microsoft.com/learning/booksurvey

Tell us how well this book meets your needs—what works effectively, and what we can do better. Your feedback will help us continually improve our books and learning resources for you.

Thank you in advance for your input!